Driving

T0273128

Your Car, Your Government, Your Choice

James D. Johnston

The AEI Press

Publisher for the American Enterprise Institute
WASHINGTON, D.C.

1997

. To order call toll free 1-800-462-6420 or 1-717-794-3800. For all other inquiries please contact the AEI Press, 1150 Seventeenth Street, N.W., Washington, D.C. 20036 or call 1-800-862-5801.

Library of Congress Cataloging-in-Publication Data

Johnston, James, 1930–
    Driving America / James Johnston.
      p. cm.
    Includes bibliographical references and index.
    ISBN 0-8447-4024-1 (pbk.)
    1. Transportation, Automotive—United States. 2. Automobile industry and trade—United States. 3. Air—Pollution—Economic aspects—United States. I. Title.
    HE5623.J63   1997
    388.3'21'0973—dc21   97-45846
                                              CIP

THE AEI PRESS
Publisher for the American Enterprise Institute
1150 17th Street, N.W., Washington, D.C. 20036

ISBN 978-0-8447-4024-9

CONTENTS

PREFACE

This book is an attempt to provide a useful background for those who care about personal mobility, and to better prepare them to become involved in shaping government policies that affect our cars and their use. My fondest hope is that more people will become involved. If not, these issues will be decided by the "special interests."

For nearly twenty-five years, I was an executive representing an automobile manufacturing company—definitely a special interest in Washington, D.C. Before that, as a foreign service officer with the U.S. Department of State, I represented the United States of America—definitely a special interest in the countries to which I was assigned. Much of what I have written about comes from my own personal knowledge, gained as a participant in the events described. I have sought to be accurate, fair, and objective, but I know that everyone, including myself, is a captive of his or her own experience. This is true for all special interests, and Americans are learning that special interests are not just limited to manufacturers, businesses, mining companies, farmers, and others in the private sector. Government agencies have their own very special interests, as do politicians, the news media, and all human organizations, including the dozens of professional environmental and other activist groups that play an active role in public policy formation. It is valuable for the public to receive information from these and all special interests. People make better decisions about public policy issues after listening to all sides, but also by recognizing that all groups involved have their own axes to grind.

Not surprisingly, I strongly value and endorse the freedom and independence provided by the automobile. At the same time, my wife and I live in a condominium apartment at the center of the city. I generally walk to my office. We frequently walk to restaurants, shops, and theaters in our diverse neighborhood. We also each have a car (one large and one small), and we use them to visit our grandchildren and our children, and like the vast majority of Americans, we use them to shop, visit the doctor, get to church, go on vacation, and generally get around.

Cars bring problems as well as benefits, and like most Americans I want to minimize these problems. Again, like most Americans, I recognize the benefits of personal mobility and believe they outweigh the costs. My intent in this book is to examine the environmental issues involving our cars and the policies that the government is adopting to deal with those issues. The outcome of the debate will determine the future of the car and truck.

The views contained herein are my own and do not necessarily represent those of any of my associates in the automobile industry or elsewhere, who in fact may well disagree. I am grateful to the many people who have helped me complete this project, especially the outstanding interns at the American Enterprise Institute.

· 1 ·

INTRODUCTION

Virtually every young person in the world wants a car, and a car is what the aging tenaciously resist giving up. Many people love cars, a few may hate them, and others may take them for granted; but people will not do without them.

The desire for a car comes as no surprise. It is simply the latest, best way available for humankind to get around. It is not a car—the one or two tons of metal, plastic, glass, and rubber—that people want. What they want is this ability to get around. They want mobility—personal mobility.

Throughout history, people everywhere—especially the young ones—have eagerly adopted any new form of transportation that is an improvement over the old. We started on our own two feet and progressed to the backs of lesser animals. The wheel, experts say, came along around 7,000 years ago in Mesopotamia and enabled us to be pulled in ox carts at 2.5 miles per hour. The introduction of the horse from the steppes of Asia provided a great leap forward in transport speed. The horse itself quickly became the most popular means of getting around, and chariots, introduced around 2800 B.C., soon became the vehicle of choice. A horse-drawn chariot, around 2000 B.C., could cover about eighteen miles per hour, a speed not exceeded until the steam engine was developed more than three-and-a-half thousand years later. Four-wheeled wagons carried cargo but had no swiveling foreaxle that would make them steerable. A swivel device was not widespread until the seventeenth century. From that time, steerable, horse-drawn vehicles with continuously improved suspension, more effective harnesses, and enlarged carrying capacity became the mainstay of personal mobility, and they remained so until the development of the internal combustion engine in the late nineteenth century.

It may have been satisfying, as the twentieth century began, for the man without a car to come upon an "automobilist" stranded with a flat tire or a dead engine, or just plain stuck in the mud.[1] He could shout, "Get a horse!" and relieve his envy—momentarily. In his heart he knew the car was the wave of the future. The Century of the Car had just begun.

1

Personal Mobility—Good or Bad?

Having the benefits of personal mobility is not something that just happens. All governments or societies make overarching decisions about the mobility of their members. Essentially, they decide how to address the very basic drive of humankind to move about and to do so in the fastest, most flexible, most affordable mode possible. The question for society is whether to accommodate this human drive or to attempt to contain it.

Personal mobility for others has always been worrisome to those who believe they should control the wayward inclinations of their fellow men and women. It is no accident that there is a direct relationship between personal mobility and freedom. No authoritarian leader really wants to see his people able to move about freely, associating with whom they please, with the inevitable exchange of ideas and information and the independence these freedoms bring. The shortage of cars in the Soviet Union was not caused by an inability to build them. The Soviets had the first satellite in space and some of the most advanced aircraft and other instruments of war the world has ever seen. There were no cars for the people simply because the leadership did not believe that personal mobility was a desirable goal. It is much easier to control people if they stay put or move about only on mass transit.

On a trip to the United States, Premier Nikita Khrushchev was appalled at the number of automobiles in the hands of the American people and announced that this was certainly not what the people of the Soviet Union needed.[2] Ironically, he was succeeded by Leonid Brezhnev, who turned out to be a car buff (but no democrat). Today the former Soviet Union countries are scrambling to acquire the cars Khrushchev disdained.

In the United States, the decision of society was to accommodate personal mobility—more a consensus than a decision, as befits a democracy. For the first half of the Century of the Car, every level of government in America gave its support to meeting the desire of all Americans to own and use a car or truck. The government's most important accommodation was to avoid getting between the people and their cars. The motor vehicle was regulated not by government but by what the customer demanded, what competitors offered, and what science and good engineering could produce. In Europe, the early automobile was a trophy for the nobility and the wealthy. In America, it became everyone's means of getting around. Henry Ford showed the way by dropping the original price of the Model T from $825 in 1908 to $440 by 1914 and then to $345 by 1916.[3] Alfred P. Sloan determined that General Motors would provide a car "for every purse and purpose." Walter Chrysler, John and Horace Dodge, Ransom E. Olds, James Packard, Billy Durant, Henry Leland, Charles "Boss" Kettering, and literally thousands of America's most creative and energetic citizens were instrumental in the development and production of the machine that transformed America.

Responding to popular clamor, elected officials improved the existing roads. (Yes, roads were essential before there were cars.) In 1910, there were 2.4 million miles of roads and streets in the United States, mostly dirt roads, in the service of farming. By 1950, road mileage had grown by 38 percent to 3.3 million miles, with much of it built to "get the farmer out of the mud." Officials who got in the way of mobility soon became former officials.

In 1950, 24 percent of American streets and roads were paved. Today 61 percent of the 3.9 million miles are paved. Credit goes to Amzi Lorenzo Barber, a teacher at Howard University in Washington, D.C., who pioneered the development of asphalt for the roadway. In 1877, Barber obtained a franchise to take asphalt from the island of Trinidad, and a year later he began changing the streets of the nation's capital from the worst to the smoothest anywhere. Buffalo, Chicago, Manhattan, and other cities followed.

Another major breakthrough was the pneumatic tire, patented in 1889. Developed almost simultaneously by a Scot named John Boyd Dunlop and by the Michelin brothers in France, these tires provided a cushion of air between the driver and the rough road, thus making the auto a practical mode of transportation. In the same era, a number of brave experimenters found that the by-products from refining petroleum for the production of kerosene and lubricants were not useless. The obvious power of these so-called by-products drove curious and inventive men to harness them to practical use. The power of one by-product, gasoline, in the internal combustion engine soon brought about the most radical change in personal mobility, at least since the introduction of the horse.

In 1903, sixty or so companies were building automobiles and had sold around 11,000. In 1923, the *National Geographic Magazine* published a comprehensive article on the auto industry. "Thirteen million motor cars! Who can visualize them!" the author wrote, and then speculated that market saturation might come at 18 million."[4] By 1930, there were 26.5 million private motor vehicles registered in America. The Great Depression cut back temporarily on the expansion of vehicle ownership, but not on the enthusiasm. In their classic study of America's so-called Middletown, Robert and Helen Lynd wrote that "while some workers lost their cars in the depression, the local sentiment, as heard over and over again, is that 'People give up everything in the world but their car.' " The Lynds quote a banker as saying, "The depression hasn't changed materially the value Middletown people set on home ownership, but *that's* not their primary desire, as the automobile always comes first."[5] At the depths of the depression, private motor vehicle registrations declined by only around 300,000, to 26.2 million in 1935. By 1940, registrations had bounced up to 32.0 million.

Only war could seriously stop the growth of the industry, and then only temporarily. As Detroit became the "arsenal of democracy" during World War II, turning out military equipment instead of cars, private vehicle ownership dropped by nearly 1.4 million vehicles. When the war ended in 1945, pent-up demand had customers clamoring to buy cars, and registrations jumped from 30.6 million to 48.6 in 1950, a growth of 59 percent in five years.

Why the Car Is King

In 1996, a century after the Duryea brothers brought the first production cars to the market, nearly 200 million cars and light trucks were registered for operation in America—more than seven vehicles for every ten men, women, and children. That is an average of two cars, vans, sport-utilities, or light pick-ups for each of the 97 million households of America. There are now more of these personal vehicles registered in America than there are Americans who are licensed to drive them. In the mid-1990s, we Americans were driving our vehicles nearly two-and-a-half trillion miles a year. We use our cars for almost 90 percent of our commuting, but only about 35 percent of the miles we drive are to get to and from work. The rest we drive to shop, visit friends, go to church, see the doctor, take the kids to day care, and accomplish other family or personal business and pleasure, including more than 70 percent of our vacations.

Getting into our cars is about like getting into our clothes—a daily necessity. Where we go, our cars go. Where our cars cannot go, most of us simply do not go. There are no possessions, other than our homes, upon which we Americans rely more than on our cars, vans, and trucks.

In what they buy and what they use, Americans make clear that they prefer the motor vehicle to any other mode of "getting around." The car is king because it has given people the freedom to move about for pleasure or for profit. The car provides an escape from unemployment. It has freed countless people from regional poverty, permitting them to take advantage of new opportunities in where to work and how to live. It frees people from repression. The private car, voluntarily mobilized to shuttle people to work, enabled the bus boycott in Montgomery, Alabama, to succeed, spelling the end of segregation in public facilities. The car has made it possible for people to live outside the crowded cities, in single-family homes with flowers, green grass, and safer streets. It takes people to the shore, to the mountains, to Grandmother's house. It gets people to church, the store, the doctor, the schools, and a hundred other places they need or want to be. It is the flexible, comfortable, reliable, affordable means for achieving freedom and independence.

An unexpected endorsement of the joy of driving came from First Lady Hillary Rodham Clinton in her first newspaper column, published in several newspapers on July 23, 1995. She wrote, "On a recent trip to Arkansas, I had a sudden impulse to drive. We were staying at my mother's house in Little Rock and I needed to run some errands. So, on a quiet Friday afternoon, I jumped behind the wheel of a car and, much to the discomfort of my Secret Service detail, drove around town. For several hours, I enjoyed a marvelous sensation of personal freedom."

Unfortunately, in the United States, an effort is underway to take us in the opposite direction. Today, professional activists and their political allies see the car as a ton or two of nonrenewable resources burning foreign-source fossil fuel, spewing tons of pollutants into the air while endangering life and limb on congested highways that are paving over America and drawing people out of the center city into suburban sprawl. Some see the car as a threat more dangerous than any military adversary they can imagine. They have plans to put an end to its dominance—and, not incidentally, the personal mobility that goes with it. No matter that the car is what the people want—overwhelmingly.

According to Alvin Toffler, elitists have concluded "that the masses are too bourgeoisified, too corrupted and addled by Madison Avenue to know what is good for them." The elite, he wrote, will fix the world, "even if it means stuffing it [the fix] down the throats of those who are too stupid to know their own interests."[6]

Stop That Car!

The World Resources Institute's "guide" to the environment prescribes what is good for us: "We can no longer assume it is our God-given right to drive, alone, anywhere we please," and adds, "New criteria are also needed to influence buying choices and driving behavior." How will this be accomplished? "Planners and developers will have to interest mainstream Americans in the kind of high-density urban developments where walking, bicycling, and public transportation are both possible and enjoyable," says the Institute. It adds that, "It's safe to assume that most Americans will continue to drive as frequently as ever unless they are given sufficient reason—whether threats or financial inducements—to do otherwise."[7] In other words, we are too stupid to know our own interests and must be coerced or bribed into the paths of righteousness.

Taming the car and corralling the truck have some popular appeal for a variety of reasons. Along with the joys of owning a car, Americans became more aware of the problems that come with it. As people became more dependent on their cars, especially for getting to work, the romance of cruising the open road was often replaced by the tension of fighting heavy traffic at both ends of the day. And so for many, driving their cars, at least for that chore, was no longer an altogether pleasant experience.[8] And when a car failed to do its duty, the consequences were increasingly important—failure to get to work, missed doctors' appointments, doing without milk from the store, and worse yet, the necessity of a trip to the repair shop. For some, the car became more like an appliance than a prized possession.

By the 1960s, owning a car had become common. Not only did the banker, the butcher, and the baker own them, even welfare recipients were driving. When everyone can have something, it may be a mark of success for democracy in the marketplace, but it disappoints a set of people who prefer exclusivity. For them, joys that become common lose their attraction. Not that these people give up their cars; they may even drive the latest upscale models with luxury cup-holders. They just quit speaking about them kindly. The cutting edge of their commentary is no longer about the benefits the car provides, but rather about the problems that come with it.

The young people not only *wanted* their cars as much as the youth of any period; to an unprecedented degree, they fully *expected* to have them. Cars had become an entitlement for many affluent and middle-class young people. Getting a car did not necessarily require that part-time job during the school year and full-time in the summer. They got the old family car—or even a new one from Mom or Dad. And what is acquired too easily is accorded too little respect.

The general disaffection of the 1960s brought institutions of all kinds under sharp attack. The automobile was not spared. While cars have always had their opponents, for the first fifty years of the twentieth century the naysayers had been in a distinct, eccentric, and even disparaged minority. Since the 1960s the car has been in retreat—not in numbers or use, but in intellectual justification, moral support, and approbation in the popular media. Concerns about safety, energy conservation, and most especially, the environment have dominated public policy affecting the automobile. Laws were passed, regulations promulgated, vehicle costs increased, choice reduced, and new roads blocked.

In his 1975 book *The War against the Automobile,* B. Bruce-Briggs made the case:

> The automobile-highway system is an unequaled complex of structures, machines, and techniques for maximizing the mobility of the individual American and American families. . . . So it seems strange that over the last generation a concerted and comprehensive attack has been made on the auto-highway system by a small band of publicists and politicians. The number of these opponents of the automobile is very tiny, but they have been powerfully placed, and have strongly influenced—indeed dominated—public discussions of personal transportation in general, and the automobile in particular."[9]

His concerns are at least as relevant today as they were twenty years ago.

Critics and professional activists no longer constitute the small group Bruce-Briggs encountered. They have grown in numbers and in influence and have spawned regulatory programs staffed by thousands. Government regulation of cars and trucks is now so comprehensive and detailed that the ability to choose the vehicle that provides what the customer wants is increasingly limited. The result is a regulated consumer—one who is no longer offered the choice he or she once had. This spectacular growth of government regulation now covers every aspect of the design, manufacture, sale, service, and use of motor vehicles. In the past forty years, the federal government has issued dozens of standards with thousands of separate requirements and test procedures governing motor vehicle fuel economy, emissions, safety, damageability, theft prevention, and consumer information. Regulations extend from bumper to bumper—including standards for the front and rear bumpers.

At the same time, road building and improvements have been neglected or actively blocked. The growth in road mileage from 1950 to 1994 was only 9 percent, including the new Interstate Highway System. Only 2.5 percent of that growth was added since 1975. The streets and roads of America are deteriorating precipitously, while the unmet demand for more road capacity rapidly expands. This combination of factors means that the ability to get where you want to go when you want to go there and in the vehicle of your choice is steadily being eroded. Politicians are regularly falling prey to the temptation to raid road money to fund other programs. Maintenance in public budget planning is most often of the "deferred" variety. In contrast, the increasingly stringent regulation of cars and trucks is motivated not only by laudable goals, like having safer cars and cleaner air, but also by the belief of some people that the personal vehicle as we know it should be driven off the road. These are the same people who applaud the raid on highway funds. They make the claim that, down deep, people agree with their position and really do not want cars. In one way, they are right.

A Basic Drive

As noted above, it is a not a car that everyone wants. What people want—as the critics and their political allies forget—is mobility, the ability to get around. To forget this is dangerous, because it is basic to our very nature to move, to explore, to travel.

Some Darwinians might say we started that way: germ cells, in order to fuse, had to move about to meet. Certainly, the lemurs and apes were foraging animals, moving about to find a better meal, or a mate, or to avoid a predator. Some Biblical literalists might say that man was created mobile, and that mobility became even more necessary when Adam and Eve were

7

expelled from the Garden of Eden and required to move about to fend for themselves.

To the early Greek philosophers, mobility was a critical factor in classifying the world's physical contents. The lowest category consisted of inanimate or lifeless objects, such as minerals or stones, with no mobility. Plants made up the next group—living, but also immobile. At the next level were the animals, able to move themselves from place to place. At the highest level of the animal world was humankind, possessing life and mobility and, specifically, able to move about by conscious plan, not just instinct. This quality of auto-mobility, to the Greeks and to subsequent thinkers, was a defining characteristic of the human race.

Aristotle went further, saying, "All men by nature desire to know." This desire, he believed, exists apart from any other purpose. Because it became strongest after the necessities of life had been secured, he believed knowledge was not sought for any advantage other than its own sake. From our experience, we know that humans are insatiably curious. Like other animals, we are inclined—or compelled—to explore the unknown and investigate what is different. We have a "need to know" and a desire to experience the unusual. Our curiosity, like the cat's, can get us into trouble—and it can also take us to the moon and, we hope, beyond.

Robert A. Butler of the University of Chicago wrote about a curiosity drive, saying, "The strong tendency to manipulate, look, and listen certainly appears to be basic to the motivational system of the higher organisms."[10] Other social scientists have argued that boredom or the search for stimulation is the basic drive that causes people to move about and explore. Robert Louis Stevenson captured the reason for mobility in a more poetic way: "I travel," he said, "not to go anywhere but to go. I travel for travel's sake."

Whatever the explanation, we know that the need to be mobile is deeply imbedded in human nature, and as with all other drives or instincts, we will make every effort to satisfy it. It is inevitable, also, that humankind will seek out the way to achieve personal mobility that best combines speed, comfort, convenience, and affordability. In our world today, the mobility method of choice is the private motor vehicle, powered by the internal combustion engine. James Q. Wilson explained: "If people can afford it, they will want to purchase convenience, flexibility, and privacy. These facts are as close to a Law of Nature as one can get in the transportation business. When the industrial world became prosperous, people bought cars. It is unstoppable."[11]

The car is king today, but it would be foolish to believe that this is the last mode of personal mobility this world will ever see. Change in transportation is inevitable, as it is in all other aspects of life. What people want is an affordable way to go from where they are to where they want to be, and to do it at the time they choose. They want to go in private, either alone or with the people they choose. They want to carry or pull along with them the things they think they will want. They want to do all this at optimum speed and in comfort. Today these are the good things a car, van, or light truck can do to satisfy our eternal itch for mobility.

If something else—some magic machine or force—could do these things more effectively and economically than can the current car, the assembly lines of auto plants around the world would come to a quick halt. Junkyards, side streets, and farmyards would be overwhelmed with abandoned Chevies, Fords, Toyotas, and other formerly cherished chariots. Collectors, racers, and preservationists would hang on to some cars, but people everywhere would clamor for the new mode of mobility with hardly a backward look.

Any Star Trek fan can tell you about the excellent new ways to achieve personal mobility the television show's writers have imagined. ("Beam me up, Scottie" suggests a pretty good travel mode, especially in a pinch.) More down to earth is the speculation about new modes of personal transportation such as vehicles powered by batteries, fuel cells, or hybrid systems, all believed to be possible technologies that might get us out of our current cars. Some politicians, impressed with their power to legislate, have tried mandating the existence of new technologies. They have done so with poor results. No replacement has yet been found that provides the mobility we get from today's magic machine, the motor vehicle.

More worrisome are those people who believe that there is no need for so much wasteful mobility and who strive to limit the availability and use of our current vehicles. Their vision is one of dwindling resources, an endangered Earth, and a need to lower our expectations in preparation for lowered standards of living. In their vision, people should live in highly concentrated population centers, close to places of employment, and they should be able to travel on foot or bicycle or by mass transit if they have a need to move beyond their immediate neighborhoods. This, obviously, is not the vision of the vast majority of Americans, who care about the environment but who also prize their mobility and the means they use to enjoy it—the car.

The car is just one factor in a struggle of visions, but it is a prime target for those who fear the future. The problems the car causes are being addressed—with notable success. The government has a role in ensuring that this progress continues, but it has overstepped the line in its enthusiasm to regulate. Proposals to restrict the use and utility of the personal vehicle, if successful, would represent the first instance in history of a limitation placed on the best available means of personal mobility without the availability of a superior substitute. The American people, if they continue to care about their personal mobility, must become aware of the issues and must engage in their resolution.

PART ONE

Miles per Gallon—
The Government Rules

· 2 ·

MILEAGE RULES—
FOR THE PEOPLE

When the president of the United States decides to play golf, he gets in his car and heads for the course, like any other golfer. His trip to the course, however, is considerably different from yours or mine. The car in which he rides is necessarily large and heavy, to provide the protection and performance the president should have. It is fully armored and has plenty of horsepower to move all that weight and move it fast in the event of an emergency. It has room for guards, aides, or friends.

The president does not go to the golf course, or anywhere else, in a compact car, and secret service agents do not accompany him in vans equipped with four-cylinder engines. With safety as the primary concern, they know that size and weight—and the power to move it—count more than any other consideration. Fuel economy is not a factor in deciding what vehicles to use. The president's limo may get somewhere between 7 and 10 miles per gallon (mpg), which is understandable considering the service it is expected to provide. The secret service vans may get around 10 to 15 mpg.

For all other Americans, however, the fuel economy of all the cars available to buy—when averaged together—must, by federal law, be 27.5 miles per gallon. All light trucks, sport-utilities, and vans, taken together, must average 20.7 mpg. This means they are smaller, lighter, and therefore less safe than they would be in the absence of the government rules.

How did this gap between the president's car and cars for the people, and their gasoline mileage—and safety—occur? It happened because of an old, entrenched, and very complicated government regulatory program that provides a classic example of the unintended consequences of well-intended policies. The intention was to achieve "energy independence" by reducing America's dependence on foreign oil, but the consequences are more injuries and deaths on our streets and highways.

The Infamous CAFE

This old and complex regulatory program is known as CAFE, for Corporate Average Fuel Economy. The CAFE law has the effect of requiring that for every larger, lower-mileage car a manufacturer sells, it must sell enough smaller, higher-mileage cars to ensure that the fuel economy of all the cars that manufacturer sells in one model year averages at least 27.5 mpg.[1] This means that for every Cadillac or Town Car that is sold, enough Cavaliers or Escorts must be sold to keep the average at or above the legal level. Under another CAFE rule, each manufacturer must sell enough smaller, more fuel-economic light trucks (including sport-utilities and vans) to ensure that its total light-truck fleet averages 20.7 mpg.

Since American consumers today prefer larger vehicles, auto manufacturers must offer smaller, lighter vehicles to the president's fellow Americans—and then find ways to make sure that they buy enough of them to keep within the CAFE rules. Because of CAFE, Americans are driving cars that give them less protection than would those cars they *could* buy if there were no CAFE rules. The car for the people, thanks to the CAFE law, has been reduced in size, weight, and performance—exactly the factors that give added protection to the president when he is riding in his official car.

Some professional activists and their political allies deny that CAFE has diminished automobile safety. It should be difficult for them to keep a straight face. As any serious student of Newtonian mechanics knows, when all other things are equal, smaller and lighter means less safe. People know this intuitively. Denying the laws of physics will not change the fact that people are killed at a much higher rate in small cars.

In the years after CAFE was implemented, manufacturers found it necessary to downsize virtually all their vehicles. Cutting weight increases mileage by decreasing rolling resistance and lowering inertial forces during acceleration. Reduced aerodynamic drag is also a factor. Engineers trimmed an average of 1,000 pounds from the new models and replaced the V-8 engine with six- and four-cylinder engines in most vehicles.[2]

Unintended Consequences—More Death on the Highways. On May 6, 1996, the headline of the lead story in the newspaper *Automotive News* announced, "Smaller Cars, Bigger Risks." The story reported that three new federal studies "confirm the link" between size and safety: "Suspicions—and common sense—confirmed: The chances of dying or being injured in an automobile crash increase substantially as vehicle weight decreases."[3]

This was not the first report that CAFE was a killer. In a joint study, John D. Graham of the Harvard School of Public Health and Robert W. Crandall of the Brookings Institution analyzed the estimated effect of the

CAFE law on the weight of new cars and the consequent effect on safety. In the April 1989 issue of the *Journal of Law and Economics*, they reported their conclusion that "CAFE will be responsible for several thousand additional fatalities over the life of each model year's cars." Studies by Graham and Crandall and others, including Leonard Evans, a safety expert with General Motors, suggest that the effects of CAFE may have been responsible for 2,200 to 3,900 additional fatalities for each model year's passenger cars over a ten-year period beginning in the late 1980s.[4] Using generous estimates of fuel saved by CAFE, Pietro S. Nivola and Crandall suggest that "the entire value of the fuel saved by CAFE may be squandered in additional highway fatalities."[5]

The Insurance Institute for Highway Safety (IIHS), funded by the auto insurance companies that have a direct business interest in lower fatalities and injuries, has conducted several small-car safety studies of this issue. In 1990, it found that "comparisons of 1985–87 model cars in 1986–88 show that each one mile per gallon increase in the fuel economy of these cars was associated with a 3.9 percent increase in the occupant fatality rate." IIHS analysis revealed that, as a result of the downsizing of the 1988 model vehicles, "The actual occupant death rate for 1988 models was 2.2 per 10,000 registered cars in calendar [year] 1989, but if the mix of cars by size had been the same as it was for the 1975 models, it would have been much lower—1.8 per 10,000. . . . What this means is that during 1989, 425 more people died in crashes of 1988 model-year cars than would have if these cars had the same size mix as the 1975 models." The loss of 425 lives in 1988 model-year cars alone is a high price to pay for a misguided government regulation. Notably, 65 percent of the lives lost in traffic accidents are those of people under forty-five years of age. At least 33 percent are those under twenty-four years of age. These are not the ill and the aged; they are people in or nearing their most productive years.

Why is there no outrage over these consequences of a federal regulation? A major reason is that these numbers are developed by statistical analysis. These fatalities are not identifiable men, women, and children whose photos can be shown on television or in the newspapers. Also, statistical analysis can be flawed; accuracy is highly dependent on whether all the variables are properly considered.

The relationship between car size and safety is made clear in table 2–1, prepared with data from IIHS. It shows that the fatality rate increases by more than 150 percent when an occupant of a larger car with a wheelbase of more than 114 inches switches to a car with a wheelbase of fewer than 95 inches. While the differences among the drivers of vehicles of varying sizes would have some bearing on the numbers, the critical difference is in the protection provided by the size and weight of the vehicles. Study after study by scientists and engineers has confirmed what most people know

TABLE 2–1

OCCUPANT DEATHS PER MILLION REGISTERED VEHICLES
ONE TO THREE YEARS OLD, 1995

	Cars	
Vehicle size	Wheelbase (inches)	Occupant deaths per million registered vehicles
Small	< 95	250
Small	95–99	210
Midsize	100–104	180
Midsize	105–109	130
Large	110–114	106
Large	> 114	97
	Utility Vehicles	
Vehicle size	Wheelbase (inches)	Occupant deaths per million registered vehicles
Small	< 100	278
Midsize	100–120	144
Large	> 120	75
	Pickups	
Vehicle size	Weight (pounds)	Occupant deaths per million registered vehicles
Small	< 3,500	214
Large	> 3,500	149

SOURCE: Insurance Institute for Highway Safety.

intuitively—assuming both cars are equivalently equipped with safety technology, a larger, heavier car is safer than a smaller, lighter one.

Newton's Law—Still at Work. For engineers, the safety-related issue is one of simple Newtonian mechanics, where the law of conservation of linear momentum shows that when two objects crash into each other, the change in speed that each object undergoes is in inverse proportion to its mass. Thus, when a vehicle weighing half as much as another going at the same speed crashes head-on with the heavier car, the lighter car will undergo a change of speed about twice that of the heavier car. Forces from the more abrupt speed change are transferred to the occupants of the smaller car, with predictable and tragic results.

In 1988, James Burnley, U.S. secretary of transportation for President Ronald Reagan, said, "The CAFE statute was well intentioned at the time, but it is clear that this has become an ineffective, damaging law that ought to be repealed. CAFE is a dinosaur which ought to be extinct."[6]

In 1991, President George Bush's secretary of transportation, Samuel K. Skinner, said more stringent CAFE rules "would kill and injure thousands."[7] Diane Steed, former administrator of the National Highway Traffic Safety Administration, agreed, calling CAFE "a measure that will kill and injure thousands of Americans each year."[8] Thomas Sowell, senior fellow at the Hoover Institution at Stanford University, wrote that "lighter cars mean more fatalities in auto accidents. That's really trading blood for oil."[9] Sam Kazman of the Competitive Enterprise Institute called the effect of CAFE "death by regulation."[10]

Why, then, is CAFE still on the law books? Aside from normal, bureaucratic inertia (not many regulatory programs are ever repealed), there are several reasons. A principal one is that CAFE is an ingenious method for interjecting the government, by stealth, into the process of determining what kind of vehicles Americans should be able to buy. Very few people know it exists, and fewer understand it.

Needless Mobility?

Despite the overwhelming popularity of the car as the way to achieve personal mobility—or perhaps because of this popularity—a growing number of well-funded professional activist groups and well-placed individuals are determined to get people out of their cars and into buses and subways, or back on their feet, or on bicycles.[11] These activists want to stop major road construction, and to a large degree they have succeeded. They are not interested in relieving congestion; they generally oppose any relief, on grounds that it would encourage more people to do what people obviously want to do, travel by car. They want to reduce the choices of cars and trucks available to the American people—and they are succeeding. They are not concerned about forcing more people into smaller, less comfortable, and lower performing vehicles. It is their purpose to do so. CAFE is one of the most important mechanisms by which they can accomplish their goals.

Here is the way a publication of the World Resources Institute sets the issue: "A broad look at our car-dominated transportation system reveals environmental, economic, and safety problems at every link in the chain—from the extraction of crude oil from the ground to the burning of carbon-based fuels in vehicles that jam our city streets, befoul the air, and not infrequently crash into each other."[12]

Beyond the environmental issues, many critics of the automobile also believe that so much mobility is unnecessary and wasteful. They think about the automobile in much the same way that the Duke of Wellington felt about railroads in the early 1800s. He opposed their construction in England because, he said, they would "only encourage the common people to move about needlessly."[13]

In a book aptly entitled *At Road's End,* the authors assert,

> Awareness is growing that mobility for mobility's sake has inherent flaws. Making it easier to move people around simply encourages more moving around, just as making it easier to move vehicles around means more vehicles will be moving around. It is impossible to provide unlimited mobility, and if it were, it would have indirect consequences that are undesirable. What is important is that people have access to what they *need* [emphasis added].[14]

What they "need," not what they want. Shades of the Duke of Wellington!

Caesar, the Red Flag Act, and Other Governmental Help. Attempts to curtail personal transportation did not begin with CAFE or other restrictions on the automobile enacted since the 1960s. In 45 B.C., Julius Caesar banned all vehicles, "numerous litters and noisy chariots," from the center of Rome.[15] The ban made transit less bothersome—at least for Caesar.

A more complicated government regulation came in the 1800s, when steam power brought the first self-propelled vehicles to the highway.[16] In Great Britain, Richard Trevithick put a steam engine on a simple chassis in 1801 and achieved speeds of 15 km per hour. By 1825, Scotsman George Stephenson was hauling coal overland with a steam-powered vehicle, and in 1828, Walter Hancock had developed a three-wheeled steam tractor used to pull a coach. By 1830, he had a four-wheeled car, capable of carrying six passengers, in service on the road between Stratford and London. In 1833, John Scott Russell built a steam-powered carriage and, within a few years, had six steam buses in service between Glasgow and Paisley.

As self-propelled transport on British roads began to pick up steam, it is no surprise that the urge to regulate welled up. These vehicles belched smoke, threw up dust, made loud noises, and scared the horses. Turnpike trustees, in charge of most roads, began to ban them. Worse yet, politicians became involved.

The landed gentry, offended by these grotesque machines, saw them as inimical to their preferred lifestyle. Joined by stagecoach and railway interests, they lobbied successfully for a select committee of the British

House of Commons to investigate. Walter Hancock and others were called for a hearing, after which Parliament began to set limits on the weight, carrying capacity, and speed of these first automobiles. In 1836, heavy taxes were levied on steam road coaches. According to Peter Roberts, "By 1835, they [steam vehicles] were being forced out of business, as stagecoach and railway companies put on parliamentary and private pressure that caused the tolls for steam vehicles to be levied at something like twelve times those for horse-drawn vehicles."[17]

The culmination of the effort to get those early automobiles off the roads came in 1865, when the infamous Red Flag law was enacted. Section 3 of the law (officially, the Locomotive Act) required that

> every locomotive propelled by steam, or any other than animal power, on turnpike, road or public highway shall be worked according to the following rules and regulations amongst others, namely: Firstly, at least three persons shall be employed to drive or conduct such locomotive; secondly, of such persons while any locomotive is in motion one shall proceed such locomotive in motion of foot by not less than 60 yards, shall carry a red flag constantly displayed, and shall warn the riders and drivers of horses of the approach of such locomotives.[18]

The act further limited the speed of the vehicle to four miles per hour on the highway and two miles per hour through villages, towns, or cities.

Automobile historian Ernest Henry Wakefield wrote that the Red Flag act, passed in 1865 and not revoked until 1896, "is one of the best documented examples of government regulation limiting progress, for by 1896 France was alight with the personal automobile." In Great Britain, he wrote, "the King's highways were largely limited to horses and horse-drawn liveries and conveyances."[19]

It turned out that the Red Flag act and the opponents of motor vehicles were ultimately overwhelmed by the innate desire of humankind to find faster, more comfortable, and more efficient means for getting around. The law kept the stagecoach and stable people in business longer, and it kept the "common people" walking and cleaning up after the horses.[20] But the consequences were not in the same league as those of the CAFE law.

How We Got into This Mess

Why would Congress pass and the president sign a law that would increase the risk of injury and death on the highways of America? In October 1973, Egypt launched a surprise military attack against Israel. Other Arab countries soon joined in the conflict, including Syria, equipped with substantial armaments supplied by the Soviet Union. (Occurring on the eve of the Jewish calendar's holiest day, it is known as the Yom Kippur War.) With the help of military supplies from the United States and other countries, the Israelis defeated the Arab forces, for the third time since the end of World War II. In their frustration, the Arabs, seeing the United States as responsible for Israel's existence, imposed an oil embargo under the auspices of the Organization of Petroleum Exporting Countries (OPEC).

By March 13, 1974, when the embargo ended, the price of gasoline had jumped by 37 percent, and in many areas it was in short supply. Long lines of desperate motorists formed at the pumps. People aggravated the problem by hoarding gasoline—some in their garages, but most by "topping off" their fuel tanks, thus carrying around in their vehicles much more fuel than had been their habit before the embargo.

Believing their personal mobility to be under severe threat, Americans were immediately angry. In Washington, the answer to any new problem is to propose a new law. When the voters are angry, even the ingenious constitutional system of checks and balances, designed by the founding fathers to avoid hasty and ill-conceived actions, is not always sufficient to protect the country from bad law. CAFE, Washington's response to the oil crises of the 1970s, is a prime example.

As a rallying call for legislative action, "Energy independence!" was first used by President Richard Nixon in late 1973. It was not until the end of 1975 that the Democratic-controlled Congress completed action on the bill that became the Energy Policy and Conservation Act (EPCA). By then, President Nixon was gone and Gerald Ford was in the Oval Office. As president, Mr. Ford had proposed to remove the government's oil price control system, imposed in 1971 by President Nixon and his Treasury secretary, John Connally. This program had subjected domestic oil producers to mandatory price lids on their producing, refining, marketing, and retailing operations. President Ford believed that lifting those controls and letting the market set fuel prices would give oil companies an incentive to produce more in the United States, thus reducing the demand for foreign oil.

Congress saw things differently. Rather than agreeing to less regulation, Congress wanted to regulate everything from the thermostat settings in public buildings to the energy use of refrigerators. The major energy savings, however, were supposed to come from the CAFE scheme, added by Congress to the EPCA bill. CAFE advocates claimed that it would lower oil imports by reducing gasoline use by America's cars and trucks.

A Failed Policy from the Beginning

Paradoxically, the same bill contained another provision that had an opposite and perverse effect. Rejecting the Ford administration's proposal to lift oil price controls, Congress added a provision to the EPCA bill requiring the federal government not only to maintain controls but to roll back the price of domestic oil by a dollar a barrel before February 1976. This roll-back meant gasoline prices would be lower, giving an obvious incentive to motorists to burn more fuel, not less, and it put the burden of conserva-tion on the back of an untested, complex regulatory scheme—CAFE.[21] Since foreign oil was considerably cheaper than U.S.-produced oil, the congressional action was an incentive to import more, not less, oil. In this regard, EPCA's effect was in conflict with conservation. As economist Murray L. Weidenbaum points out, "A freely determined market price for gasoline would have produced far greater conservation than [would] regu-lating [through CAFE] only a small portion of the fuel users: new car owners."[22]

EPCA was passed by Congress and sent to the president in December 1975. Auto manufacturers and others pressed for a veto but were told that, along with EPCA, Congress had sent to the president a union-sponsored "common-site" picketing bill, allowing picketing of entire construction sites in disputes with one contractor. EPCA opponents were told that the presi-dent had been advised he could make only one veto stick. Since the picket-ing bill was opposed by virtually every business organization in the country, the president chose to veto it and reluctantly sign EPCA—and with it, CAFE—into law.[23]

Of course, CAFE has done nothing for U.S. energy independence. Today nearly 50 percent of U.S. oil requirements are imported, up from 35 percent in 1973. Unless it is blocked from entry, cheaper foreign oil will always flow into the U.S. market. That is exactly what has continued to happen. CAFE has not only produced the unintended consequences of higher vehicle costs and higher fatalities and injuries, it has completely failed in achieving the goals for which it was intended. It had no chance of success; when the use of a commodity (such as gasoline) becomes more economi-cal, the natural effect is for more of it to be consumed. When someone can drive more miles with the same amount of fuel, the incentive is to drive more, not less.

Throughout history, American example has often been followed by other nations. Foreign countries, some totally dependent on outside sources for their oil, have had the benefit of observing how CAFE has worked out for the United States over the past two decades. Not a single nation has followed the U.S. lead by adopting a CAFE-type program.

Double Jeopardy—the "Gas Guzzler" Tax. After the regulatory commit-tees of Congress took their bite out of the American automobile with CAFE, the taxing committees wanted their turn. The Carter administration gave them their chance.

At the beginning of the oil shocks, there was much discussion about the most effective way to conserve fuel through government action. There was some talk about a gasoline tax, but elected politicians saw that route as one of high risk—to themselves. (Not only was this route not taken; Congress, as noted earlier, actually rolled back the price of oil when it passed the Energy Policy and Conservation Act of 1975.) The other two routes considered were taxation of cars on the basis of fuel consumption and command-and-control regulations, requiring cars to meet specific fuel use standards. With the passage of EPCA, containing the CAFE regulations, some people assumed that the argument was over. It just took the tax writers longer.

In 1977, the Carter administration proposed a tax based on fuel use. In hearings before Senator Russell B. Long, chairman of the Senate Finance Committee, S. L. Terry of Chrysler called it a "punitive tax on family cars." Fred Secrest of Ford said it would be unfair to a family needing one large car. Senator Long observed, however, that big cars should be taxed "so consumers won't demand them so much." "People would expect to pay a premium for a Cadillac or Lincoln," Senator Long explained, adding, "They should have the privilege of buying a big car but should pay the tax."[24] Of course, most large cars were not luxury models: they were Plymouth, Chevrolet, and Ford sedans or station wagons. Nonetheless, Congress passed the Energy Tax Act of 1978, placing an excise tax on cars under 6,000 pounds in curb weight that did not meet specific mpg levels. This addition of taxation "suspenders" to the CAFE "belt" was meant to get people into more fuel-economic—and therefore smaller—cars as quickly as possible.

In 1980, any car getting below 15 mpg was taxed $200 dollars. The stiffest tax was $550, levied for cars getting 12.5 mpg or fewer. In 1991, this tax was raised to $1,000 for cars getting fewer than 22.4 mpg (using government test procedures). The tax increases incrementally. For example, below 17 mpg, the tax is $3,000 per car; under 12.5 mpg, it is $7,700. Through 1993, this tax added about $1.5 billion to the cost of vehicles purchased by the American public. Now, of course, it is a fiercely defended federal revenue source. As a concept, the excise tax does not prevent consumers from buying the vehicle they think they need—if they are willing and able to pay the extra dollars. The result of CAFE, however, has been that the entire fleet of cars offered to the public is made up of smaller and therefore less safe vehicles.

Who Can We Blame for the Consequences of CAFE?

Congress and the president did not anticipate, when CAFE was enacted in 1975, that it would reduce safety in motor vehicles. The country had just gone through a wrenching period of fuel shortages, and our thoughts were on "energy independence" rather than on the unexpected consequences of this complex set of regulations. Who should have raised the alarm? The car companies saw the problem and testified that CAFE would force the reduction of the size and weight of their cars, but their credibility had been continuously and thoroughly attacked for years by the professional activists and their political allies. The manufacturers may have had the technical experts, but ridicule by the critics received more attention than industry views.

Critics still say that the auto industry "cried wolf" about the potential effect of fuel economy regulation. They refer to an industry representative who, in testimony before Congress in 1974, said that CAFE would force manufacturers to downsize their cars to the size of 1970s compacts like Ford's Pinto or Maverick. The industry is slow and sometimes inept in getting the facts across to the public, but on this point its testimony turned out to be on target. By the 1990 model year, the average auto for sale in the United States had the outside dimensions of a Pinto station wagon and the interior space of a Maverick sedan. Based on exterior dimensions, most 1990 cars would be classified as small cars by 1974 standards. Even the 1996 Cadillac DeVille is the size of the average mid-sized car of the earlier period, and its engine is around 140 cubic inches smaller.

Keith Crain, publisher of *Automotive News*, recalls that when fuel standards were being considered in Washington "some very sober folks mentioned that, yes, you just might be able to save some fuel, but you're going to kill some people in the process." He adds, "Those sober people were laughed out of town, and the problem was ignored ."[25]

Where Were the Safety Advocates?

Where were the professional activists on the issue of small-car–large-car safety? Actually, some of them had recognized the problem and had written about it. Ralph Nader, who made his initial reputation as an advocate of government regulation of auto safety, made the point about small-car safety problems when he attacked the popular Volkswagen Beetle in 1972. In his introduction for a report by the Center for Auto Safety (CAS) entitled "Small—On Safety, the Designed-in Dangers of the Volkswagen," Nader called attention to a study showing that the total weight of major replacement parts (doors, hood, fenders, and rear-quarter panels) of the Beetle was the lowest of those cars considered. This, he wrote, was "a hint, of the VW's abysmal crush characteristics. What may be an economy in a minor collision may lead to a staggering loss in a more serious crash."

The text of that CAS report included this conclusion: "Small size and light weight impose inherent limitations on the degree of safety that can be built into a vehicle. All known studies relating car size to crash injury conclude that occupants of smaller cars run a higher risk of serious or fatal injury than occupants of larger cars." Clarence Ditlow, now head of the Center for Auto Safety, was a contributor to that report. Although the laws of physics have remained unchanged, and there are no studies that show that smaller is safer, Nader and Ditlow have since changed their views.

Another prominent professional activist, who served as President Carter's vehicle safety chief in the late 1970s, was also concerned about the small-car safety problem. Joan Claybrook, a close associate of Ralph Nader's before and after her government service, told the Fifth International Congress on Automotive Safety in 1977, "The most serious general problem is one dictated by the fundamental laws of physics. How do you protect a smaller object from the violence of a collision with a larger one?" At that time, she reflected an understanding of the underlying laws of physics.

When focused on vehicle size and safety, these activists were on the right track. They were in a position to help steer the nation away from a policy that has resulted in the very problem they had exposed—that is, the effects of forcing greater numbers of smaller cars on the American public. Unfortunately, Nader, Claybrook, and Ditlow failed to meet the challenge. Ignoring their own work—and all serious studies of the issue—they left safety behind and became three of the most vocal advocates of CAFE.

Motives are always difficult, if not impossible, to discover. Perhaps the lure of CAFE, a program that gave government extensive control over the personal motor vehicle, was too tempting. Perhaps the thought of using fuel economy regulation as a modern-day Red Flag act to get more people out of the automobile was an adequate trade-off for the general reduction in vehicle safety that would result from CAFE. Certainly it was not global warming that drove the issue; at the time CAFE was enacted, scientists were concerned about global cooling. It is hard to believe that the elusive goal of "energy independence" could have lured serious safety advocates to throw out what was well known—and what they themselves had said— about small-car safety. It is all the more remarkable because knowledgeable analysts knew that energy independence could not be achieved without oil import barriers, escalating fuel prices, and a consequent radical reduction of energy use.[26]

Today, CAFE advocates argue that smaller cars can be made safer with new technology. They are right. Safety belts when properly used have helped, and air bags have provided supplemental protection (although they, like CAFE, have drastic, unintended consequences of their own). Improved structural integrity and programmed crushability have made small cars safer. A new small car may offer more safety protection than did many larger cars of past decades. In her lobbying effort on behalf of tighter CAFE standards in 1991, however, Joan Claybrook took liberties with this fact. "Small cars," she said, "are designed to crumple on impact, absorbing the energy of the crash and saving the lives of those within."[27] Of course, what she did not say is that large cars are designed in the same way. The fact remains that large cars with belts, bags, and other technologies are safer than smaller cars equipped with the same technologies.

The Nader-founded Center for Auto Safety (CAS), headed by Clarence Ditlow, made the same slippery argument in a report released April 9, 1991, to support pending legislation that would have set CAFE standards at 40 miles per gallon. In attempting to explain how this proposal would not increase safety risks, the report said, "Recent contributions to improvements in vehicle safety include the greater use of available restraints, particularly in small cars, the greater number of mid-size cars, the 1977 to 1986 reduction in the number and weight of large cars and the introduction of passive (padded) interiors." The theme again is that if these same technologies are not added to larger cars, smaller cars are comparatively made safer, thus compensating for their smaller size and weight. The additional suggestion that a "reduction in the number and weight of large cars" is among "recent contributions to improvements in vehicle safety" is a cynical rejection of Ditlow's earlier views about safety problems of small, light cars, views that were consistent with the laws of physics.[28]

Two often-quoted critics—John DeCicco of the American Council for an Energy-Efficient Economy (an activist group), and Marc Ross, a professor at the University of Michigan—try to take the argument a bit further. They have said, "Some opponents of fuel economy regulation assert that decreasing mass decreases safety."[29] (That is certainly true.) They added: "But the protective benefit of heavier automobiles" (so, mass must protect the occupants of the larger car!) "comes at the expense of greater damage to people." The sum of their argument is that people who protect themselves and their companions by driving larger cars are endangering those who choose to drive smaller cars—if the two vehicles should collide. They assert that "cars built with lightweight but strong materials can shield passengers more effectively than can many heavier vehicles of today, yet they pose less risk to the occupants of other cars during collision."

This statement is partially true, but DeCicco and Ross cannot escape Newtonian mechanics that explain the advantage for an occupant of a larger, heavier car. Also, if a car is built with lightweight, stronger materials yet retains its size and weight, it would be even safer.

Larger Is Safer

More to the point, studies also show that when two smaller cars of equal weight crash head-on at equal speed, the risk of driver death or injury is about twice as great as when two cars, each twice as heavy as the first cars, experience the same type of crash.[30] This means that even if all cars were of the same size and weight, thus eliminating one car's advantage over another, occupants would still be safer if all those cars were larger and heavier than if they were smaller and lighter.

Twenty-two percent of occupant fatalities occur in two-car crashes. Twenty-five percent occur when cars crash into other vehicles—mostly trucks. In a crash with a truck, mass is a critical factor. All other things being equal, a vehicle with more weight and size offers more protection to its occupants.

Around 45 percent of fatalities result from single-car crashes, and of these, 27 percent are deaths in non-rollover crashes. Eighteen percent occur in rollover crashes. In addition to the added safety larger vehicles by their mass provide to their occupants, greater vehicle length and width (between the left and right wheels) provide greater stability and help to prevent rollovers. Studies also show that in both rollover and non-rollover crashes, the lighter and smaller the car, the greater the risk to the occupant.

There appears to be no precise way to measure the individual or relative importance of size as compared with weight. Each factor brings important characteristics to a crash. In a head-on crash of two identical cars, an occupant changes his or her forward speed instantly, going from the prior speed of the vehicle to zero in a fraction of a second. The forces that result from that abrupt deceleration can determine the degree of harm the occupant may suffer. Larger-sized vehicles provide more structure to absorb the forces of the crash, giving the occupant a more constant rate of deceleration and, consequently, reducing the harm to that occupant. The mass, or weight, of the vehicle also generally gives the occupant more time to decelerate at a less harmful rate. A heavy car does this by moving, bending, or breaking the object struck in the crash, whether it is a tree or a wall or another vehicle.

In his book on alternative cars for the future, Robert Q. Riley writes, "In a two-way crash the vehicle with the lowest mass receives the greatest blow, and matters get worse as mass differential increases. Smaller cars also overturn more often as a result of an accident."[31] Riley also says that "designs for increasing low-mass vehicle safety must ultimately rely more on crash avoidance countermeasures." As an authority on energy-efficient automobile design, Riley is an enthusiast for small cars. He reluctantly adds that, "Given equal technology, a low-mass car will likely remain the less crashworthy design."

DeCicco and Ross point out, correctly, that cars built with "lightweight but strong materials" can be structurally better than current cars. As Riley and other safety experts know, however, larger cars built with those same materials will be safer than smaller ones, and they can provide the "protective benefit of heavier automobiles." Safety experts advise that there are no crashes in which the occupants are at a lower safety risk in a lighter or smaller car than in a heavier, larger one with *equivalent safety features*. As the National Highway Traffic Safety administrator Jerry Ralph Curry said in 1991, when more stringent CAFE laws were being considered in Congress, "The laws of physics cannot be legislated away."

One of the attributes of safety technology most prized by activists is that it be "passive." In vehicle safety, passive equipment refers to a device or structure that would do its job with no action needed by the vehicle occupant. This feature attracted early supporters of the air bag. These same activists, however, fail to acknowledge that size and weight provide built-in safety. In fact, together they are the most important passive safety features available.

From the data on deaths in cars of different sizes, we can see that, compared with a car that has a less-than 95-inch wheelbase, a car with a wheelbase of 95–99 inches offers a 21 percent reduction in the risk of death in a crash. In a car with a wheelbase greater than 114 inches, the reduction in risk of death as compared with that of the car with a wheelbase of under 95 inches is about 60 percent. That is excellent passive protection.

By contrast, air bags reduce a belted driver's risk of death in a crash by only 9 percent.[32] Unfortunately, air bags also kill people. Since 1990, eighty-three people, including forty-five children, have died from the effects of air bag deployments. The adults who died were predominantly women of small stature, and the children were younger than thirteen years of age. Since the federal government rules mandate that all cars and most light trucks will come equipped with air bags, these very identifiable groups of vehicle occupants are put at serious risk of death.

The response by the government to this risk is to say that all children under thirteen should never sit in the front seat of a vehicle.[33] They should sit in the back seat, first, to avoid a mandated safety device—the air bag—that may harm or even kill them. Second, they should sit in the back because the rear seat is safest when the vehicle is involved in a frontal crash. It isn't just children who are safer in the back seat. All occupants of the car would be safer in the back seat. It is safest precisely because there is more vehicle structure in front of the occupant. More structure will absorb more crash energy, preventing it from causing harm to the occupant. Ironically, it is vehicle structure that is reduced to build the smaller and lighter cars required to meet another government mandate—CAFE. What a tangled web we weave when first we regulate!

The Right to Choose

Even if President Gerald Ford had successfully vetoed the bill setting up CAFE, people would still buy small cars. They should have that choice. The fatality rate for motorcyclists is seventeen times higher than the rate for occupants of other motor vehicles, but there is no plan to outlaw motor-cycles—as there should not be. Bicycling in traffic can be dangerous, but it is permitted, even encouraged. Helmets, safe driving habits, and other concepts can save more lives, but people, not government, should have the basic right to choose their mode of transportation.

When the price of gasoline spiked upward in the 1970s and gasoline was scarce at the pump, car buyers rushed to acquire smaller, more fuel-economical cars. As the oil scare subsided the demand for larger cars returned, but many people continue to buy small cars; they are generally cheaper, they take up less space and so are easier to park, and they can usually save money on gasoline.

People on tight budgets are highly sensitive to the price of gasoline and the mileage of the cars they drive. They also have a pretty good idea of the trade-off between more economical cars and larger ones, including the question of safety. Instinctively, they know that a larger vehicle has a safety advantage over a smaller one.[34] All car buyers should and generally do take these factors into consideration when they choose the vehicle that best meets their needs. Some will buy small cars; others, even some with tight budgets, prefer larger, less fuel-efficient vehicles. They may do this to accommodate their families and to provide comfort, utility, and safety. They may balance the higher purchase and operating costs of larger cars by planning their trips more carefully and driving less. These are the choices and decisions made every day in the marketplace.

The CAFE program, unhappily, takes these decisions away from the citizen and places them under the control of the government. There is an enormous difference between an individual's choosing to accept the risks of driving a smaller car and the government's forcing that decision on the individual. Under CAFE, this loss of personal choice is accomplished by stealth. The government sets the fuel-use rules, and the automobile manufacturers must become the agents of the government in implementing those rules. To do so, the manufacturers have had to reduce average vehicle weight and performance. As a result, they must offer the public cars and light trucks that meet what the government wants, not what the customer wants.

Because people do not want to buy smaller cars in the numbers necessary to meet CAFE standards, manufacturers must price their vehicles to ensure that they sell enough small cars to offset the sales of larger ones and keep their fuel-economy average above the government requirements. They do this by lowering the prices of small cars, often losing money on them, while raising the prices of larger cars. Their purpose, driven by CAFE, is both to drive customers to smaller cars and to subsidize those cars.[35] This is an unhappy circumstance for the auto manufacturer, worker, and stockholder, but it is an even more unfortunate arrangement for the customer. If car buyers want their families to have cars with the safety provided by adequate size, weight, and performance—those factors that give the president of the United States the protection he needs in a car—then they must pay a premium to do so. Those who can afford it pay the price. Those who cannot are paying another kind of price—settling for a vehicle that is less useful and less safe than they would otherwise have chosen. All this is done by a regulatory program that attempts to accomplish its goals by indirection, not with full disclosure.

The downsizing of America's vehicle fleet and the attendant reduction in the protection offered by these vehicles were not the result of the conscious decisions of Americans to buy smaller cars. Most citizens have no knowledge of the CAFE program or how it works, nor do they understand that it is limiting their ability to buy larger cars. The advocates of CAFE have sold it as a free lunch, suggesting that it is providing car buyers with higher mileage cars, at no additional cost or penalty. But CAFE is in fact a public policy of the U.S. government that deliberately forces car manufacturers to offer cars that are less safe than they would be if those manufacturers were permitted to listen to the voice of the customer. Instead they must listen to commands of the government.

What most Americans actually want in a car is quite clear. It is reflected, appropriately, in the evaluation of new models by *Consumer Reports*. One of the magazine's 1995 "recommended" vehicles was the Buick Regal, about which the magazine's evaluator said, "The 3.8-liter V-6 performs better than the standard 3.1-liter V-6 and is worth the modest penalty in fuel economy." Another "recommended" car was the "big, quiet, softly sprung" Buick Le Sabre. The Chrysler Cirrus "offers roomy seating." In the Camaro, "The V-8's effortless thrust makes the adequate V-6 seem sluggish." For the Dodge Stratus, "The optional 2.5-liter V-6 provides lively acceleration." In the Ford Aspire, "The 1.3-liter Four is painfully slow." In the Volvo 940, "The base 2.3-liter Four is sluggish," and "an optional turbocharger increases performance dramatically." In the Oldsmobile Eighty Eight, "The V-6 accelerates responsively." The "recommended" Nissan 300ZX has "blazing acceleration."

This theme is continued in the *Consumer Reports* evaluation of 1997 models. With the Buick Park Avenue 240-hp supercharged V-6, "Acceleration is effortless." The "roomy" Chevrolet Malibu offers both a "2.4-liter Four and 3.1-liter V-6 (a better choice)." The large Chrysler LHS V-6 delivers "spirited acceleration," while the small Ford Aspire "accelerates painfully slowly." The large Ford Crown Victoria's V-8 "cruises effortlessly," while the small Geo Metro's "three-cylinder engine is underpowered."

The editors of *Consumer Reports* understand what their readers want to know about cars. But the features that the magazine has pinpointed as being of interest to car buyers—good performance and adequate size—are in direct conflict with the CAFE requirements. That is why the auto manufacturers say that meeting those legal requirements puts them in "conflict with the customer." Interestingly, *Consumer Reports* is published by Consumers Union, whose Board of Directors includes Joan Claybrook and Clarence Ditlow and once included Ralph Nader, all of whom advocate policies that deny the customer the attributes he or she wants in a vehicle, and all of whom have lobbied for passage of a bill that would have increased fleet-average fuel-economy requirements to 40 mpg or more.

How the American people *want* to travel and what vehicles they *want* to drive is not important to professional activists and their political allies, who want to reengineer our society. They would prefer that people walk, bicycle, or take mass transit.

Since the critics cannot accomplish their goal directly, their first step has been to attempt to require Americans to drive cars that get 40 or more miles per gallon. In session after session of the U.S. Congress, these critics have consistently pushed for legislation that would raise CAFE standards to that level or higher. Ironically, if these activists and the politicians who sponsor such legislation want cars that get 40 mpg, there is no need to pass a law. They can buy them today. Unfortunately, the manufacturers that have produced these cars have immediately encountered that "conflict with the customer." In other words, they don't sell so well, even to the activists and politicians, and even when the manufacturer offers them at a money-losing price.

No Free Lunch at This CAFE

If asked whether he or she would like a prospective new car to get 40 miles per gallon and still meet all his or her other needs, any consumer would say "Yes." This is what CAFE advocates promise—a no-cost, penalty-free boost in fuel economy provided through government regulation. Of course, like all purveyors of the proverbial free lunch, they cannot deliver. The most important cost of CAFE regulations is the loss of safety. As Ralph Nader said in an interview with *Women's Day*, "Larger cars are safer—there is more bulk to protect the occupant."[36] The costs of CAFE include a loss of the protection by that "bulk."

American car buyers also are paying hidden "taxes" as a result of CAFE. In the attempt to cut sufficient weight to meet CAFE standards while retaining the size people want in a car, manufacturers are using lightweight and higher-cost materials. Peter Pestillo, executive vice president of Ford, pointed this out, saying, "To help meet CAFE requirements, Ford is using aluminum mini-spare tires to reduce weight in products like the Ford Taurus—at a customer cost of $70, for a savings of less than a gallon of gas a year. Many such CAFE-driven actions amount to a hidden tax on consumers."[37]

Saad Abouzahr, a materials executive at Chrysler, says weight reduction, by substituting aluminum and other lightweight materials for conventional steel, can provide "dramatic gains" in fuel efficiency, but pound for pound, aluminum can be up to four times as expensive as steel.[38]

Penny Wise and Pound Foolish. CAFE proponents make the claim that increasing fuel economy is cost-beneficial to the consumer. Studies have shown that an 8 percent increase in fuel economy can be achieved by reducing a vehicle's weight by 10 percent. To reduce vehicle weight, auto manufacturers substitute aluminum parts for iron ones. While these substitutions do increase fuel economy, the amount of money consumers save in fuel over the lifetime of their vehicles is often less than the added fixed cost of using aluminum components. For example, if the manufacturer of a 3,500-pound car that achieves a CAFE rating of 28 mpg elects to reduce vehicle weight by 4 pounds by replacing a $5 iron component with its $20 aluminum counterpart, the added fixed cost amounts to $15. A 4-pound weight reduction increases mileage by only 0.09 percent. If the average car travels 12,000 miles per year and gasoline is priced at $1.20 a gallon, the consumer saves only 55 cents a year in fuel. At this rate, it would take more than twenty-seven years for the switch to prove economically beneficial. By that time the car would have been junked and recycled.

Car buyers are not being compensated in gasoline savings what they are paying to get fuel savings from high-cost materials substitution—but they do not know that. The government has made the decisions requiring these costs in a manner never fully revealed to the public for validation.

Equally hidden from the public view is the additional cost that family-size–car buyers must pay to get a car that meets their needs. A customer wanting a larger car frequently must pay an additional cost hidden in the price of that car, the purpose of which is to induce him or her to buy a smaller car or a less powerful engine, so that the manufacturer can meet the CAFE law. In effect, the buyer must override the voice of the government by paying more than he or she would pay if there were no CAFE. There is no free lunch.

There are no available figures to demonstrate just how much car buyers are paying in penalties for cars that meet their needs rather than meet the requirements of the social engineers who think they know what people should have. Pricing a car or truck is an art, not a science, and it involves many factors. Also, of course, the manufacturer's suggested retail price is often only the beginning of the process of establishing the final price of the purchase. Manufacturers are not anxious even to discuss how much they spend to subsidize the sale of their small cars with revenue from larger cars or trucks and vans, but the number is very likely in the billions of dollars.

Michelle Malkin, columnist for the *Seattle Times*, said it well: "Large-car buyers (regardless of how little they drive) end up subsidizing small-car drivers who benefit from artificially lowered prices (regardless of how much they drive)."[39]

A figure that *is* available is the cost to the car buyer of fines paid by foreign manufacturers for *not* meeting CAFE requirements. Mercedes Benz, for example, has never met the CAFE standards, and since 1987 it has paid more than $135 million in fines. Volvo is another company that does not meet the standards, and it has paid $32 million in fines. Other companies paying fines include Porsche, BMW, Range Rover, and Jaguar.[40] These companies, which supply a small percentage of the U.S. market, simply plan not to meet the CAFE rules. As foreign-based companies, they are not vulnerable to the same range of civil lawsuits as U.S. companies. The costs of their fines, of course, are offset by charging higher prices to American purchasers.[41]

Another cost of CAFE is the value of those features the car buyer wants but cannot get because of the regulations. Called *deadweight losses* by the economists, these costs are exceedingly hard to estimate. If someone wants a car that will carry himself, his wife, four children, and the family dog, he may be willing to leave the dog at home, but he still needs a six-passenger vehicle with the power to move it at an adequate rate of speed and with enough size and weight to protect his family. Thanks to CAFE, he will not have the full range of vehicles and power trains to choose from—at the price he would pay in the absence of CAFE. How much deadweight loss he incurs by buying a vehicle slower and smaller than he wanted is hard to calculate, and it may be a loss that some social engineers (who would prefer that he not drive at all) believe to be desirable.

The most effective way to achieve conservation is to raise the price of what we are trying to conserve. Most economists argue that increasing the price of gasoline would be the most effective way of conserving it. If our political leaders really want conservation, then, why doesn't Congress raise taxes on energy? In their 1995 book *The Extra Mile*, Nivola and Crandall explain: "Representing an overwhelmingly automobile-dependent urban population, Congress cannot comfortably vote to impose highly visible costs on motorists. Hence, it finesses its commitment to conserving motor fuel by resorting to indirect techniques, such as CAFE standards, with delegated enforcement functions (to auto manufacturers) and concealed costs."[42]

Not only are the CAFE standards driving America into unnecessary highway fatalities and injuries: customers are paying extra for the privilege.

There is much talk about the adverse externalities, or side effects, of cars and trucks. The prime example is pollution of the air, which is not paid for by the car buyer or seller. While there are legitimate concerns about these externalities, there is another set that receives little attention—the adverse side effects or externalities of government programs and policies. Loss of safety through CAFE is a major example.

· 3 ·

CAFE, IMPORTS, AND JOBS—MORE UNINTENDED CONSEQUENCES

Any discussion of international trade in recent years includes a call for "fairness." Protectionists and free traders alike call for access to the markets of those who sell in this country. Democratic House Leader Dick Gephardt, Pat Buchanan, Ross Perot, labor unions, many industries, and even Ralph Nader have all expressed concern over any disadvantage American products, and the jobs to produce them, might suffer as a result of America's trading relationships. With this background it is hard to imagine that the federal government would adopt a policy that actually gives foreign products a substantial advantage over competing products made in America.

Just as it is reasonable to assume that the government did not intend to make cars and trucks less safe by passing CAFE, it should be reasonable to assume that the government did not intend to put American industry at a competitive disadvantage with foreign producers. Nonetheless, that is exactly what happened. The beneficiaries were the Japanese car manufacturers. That is no cause to bash the Japanese. They merely took advantage of a public policy that the U. S. government unwittingly handed them on a silver platter. It takes a little history to show how it worked.

In the early 1970s, automobiles made in Japan were predominantly small, for a set of good reasons. Space is at a premium in Japan, a country with a total area smaller in size than California. The surface of the main islands of Japan consists mainly of mountains and narrow valleys. There are 701,000 miles of roads and streets in Japan; in the United States there are 3,900,000 miles. Parking is at a premium in overcrowded Tokyo. In order to license a vehicle there, the owner must show proof of the rights to an adequate off-street parking space. Most important, for many years gasoline in Japan has been around three times as expensive as in the United States, thanks largely to very high Japanese fuel taxes. Also, until the 1990s there was a substantial tax penalty for larger cars with larger engines.

For all these reasons, the cars traditionally bought by the Japanese consumer were small. When the Japanese manufacturers began to export motor vehicles, those small cars were the first they sent to the United States and other world markets. In the 1960s and early 1970s in the United States, which had a cheap oil policy, they sold poorly.

In early 1973, small Japanese imports were piling up on the docks of American ports. The supply of all small cars—already built and on the way to market—was sufficient to meet U.S. demand for about 120 days. By contrast, the target of car manufacturers was to have about a 60-day supply in the pipeline. Large cars, however, were in great demand, with a "day-supply" rate of about 40. Clearly the American industry, at that point, was more successful in offering what American consumers wanted—large cars. While U.S. automakers were full-line manufacturers—making cars of all sizes—they were overwhelmingly concentrated in the larger cars their customers were demanding.[1]

War, Oil, and Imports

Interventions by governments thousands of miles away changed the American market swiftly and radically. When the Arab oil embargo following the Yom Kippur War drove the price of gasoline from around 38 cents a gallon to 52 cents a gallon by March 1974, it also drove customers out of new car show rooms. The president of the American Petroleum Institute predicted that the so-called energy crisis would last "as long as most of us will live," adding, "We will have to adopt a whole new way of life. The love affair of the American with the large car," he said, " has come to an end."[2]

For a while, he appeared to be right. Sales of large cars dropped by 35 percent. Auto stocks fell. Some 135,000 auto workers were laid off. Skyrocketing energy prices brought both high inflation and high unemployment. A new term—*stagflation*—was coined to describe the economy, which had quickly sunk into the worst slump since the Great Depression.

The people needing to buy cars generally wanted more fuel-economic and, therefore, smaller models. Almost overnight, the Japanese manufacturers had an unexpected edge—not because of any brilliant planning or superior technology, but because small cars were what they traditionally made and what they had on hand. And the price was right. While the total U.S. car market was sharply declining, Japanese passenger cars began to take a larger share. In 1973, the Japanese manufacturers had 6.5 percent of the U.S. passenger car market. By 1975, they had increased that share to

9.4 percent, and in 1977 it reached 12.4 percent. In fuel economy, the Japanese car fleet led the U.S.-made fleet of passenger cars in the 1975 model year with an average of 23.4 mpg, the American-made cars averaging 13.2 mpg. The average weight of the 1975 U.S. car was 4,400 pounds, and 58 percent of them were powered by an eight-cylinder engine. The Japanese models were considerably smaller, with an average weight of 2,500 pounds, and they were powered predominately by four-cylinder engines.

Then came the next governmental intervention, this one from Washington. As mentioned above, the government wrung its hands over the "crisis" and produced the Energy Policy and Conservation Act (EPCA), with its CAFE scheme and with its anticonservation rollback of domestic oil prices. While the auto industry vigorously opposed the enactment of the complex regulatory structure of EPCA, there was a consensus in the industry and throughout the country that oil supply was in decline. Despite the U.S. government's cheap oil policy, analysts believed prices would be forced steadily upward and would move car buyers to buy more fuel-economical vehicles.

Experts in the Nixon, Ford, and Carter administrations, as well as those in Congress and in the private sector, had predicted a growing worldwide oil shortage and ever-higher gasoline prices. Small-car sales went up dramatically, and the average fuel economy of the fleet of cars sold in America rose accordingly. This was before CAFE was in effect; it was the marketplace at work.

Very few people saw the oil crisis as a temporary phenomenon. Even former secretary of state Henry Kissinger as late as 1982 wrote, "Since the first price explosion of 1973, we have learned that the energy crisis is not a mere problem of transitional adjustment: it is a grave challenge to the political and economic structure of the free world."[3] A task force of representatives from business, academia, and labor formed by the Twentieth Century Fund reported that it was "convinced the challenge posed by the energy crisis requires the same kind of response that motivated the nation in organizing economic recovery during the Great Depression and mobilization for war following Pearl Harbor."[4]

An exception to the chorus of doom came from the *Economist* magazine, and the reasons for the magazine's dissent are noteworthy. In a 1974 editorial entitled "The Coming Glut of Energy," the *Economist* observed, "There is a case for arguing that the world is likely to be glutted with energy before the end of this decade." The writer turned out to be correct in this, but the main point of the article was that if the world would allow the market for energy to function and governments did not meddle too much, the energy supply would soon be quite adequate.[5]

Other, less serious-minded skeptics believed the oil shortage was the product of a conspiracy of oil company executives. Rumors abounded about fleets of oil tankers anchored just beyond the horizon off the East coast, waiting until prices soared before landing their cargo. (One oil executive's private comment was especially memorable. He said, "If only the charges were true! Then the government could just take a few of us out and shoot us and the energy problem would be solved.")

In the midst of this national anxiety, Jimmy Carter was elected president. He saw energy as his priority problem, and in April 1977 he announced his program, calling it the "moral equivalent of war" (unhappily dubbed with the acronym "Meow" by the media). The program was a hodgepodge of proposals, but one made very good sense—the decontrol of oil prices. The good advice from the *Economist* seemed to have been heard. At the same time as the president announced decontrol, however, he called for a "windfall profits tax" on the "excess" of oil company earnings. Thus he managed to irritate the liberals with prospects of price decontrol, which would stimulate oil production as prices went up, but he also irritated the conservatives with the tax, which would dampen the oil production incentives of decontrol.

Contrary to expectations, the supply of gasoline returned to normal after the Arab oil embargo ended and American consumers again began to buy larger cars. By December 1978, imports were again stacking up in the ports and in the dealerships. The day-supply rate of imports hit 154. Large-car supplies were at around 60 days, the target that most manufacturers attempt to maintain.

The Ayatollah Weighs In

In January 1979, a third government-related action turned the energy world on its ear. The shah of Iran was deposed from his Peacock throne and the Ayatollah Ruhollah Khomeini seized power.[6] As turmoil took over Teheran, oil exports from that country were interrupted and the crisis mentality about the oil supply returned. While the effect on oil supplies was significant—Iran was the second-largest exporter of oil—it was not as serious as many in the U.S. government claimed. The ensuing worldwide disruption was driven not by reality but by panic. Buyers around the world, fearing a repetition of the shortages experienced during the Arab boycott, scrambled to build up their inventories. They bought not only to ensure they would have oil but also because they believed oil prices would soar. In effect they created the shortages.

As panic spread and lines began to form again at the pumps, the call for action became overwhelming. Believing that a few smart people in Washington could handle the situation better than could market forces, the U.S. government jumped in. Instead of letting higher prices direct oil to the people and places that valued it the most, a Washington bureaucracy once more was called on to manage the very complex operations of the oil industry, attempting to decide who got which oil to refine and whether it went to heating, transportation, or some other purpose. The government also determined how much gasoline each station got to sell. (Price controls on U.S. oil, unfortunately, were still in effect. The rise in the price of gasoline came as the price of oil imports shot up.) Plans for implementing gasoline rationing were drawn up. Rationing coupons were printed and made ready, but fortunately were never used.

This meddling resulted in a completely muddled marketplace. The government's allocation system was based on historical patterns. (What other rationale could a bureaucracy have used?) As a result, some outlets, mostly rural, received more gasoline than they could use; others, mostly in growing urban areas, received too little. For example, tourist centers like Williamsburg, Virginia, had plenty of gasoline, while tourism dried up; 100 miles away, people waited in long lines to get a 5-gallon allotment. The program did not have the flexibility to adjust for changing patterns. The public returned again to hoarding by topping off their gas tanks whenever possible. (This not only took more fuel out of the distribution system than normally would be the case but also added weight to the vehicle, making it less fuel economical.)

With American consumers already angry and upset, the country and President Carter suffered another energy-related blow. On March 28, 1979, radioactive water flooded the building housing the reactor at the Three Mile Island Nuclear Plant in Harrisburg, Pennsylvania. The plant was shut down for repairs, and although there were no injuries, nuclear energy as a future source of energy independence received a public relations setback from which, unfortunately, it has never recovered. For President Carter, the worst was still to come. In November, Iranian "students" seized the U.S. Embassy in Teheran, and the U.S. staff was held in captivity until the Carter administration ended in January 1981.

Automakers Respond to "Permanent" Oil Shortage

These events had a searing effect on the car market in the United States. For the American manufacturers, there was a scramble to cut vehicle size and weight as quickly as possible and to take performance out of the powertrain. As gasoline prices in America rose, the Americans dedicated their best engineers and massive financial resources to downsizing virtually every vehicle they offered for sale.

In the first years after the "crisis," this rush to smaller cars was driven by the rapid market changes created by the disruption of oil supply from Iran and OPEC countries. The first CAFE standards were largely irrelevant. They called for an average 18 mpg for 1978 model-year cars. (Incremental increases were scheduled for later years, reaching 27.5 mpg in 1985.) Light-truck standards started at 15.8 mpg for 1979 models, and were to rise to 20.7 mpg by 1985. Because the crisis mentality drove people into smaller cars, the average fuel economy of fleets built by American manufacturers in the first few years of regulation actually exceeded the requirements of the CAFE law. Karl Hausker, then chief economist for the U.S. Senate Energy and Natural Resources Committee, wrote in 1991, "CAFE standards had little effect on fuel economy in the late 1970s and early 1980s. During that period, market forces led to fuel economy levels higher than the standards."[7]

In the auto industry, the pessimism about oil supply and gasoline prices led to optimism about meeting future CAFE requirements. The rapid consumer switch from large to smaller cars after the Iranian revolution convinced automakers that the small car would dominate the market if the government did not meddle with gasoline prices, which had risen about 50 percent between 1978 and 1980. Reflective of this view was the announcement by General Motors in 1980 that it was committed "to achieving a fleet fuel economy average of 31 miles per gallon by 1985 with a fully redesigned lineup of U.S. cars."[8]

This announcement by Elliott M. Estes, president of GM, meant that GM was committing itself to exceed, by nearly 13 percent, the government's fleet-1985 mileage standards of 27.5 mpg. In making this unusual announcement, Estes explained two points: "First, that the market is now way ahead of the government's fuel economy standards, and, second, that standards are unnecessary if the government will allow the price of motor fuel to reflect its real world value."

There were, it turned out, two major errors in Estes's analysis. First, the effect of the Iranian oil shock had already begun to wear off. Oil supplies began to increase, panic subsided, and prices stabilized. As a result, the market for small cars was beginning to slow and larger cars were gaining in market share. Americans, it turned out, did not like to be confined in smaller vehicles with less power and lower performance.

Second, while government controls of oil prices had held gasoline prices in the United States below world prices, when these controls were dropped, the "real world value" of oil turned out to be much lower than Estes or virtually anyone else anticipated. In his comments, Estes said the GM forecasts were based on $2.00- to $2.25-a-gallon gasoline. Prices never came near that level, which in 1995 dollars would have been more than $4.00 a gallon. Gasoline prices peaked in 1980 at 34 percent over 1974 levels and then began a long decline. Estes was one among many who was wrong on this point. In January 1981, Congressman Edward Markey said he was concerned with the projection that gasoline prices would reach $1.65 per gallon by spring. He also opposed the decontrol of oil prices, saying,

"Decontrol means handing a blank check to the oil companies and asking OPEC to fill in the amount."[9] The *New York Times* reported, "Consumer groups put the likely increase [attributable to decontrol] at 10¢–13¢ by the end of the summer."[10] These predictions turned out to be incorrect. In large part this was because OPEC, like most cartels, could not hold the line. To increase their own revenues, several individual members dropped their oil prices, proving once again that "real world" value is not what we say it is or wish it to be, but what willing buyers and sellers in the market determine it to be.

In congressional testimony in 1985, Marina v. N. Whitman, vice president and chief economist of General Motors, said, "Most critically, 1985 gasoline prices have not come close to the $2.00–$2.50 per gallon in 1985 anticipated by some experts just four years ago. In fact, inflation-adjusted retail fuel prices have dropped about 25 percent since 1981. Also, the projected shortage of world oil supplies anticipated by many experts has not occurred."[11] In a 1995 review of the mid-1970s, Alfred C. Decrane, Jr., CEO of Texaco, Inc., said, "Alleged experts predicted crude oil prices of $50 to $60 a barrel and beyond. Others claimed world oil reserves would dry up within fifty years. . . . Well, they were wrong. Today oil is selling for about $17 a barrel. . . . Global reserves have increased by 60 percent . . . and we continue to add to our reserve base."[12]

In 1997 there was still no shortage, and while prices fluctuate, gasoline often sells for less than bottled water in the grocery store. This teaches an important lesson in recognizing how vastly wrong the experts—private and government—can be, and how much mischief their errors can create when they are used to plan either public policies or product programs. All the best computer-run forecasting models in the world cannot compensate for flawed assumptions, and rarely do our assumptions about the future turn out to be correct.

An Object Lesson for General Motors. GM's experience with its personal luxury cars demonstrates the point. For years, the Cadillac El Dorado, the Buick Riviera, and the Oldsmobile Toronado, known internally as the "E" cars, were popular in the market and highly profitable. Faced with the so-called oil crisis as well as a consensus about rising oil prices and mindful of the impending implementation of CAFE rules, GM completely reengineered these cars—twice. The 1979 models were 14 inches shorter than the 1978s, 1,000 pounds lighter, and had 4.0 mpg better mileage. Reaching the market as gasoline prices were moving up, these downsized vehicles were a great success.

Looking to the 1980s, with gasoline prices at record highs and CAFE standards moving upward each year, GM's product planners took another 425 pounds and 16 inches off the E cars, gaining 3.0 mpg in fuel economy.

Demonstrating a textbook lesson about the effect of lead time (that is, what can happen in the time it takes to get a car from the drawing boards to the customer), when these 1986 model vehicles hit the market, gasoline prices were tumbling. In 1986, prices fell 25 percent from their 1985 level.

With gasoline availability and price no longer constituting significant concerns, customers focused on the fact that the E cars were no longer the imposing, powerful personal statements they had been, and the customers reacted by keeping their old cars or buying luxury imports. Sales of these vehicles fell from 200,000 annually to 80,000 in 1986, a severe financial blow for GM. Japanese manufacturers Toyota and Nissan jumped into the breach with their new Lexus and Infiniti models, substantially larger than any previous vehicles they had produced for export. The Germans made important gains with the BMW and Mercedes Benz. None of these manufacturers felt constrained by the CAFE law in what type of vehicles they sold in the United States. Only the full-line American manufacturers were affected, and for them, it was a severe problem.

CAFE: A Boon for the Japanese. In her 1985 testimony, Marina Whitman told Congress: "The combination of ample petroleum supplies, which has been characterized as a glut, and gasoline prices approaching $1.00 per gallon have caused a strong resurgence in consumer demand for family-size cars and cars capable of pulling trailers." As gasoline prices fell sharply, Ford and General Motors were hampered, by increasingly stringent CAFE requirements, in being able to answer the customer's call for more size and performance.[13] Instead, they had to respond to the government call for the reverse. One of the major unintended consequences of the CAFE solution to the oil crisis was to cement into U.S. regulatory law the advantage that the OPEC oil embargo and the Iranian revolution had given Japanese auto manufacturers. After the oil crisis and the enactment of the CAFE law, the American manufacturers had to scramble, investing huge resources, both money and engineering talent, in downsizing their vehicles, even though their customers were going in the opposite direction.

Over the next several years, Japanese reengineering was dedicated not to downsizing but to the reverse. Their engineers and designers were busy producing larger cars with higher performance. In some years, their fleet fuel economy actually declined. (In 1982 Japanese new-vehicle fuel economy was an average of 30.5 mpg. By 1988 it had slipped to an average of 27.3 mpg.)[14] Since their sales base was in small cars, however, they could get into the large-car business while still meeting the average mileage requirements of the CAFE standards. By 1993, the average weight of the cars sold by Japanese companies had climbed from a 1977–1983 average of 2,500 pounds to 3,000 pounds.

To show the contrast in fuel economy performance, the mileage of cars made and sold by U.S. manufacturers from 1977 to 1994 has increased by more than 75 percent, while the average of Asian imports has increased by about 3 percent.[15] This does not mean that the U.S. manufacturers had better technology or that the Japanese were unable to do better. It means that while the Americans were constrained by U.S. law from following a free-market product plan, the Japanese could build and bring to America more large cars with lower mileage and still meet CAFE rules by averaging them in with their traditional small cars.

As economist Karl Hausker put it, "CAFE standards have been binding on U.S. companies that build a full line of large, mid-size, and small cars. In contrast, CAFE has never been binding on Asian manufacturers. Their fuel economy has *decreased* over the past five years . . . as they have offered greater size and performance in what is still overwhelmingly a small-car fleet. The universal application of a 27.5 mpg standard is also of unquestionable benefit to Asian automakers in their ongoing efforts to increase market share in the mid-size and luxury markets."[16]

The Japanese deserve no condemnation for this series of events. As very able businessmen, they simply took advantage of a flawed U.S. public policy—well-meaning, but rich in unintended consequences. The Japanese also happened to have some very good products. With important help from a strong dollar, which made Japanese exports to America cheaper, they were so successful that pressure grew strong in the United States for import restrictions.

CAFE and Trade Policy

By 1980, with gasoline prices at their highest point and with the help of a strong dollar and weak yen,[17] Japanese passenger-car market share grew rapidly, reaching nearly 20 percent. In the same year, scrambling to meet government clean-air and safety regulations while also downsizing their vehicles to meet CAFE rules, Chrysler, Ford, General Motors, and American Motors together lost $4 billion.[18]

The scene was set for a strong push for legislation protecting the American auto industry from foreign competition. The Carter administration was split internally, but as the 1980 election approached, it sent clear signals to the Japanese government to find a way to restrain vehicle exports to the United States. The Japanese decided that in view of the upcoming U.S. election it would ignore the signals. When Ronald Reagan became president, his administration was also divided on the issue of import restraints. Although Reagan was a free-market advocate, in view of the U.S. auto industry's deep troubles, complicated by high interest rates and a weak Japanese currency that made imports cheaper, he agreed with his special trade representative, William Brock, that the Japanese should be asked to come up with a voluntary export restraint (VER) program.

Three months into the Reagan administration, the Japanese government announced it would voluntarily limit vehicle exports to the United States for a year or two—not more than three. These restraints, in the form of quotas established by the Japanese Ministry of International Trade and Investment (MITI), had the appearance of providing relief for U.S. car companies and workers.[19] In today's terms, the Japanese VERs would be called "corporate welfare"—good for the companies and workers, bad for the consumers. In fact, they were bad for everyone.

By limiting the availability of the Japanese cars the customers wanted to buy, the export VERs pushed up the price of those cars. This gave domestic makers an opportunity also to sell more cars at higher prices. The customer, therefore, had to pay more to both the Japanese and the Americans companies.

The quotas provided an immediate incentive for the Japanese to upgrade their vehicles. Instead of using up their quotas to bring in cheaper cars, the Japanese began to ship "more car per car." They added features and performance so that each car shipped would produce more revenue than the previous models. These higher revenues meant more dollars in the treasuries of the Japanese manufacturers, helping them to expand production. The U.S. manufacturers, at the same time, were downsizing their vehicles to meet CAFE (and the anticipated fuel price increases—which never materialized). The Japanese, with their small-car base, had no trouble meeting CAFE. The quotas provided an additional incentive for them to jump into the U.S. market with larger and, later, luxury cars. They may eventually have gone into these market segments anyway, but the quotas and CAFE gave them a faster, safer, and more profitable opportunity to do so. They followed up with a good product and well-conceived marketing.

Overcapacity—The Coming Glut of Cars? Another fallout from the quotas was a major increase in the worldwide capacity to produce motor vehicles. Since there were quotas on what could be shipped from Japan, the Japanese manufacturers began to build production facilities elsewhere. The Koreans and others also expanded. This increase in capacity, therefore, was not always a result of increased world demand but came also from the distortions caused by artificial barriers to trade. The effect was hardest on the U.S. manufacturers with their aging plants, complex work rules, growing health care and pension costs, and high wage rates.

Some managers in the U.S. auto industry began to call for the Japanese to "build where you sell." They believed the Japanese could not successfully build vehicles in America because of labor costs and work rules. Assuming that the foreign-owned plants would be unionized, they did not anticipate the competitive danger coming from "transplants," the name given to Japanese (and now German) plants built in the United States. They were wrong. With few exceptions, the transplants defeated the attempts of labor unions to organize their employees. They paid competitive wages but recruited a young work force and therefore had very low health care costs and no pension costs. (U.S. automakers had a ratio of active workers to retirees ranging from 2-1 to 1-1, resulting in high costs both for pensions and for retiree health care.) Also, the new Japanese plants had simple work rules and fewer job classifications, resulting in more flexibility and efficiency—and therefore lower costs.

While these new plants brought new job opportunities to the United States, they also hastened the closing of many existing U.S. plants. As the Japanese were hiring, the U.S. companies were downsizing their operations—as they still are. The new jobs, however, did not equal the ones lost in plant closings. The Japanese transplants were assembly operations, with many, if not most, of the components coming from Japan and elsewhere. A vehicle assembled at one of these plants, therefore, was not the equivalent in American jobs to the vehicle made by a traditional U.S. manufacturer.[20] That is not a sin, but it is a fact not always understood.

Overcapacity, stimulated by the quotas on Japanese exports, remains a major problem. The *Economist,* which correctly foresaw the truth about energy supply in the 1970s, reports that in 1997 the world has the capacity to produce 68 million passenger- and other light-duty vehicles, 18 million more than were actually made in 1996. In a cover story entitled "Car Firms Head for a Crash," the magazine says some forecasters believe world capacity may grow to 80 million by the year 2000, while demand may rise only to around 60 million. In these circumstances, the *Economist* says, "every factory in North America could close—and there would still be excess capacity."[21]

Protection—A Weak Reed to Lean On. Another flaw in the VERs was the false sense they gave to American managers and workers that the competitive pressure was off—or at least contained. That was perhaps the most harmful effect. In the global economy of the 1990s and beyond, there is no way for an industry to stay healthy by hiding behind a wall of trade barriers, especially when the foundation of the wall is a piece of paper politically arrived at and vulnerable to politically motivated change by one or more of the parties involved. A job earned by winning customers in open competition is always more secure than that "guaranteed" by a piece of paper signed in Washington, D.C., or anywhere else.

In January 1985, the chairman of General Motors called for the end of the auto quotas. In an article appearing in the *Washington Post*, Roger Smith said that "it is time to remove trade barriers—not to build them,"[22] adding,

"So let's drop the restraints and get on with slugging it out in the world marketplace." He argued that "the discipline of worldwide competition not only can assure that customers have access to the best products at the best prices, it also speeds up the pace of technological innovation and industrial modernization, which means growth and more and better jobs." GM and the other American automobile manufacturers paid a heavy price by facing the competition, losing billions in the next decade, but the struggle resulted in new vehicles that are the equivalent in quality of any in the world,[23] and the American companies have a new competitive strength they would not otherwise have. Obviously, the consumer was a winner.[24]

Smith had also said that "the Japanese government must find the will and the way to open up its domestic market to U.S. manufacturers. There are too many examples of resistance to competition in everything from high tech to agriculture and services." The Japanese have been masters at much talk and little action in meeting this challenge. (The U.S. deficit with Japan is huge—nearly $48 billion in 1996.) Removal of Japanese government-sponsored trade barriers (ranging from costly certification procedures to taxes on larger engines, typical of American cars) took years. More difficult to overcome are the cultural barriers, especially the traditional belief of Japanese customers and dealers that staying with Japanese products is the right thing to do.

More perplexing is the way currency exchange rates work. Fluctuations have tremendous effect. For example, when production in Japan's domestic auto plants dropped to about 50 percent of capacity, the yen began to depreciate in relation to the dollar, making exports to the United States much cheaper. Immediately, exports to the United States increased. Honda and Toyota reached record sales in the spring of 1997, and the trade deficit grew.

In theory, at least, the rates of exchange among currencies is determined by international market forces, unless governments (or other financially powerful organizations) intervene. When currencies "float" freely in the markets, they automatically adjust (in theory, at least) for differences in fiscal policies such as taxes and subsidies. For many policy purposes, the yen-dollar exchange rate is considered to be determined by market forces. The CEO of Mitsubishi Electric Corporation, however, in discussing what the Japanese government has done to deal with current economic problems, said that "the Ministry of Finance [of Japan] has engineered a depreciation of the yen to relieve exports."[25] This "relief" for Japanese exports to the United States came about because it took fewer dollars to buy cars and other goods denominated in yen.

In the Ministry of Finance, Eisuke Sakakibara, vice minister for international affairs, is credited with having remarkable influence on exchange rates. Sandra Sugawara of the *Washington Post* reports that "Sakakibara's ability to influence foreign exchange markets has given him the nickname 'Mr. Yen.' He has close links with U.S. Treasury officials and with prominent market participants . . . including legendary hedge fund manager George Soros."[26] In January 1996, Sakakibara and Soros appeared together on a panel in Tokyo and, Sugawara records, "Both men said the same thing—the yen was overvalued and would continue to depreciate. Wire service reporters rushed from the room and the yen fell in response to the statements." (So much for the "free float" of the yen.) This depreciation made Japanese goods cheaper in America and American goods more expensive in Japan, thus accelerating the growth of the U.S. trade deficit with Japan.

While the trade deficit with China displaced the deficit with Japan as a subject of public concern early in 1997, as Japan comes back from a serious recession, the pressure will grow for the Japanese market to be more open and accommodating to imports. Open markets benefit all consumers and ultimately all nations. Trade barriers such as the VERs are a false remedy.

CAFE and VERs together are not just alphabet soup—they are lost jobs and higher consumer costs. These schemes provided no security in energy supply or in employment. Both are flawed central government regulatory plans and programs, rife with unintended consequences of the most serious and negative kinds. Both had the effect of limiting the American consumer's ability to choose the vehicle that best met his or her needs. The business community is right to resist costly and ineffective regulations of its products and processes, but it is also obliged to resist governmental regulation in the form of trade restrictions designed to protect it from competition.[27]

But What about Energy Independence?

As noted earlier, the United States is further from energy independence than it was in 1975. We now import a much higher percentage of our oil than we did when CAFE was enacted. That leaves open, however, the question of whether we should be working toward energy independence. Michael J. Boskin, former chairman of the President's Council of Economic Advisers, addressed this issue in testimony before the National Academy of Sciences–National Research Council study of CAFE in 1991. "Given the increasing integration of world economies and the total integration of the world oil market," he said, "our energy security cannot be defined independently of that of our friends, allies, and trading partners. . . . Moreover," he added, "even the most optimistic assessment of the oil consumption effects of higher CAFE standards cannot conceivably put us past a threshold where we would no longer have a vital security interest in the major oil-exporting regions of the world."

Chairman Boskin mentioned several policies that provided "important energy security benefits," three of which are:

- *Reliance on the market.* He called attention to the absence of gasoline lines after Iraq invaded Kuwait, as compared with conditions following the Iranian revolution in 1979, and said this difference "reflects the use of markets rather than bureaucracies to allocate available oil supplies."
- *Maintenance of sound macroeconomic policies.* He remarked that during the 1979 oil shock, "import-dependent Japan fared much better than the United Kingdom [with less sound policies], which produces more oil that it consumes."
- *The continued development of the strategic petroleum reserves.*

The role of the strategic reserves administered by the Department of Energy is somewhat controversial, and the commitment to maintaining the reserves is less than sturdy. When it was established, the capacity target was 1 billion gallons. This target was cut back to 750 million barrels (and further reduced to 678 million when a sinkhole necessitated the decommissioning of a storage site). At last count there were some 563 million barrels of oil in storage. This represents an approximately sixty-seven–day supply for the United States.

During the Iraqi invasion of Kuwait, when there was concern that oil prices would surge, the Bush administration announced it would sell oil from the strategic reserves and, subsequently, 17 million barrels were sold. Prices did not soar, but there seems to be a consensus that any benefit came from the presence of the reserve and the announcement of the sale, not from the sale itself.

While the reserves reached a high of 592 million barrels after the Gulf War, there were 29 million barrels fewer in mid-1997, thanks to a requirement enacted by Congress to sell off some reserves to help reduce the budget deficit. No further sales for that purpose are currently planned, although some in Congress see it as an option. This attitude reflects either a skepticism about the need for a reserve or a belief that putting oil back into the ground is not the most effective way to deal with the energy security issue. It is true that having the reserves would not mean that the United States could look with disinterest on a takeover of the Mideast oil fields by a hostile force. It would give some protection, however, from erratic price fluctuations in periods of uncertainty. In this respect it is far more useful than CAFE.

More useful yet is the discovery and development of new oil reserves. For example, the Hibernia field below the ice-filled waters off Canada's east coast is expected to deliver its first oil by the end of 1997. Billed as "one of the largest oil discoveries in North America in decades," it and surrounding fields are expected to provide more than a billion barrels of high-quality crude.[28] Vast oil and natural gas fields are also being developed in Kazakhstan, Azerbaijan, Uzbekistan, and other former Soviet countries. According to petroleum scientists, this Caspian Sea region contains the third largest oil and natural gas reserve in the world, after the Persian Gulf and Siberia. These fields offer less energy security to the United States than does Hibernia, but all new discoveries help ensure personal mobility, regardless of political upsets in any one oil-producing area.[29]

· 4 ·

CONFUSION IN THE VEHICLE MARKET, TURMOIL IN THE INDUSTRY

Although CAFE has distorted the vehicle market, not everyone is willing to be pushed into a small or less powerful vehicle. Without even knowing there is a CAFE program, savvy customers have benefited from its loopholes. Under the law, no one has to buy a specific kind of vehicle; the restrictions are placed on what the U.S. passenger car makers can make, not on what the individual customer can buy, except in the aggregate. Customers not able to get the desired size or power in the passenger car they traditionally buy may move from dealer to dealer until they find vehicles that meet their needs. If a customer has the funds, he or she may buy a larger or more powerful car from a foreign manufacturer who can average in its low fuel economy with a small-car base to meet CAFE rules. Or the customer may buy from a European car maker who is willing to pay the fine for violating the CAFE regulations—and believes it does not have the same legal risks as the Americans do in planning to pay fines instead of meeting the rules. Or the customer may buy a van, sport-utility vehicle, or pickup truck.

Vans, sport-utility vehicles (SUVs), and light pickups are all classified for CAFE purposes as trucks. Since CAFE mileage standards for trucks are lower than those for cars, these vehicles can be larger and heavier and can have more power than a car—which makes sense for a truck. Not all buyers of vans, SUVs, and light pickups were driven to them by CAFE, but many customers went looking for more utility and performance than cars could provide and joined the stampede to those kinds of vehicles. One consequence is that if people drive the same number of miles as before, they will burn more fuel than they would have burned with the cars formerly parked in American driveways.

John Merline of *Investor's Business Daily* has observed that when gasoline prices went down, "Consumers again wanted larger, less fuel-efficient cars, but were blocked by government policy. The only escape valve was into the van and light truck market which came under separate and far less restrictive CAFE standards."[1] The *Tampa Tribune* editorialized that in the past, utility vehicles were big, bad, and ugly, "But with consumers gradually deprived of a broad selection of larger cars, the bulky vehicles quickly evolved until today they are big, genial, and beautiful." Cars have gotten smaller, the *Tribune* says, "But families by the thousands are cruising around town in tall, heavy, truck-like vehicles."[2] Professor Lester B. Lave of Carnegie Mellon University wrote, "Denying Americans the cars they want has a high social cost." If Americans believe there are reasons that justify sacrifice, they will accept it, he says, "However, without this social agreement, and without fuel prices that support the more fuel-efficient cars, American genius will figure out ways to get the cars they desire, despite the bureaucrats."[3]

As Keith Bradsher, writing in the *New York Times,* points out, "Light trucks have soared in popularity partly because, with gas prices low, Americans want bigger vehicles. A quirk in federal regulations prevents the automakers from simply selling lots of big cars like station wagons, the quirk being that federal fuel economy standards are much higher for cars than for light trucks."[4]

This rule was not a quirk. Trucks are built to carry loads and pull trailers. Tight fuel economy would prevent them from being trucks. The difference in CAFE requirements for cars and trucks was a deliberate and sensible "quirk": the flaw is that the CAFE law is designed to limit the consumer's choice of vehicles to those with lower performance and smaller size, and Americans did not agree to this restriction. CAFE was presented as a means to achieve higher mileage without additional cost in utility, size, or performance. It was wrapped in the mantle of energy independence. There was no "buy-in," no social compact between the government and the people in support of a policy that meant the people would no longer be able to obtain the vehicle that met their wants and needs. As a result, as Lave suggested, American genius has figured out a way to buy the vehicles that provide the kind of personal mobility Americans want, despite the activists, their political friends, and the bureaucrats.

Regulatory Fallout

The oil shocks, the slowdown of the economy in 1979 and subsequent recession, the effect of environmental, safety, and fuel economy regulation, and trade restraints (specifically the VERs) all had a devastating effect on the U.S. auto industry. With the total car market down and Japanese imports increasing, the U.S. auto companies were losing billions of dollars. Thousands of employees were laid off. Tiny Checker Motors, maker of the roomy taxicab with jump seats in the back compartment, went out of business. With its limited engineering capability, Checker simply could not keep up with the flood of federal regulations that hit the industry in the 1960s. Kaiser Industries also folded its automotive operations in this period, selling its Jeep to American Motors. During the 1970s and 1980s, two of the four major auto companies—Chrysler and American Motors—were in deep trouble, thanks in part to the heavy burdens of regulation (as well as product problems). Chrysler survived to become a tough competitor once again, but in the 1970s and 1980s it was touch and go.

Crisis in Chrysler. In 1969 and 1970, Chrysler had experienced serious financial difficulties, and its management held heavy regulatory requirements responsible for a major part of the problem. Along with the rest of the industry, Chrysler had struggled with the burden of new emission standards required by the 1970 Clean Air Act. The corporation had filed a lawsuit against a rule mandating air bags in cars by 1975. (It lost the suit, but air bag requirements were postponed by the Department of Transportation.) In 1972, Chrysler experienced a recovery, but in the second half of 1973, things went sour. In September, after a series of wildcat strikes, the United Auto Workers chose Chrysler as the target for the 1973 contract negotiations. A strike of all assembly plants followed and closed the company down for nine days.

In early October 1973, Chrysler announced a loss for the third quarter. Two days later, Israel and Egypt went to war and the OPEC countries announced the oil embargo against the United States and other countries supportive of Israel. Small-car sales surged. Chrysler had no subcompacts and had just spent scarce resources on restyling its large cars. Adding to the problem, inflation soared to its highest level since World War I and, simultaneously, the worst recession since the end of World War II was underway. By May 1975, 9.2 percent of the national work force was jobless, stagflation had a tight grip on the nation, and the government was shaken when Richard Nixon resigned his presidency. Chrysler's losses increased, as did its debt.

Although the company experienced a slight rebound by the first quarter of 1976, it took another severe blow when the market for its new Dodge Aspens and Plymouth Volares collapsed following major recalls for safety defects. (*Motor Trend* magazine had named the Aspen/Volare line Car of the Year earlier. Even though Chrysler found and fixed the defect, the Consumers Union and the Nader-affiliated Center for Auto Safety did not relent in their attacks. The cars were finished in the market, adding substantially to the corporation's problem.)

The regulatory effect on the company was described by Robert Reich and coauthor John Donahue in their book on the Chrysler near-bankruptcy.[5] In reviewing the explanations for Chrysler's sorry condition in 1977, the authors wrote: "There was another reason: federal regulations. The safety and pollution control requirements that had been enacted years before were now taking hold. There was also a requirement that each automaker's products must average out to specified levels of fuel efficiency."

By 1979, Chrysler faced bankruptcy. The company asked for government help, immediately characterized as a bailout. David Stockman, then a Republican member of Congress from Michigan, was quoted as saying, "If you bail Chrysler out now, you're just bailing out the Environmental Protection Agency and the Transportation Department regulations."[6] In August 1979, auto industry analyst Maryann Keller, then with Kidder, Peabody & Company, told the *Detroit Free Press,* "Chrysler probably can make a good case for government regulations getting it into the mess it's in today."

It is not possible to calculate accurately the cost of the Chrysler "bailout." The principal benefit for the corporation came in the form of loan guarantees, but other factors were present. (With concessions from the UAW, Chrysler assembly-line workers were paid around $2.60 an hour less than those at Ford or GM.) There was also enormous disruption of the lives of tens of thousands of employees of Chrysler and its suppliers. (Some executives were put on part-time pay. Many were terminated. The CEO, Lee Iacocca, was obliged to give up the corporate jet.) It is doubtful that the analysts attempting to calculate the benefits of the regulations that helped put Chrysler at risk would or could estimate these extensive costs. Without doing so, their analysis is flawed.

The demise of American Motors is also relevant. Auto writer John Peterson said,

> If American Motors Corp. and Chrysler Corp. were to eventually join Studebaker, Hudson and Packard in the graveyard of dead automakers, the federal government would have to bear a large share of the blame. That's the assessment of a number of respected market analysts who believe that the growing burden of federal safety, emission and gas mileage regulations eventually will prove insurmountable for both AMC and Chrysler.[7]

Eugene Jennings, professor of management at Michigan State University, told John Peterson that "Ralph Nader and the regulations he helped put in place have all but doomed AMC."

Chrysler, with the help of the U.S. government (as well as state and local governments, the UAW, suppliers, bankers, and others), dodged the bullet. But in 1987, American Motors gave up the ghost; most of its significant assets were purchased by Chrysler. American Motors had pioneered with smaller cars under George Romney in the late 1950s and early 1960s. It had stayed afloat until the 1980s by buying the Jeep operation from Kaiser Industries (which had acquired it from Willys-Overland, the company that first produced it for the military during World War II). Ironically, AMC's Jeep unit, which Chrysler purchased, has been highly profitable and has helped Chrysler to weather another storm in recent years. If regulations had not been so draconian for American Motors, perhaps American Motors would still be a producer today.

In 1976, Chrysler dropped virtually all pretense at being a full-line manufacturer. Its large cars were cut from the product plan, and it concentrated on the small K-car platform and, later, the minivan (classified as a truck for CAFE purposes). The government rescue effort, along with smart product planning and outstanding marketing, enabled Chrysler to foil the doomsayers. Following a difficult period from the 1970s until the early 1990s, it became for a time the most profitable U.S. auto company, producing not only small cars and vans but also full-size sedans and a ten-cylinder sports car, the Viper. It is instructive to note, however, that Chrysler now builds more vehicles classified for CAFE purposes as trucks than those classified as passenger cars. The corporation's customers have found their way around CAFE.

Shut This Old CAFE Down!

CAFE is ingenious—or insidious. It enables the central government to attempt to manipulate people's choices without their knowing it. It has been a useful tool for social engineers who believe they know best how the rest of us should act but cannot always get us to go along. It has failed to meet its objectives and its side effects are devastating, but it will last only as long as people remain unaware that it is adversely affecting their choices, reducing the safety of their vehicles, and interfering with their personal mobility. When they become aware, the elected political advocates will change their tune or find new employment.

More CAFE? A lesson was learned in 1991 when Senator Richard Bryan (D-Nev.) proposed legislation to raise the stringency of CAFE requirements from 27.5 mpg to 40 mpg. Workers in auto plants around the country were immediately concerned. Typical of the reaction was that of J. C. Phillips, chairman of the United Auto Workers Local 882 at Ford's Georgia assembly plant. At a rally in Atlanta, he said his plant and others could be hit hard because "no cars made in Georgia meet the Bryan bill's mandated average." He appealed to Georgia's senators to oppose the bill, as did other cosponsors of the rally, including the Georgia Farm Bureau Federation, the Georgia Safety Council, and the Business Council. The Business Council's representative, John R. Poole, observed that "fuel economy is a good idea, but measures like the Bryan bill would outlaw the large-size vehicles we need and force us into vehicles too small to do the job." Coalition for Vehicle Choice president Diane Steed, former chief of the National Highway Traffic Safety Administration, said, "Senator Bryan's bill is well intended, but it unfortunately would increase the cost of new cars and trucks, limit consumer choice to mostly smaller and lighter models, and seriously compromise motorists' safety."

With this evidence that people were catching on to the deep problems of CAFE, the Senate did not pass the bill. Nor did they pass a subsequent bill that would have increased CAFE stringency as an inducement to authorize oil exploration in Alaska. The most recent legislative activity on the issue includes bills proposed by Representative Fred Upton (R-Mich.) and Senator Spencer Abraham (R-Mich.). These bills would freeze CAFE standards at current levels until changed by law. Passage would at least stop the bureaucrats from making matters worse with higher standards.

Unfortunately, the CAFE system is still at work, and periodic efforts are made to defend or extend it. In the spring of 1997, Daniel Becker, director of the Sierra Club Global Warming and Energy Program (and one of the most vociferous professional activists in Washington, D.C.), said in defense of CAFE, "The shame is that the auto industry has the technology to dramatically improve fuel economy sitting on its shelves. They just aren't putting it on their cars and light trucks." He gave no reason and listed no technologies to justify this resurrection of the old canard about technology being "on the shelf." The fact is that there is every reason for companies to use all effective, affordable fuel economy technologies available. They are now using expensive, lightweight materials, such as aluminum, in applications where the fuel saved does not justify the extra cost. To meet CAFE averages, they are not providing all the features and performance customers are demanding in cars, and customers are moving to trucks, which are governed by less stringent rules. They are subsidizing their sales of small cars in order to offset sales of larger cars, to meet the CAFE averages. The Europeans are paying huge fines for missing the fuel-economy requirements. They would be grateful if Becker could identify some of these magic technologies for them. As it is, he undermines the credibility of the old and honorable organization for which he works by using outlandish rhetoric to defend a failed policy.

In business, when a product fails, it disappears rapidly. In government, a failed product often becomes a permanent fixture. CAFE failed in its mission of reducing dependence on foreign oil. That should have spelled the end of CAFE. But most government programs begin to institutionalize immediately after they are put in place. They begin to have a life of their own and to find ways to grow. If the original mission fails, or if it is accomplished, another mission is found to take its place. Preservation of the institution becomes the real mission. That is what has happened with CAFE.

Since there has been no buy-in to the notion that Americans should step down in the utility and performance of their vehicles, as witnessed by the rush to vans, trucks, and SUVs, there has been an effort to forge a new public consensus. The idea is to instill guilt in the psyche of the owners of large, family-sized vehicles, including light trucks, by suggesting that they are endangering occupants of smaller vehicles. This campaign is unlikely to persuade people that the smart thing to do is to increase their own vulnerability and that of their families by trading down for smaller, less safe vehicles. The more serious effort is global. As Michelle Malkin said, "CAFE advocates quit riding the tired horse named Energy Crisis and hopped on the back of Global Warming."[8] (Global warming is the subject of Part Two of this book.) She added, "CAFE isn't just a quaint trend left over from the 1970s. It's an indefensible law that kills."

It should be embarrassing for the president, the vice president, or others of special status to ride in larger, heavier, and safer cars while everybody else must accept limited options: the cars available to them must conform to a law—CAFE—that limits the passive protection people want. For the good of the public's health and safety, this old CAFE should be shut down.

· 5 ·

A DIFFERENT APPROACH— PARTNERSHIP FOR A NEW GENERATION OF VEHICLES

C AFE is a classic example of command-and-control regulation—the control of an activity (such as fuel use or emissions) by government, using commands (such as regulations) that require persons or organizations to take or not take specific actions. Through CAFE, the government "commands" automakers to make cars that, on average, achieve specific fuel-economy levels. (Through the same regulatory program, government indirectly commands consumers by regulating the pool of new cars they can choose from to make a purchase.)[1] Stiff penalties are levied on manufacturers for failure to obey the commands.

In recent years, an effort by many students and practitioners of regulation in and out of government has been made to replace this old and rigid method of regulation with new ways to reach public policy objectives. This effort helped to lead the government away from more CAFE.

In 1993, with the objective of finding more effective ways to approach the goals of CAFE, President Clinton, Vice President Gore, and the CEOs of the U.S. automobile manufacturing companies announced the formation of a program with the awkward title of Partnership for a New Generation of Vehicles (PNGV).[2] Under this program, the government and the U.S. auto companies joined in what they called a "unique research and development effort" to develop a commercially viable vehicle "which could achieve fuel efficiencies up to three times today's automobile, while at the same time cost no more to own and drive than today's automobile, maintain the performance, size, and utility of comparable vehicles, and meet or exceed safety and emission requirements."[3]

The purpose of the partnership was to "permit dedication of private and public resources to programs designed to achieve major technological breakthroughs that can make traditional regulatory interventions irrelevant." This statement in the agreement between the Clinton administration and the auto industry was intended as a clear reference to the opportunity PNGV provided to move away from the flawed CAFE program. Instead of arbitrarily setting more stringent mileage requirements, the government would work with the auto industry to see if better fuel economy could be achieved without compromising safety, performance, size, and utility while keeping consumer cost at or below that of current (1993) cars.

At a White House ceremony on September 29, 1993, President Clinton said, "Today, we're going to try to give America a new car-crazy chapter in her rich history, to launch a technological venture as ambitious as any our nation has ever attempted." Harold "Red" Poling, CEO of Ford Motor Company, said, "This partnership will push the theoretical limits of energy efficiency, and there's no promise that the desired technologies will be found. But the opportunity for making this leap forward is unprecedented." Jack Smith, CEO of General Motors, called the program "revolutionary" and said it would bring "new energy and excitement to our industry and will help unlock some of the doors that may lead to fuel cells, advanced hybrids, and other technologies needed to meet these ambitious goals." He added, "Crucial to this revolution is the way in which we plan to achieve it—through partnership and cooperation rather than the old command-and-control adversarial approach of the past." For Chrysler, CEO Robert Eaton said, "We are going to push every aspect of vehicle technology to its limit—from lighter materials to new power train concepts."

Coordinating the program within the auto industry is the United States Council for Automotive Research (USCAR), made up of Chrysler, Ford, and General Motors.[4] For the government, the Department of Commerce serves as coordinator, under the leadership of the undersecretary of commerce for technology. Since PNGV was formed, more than 400 organizations have become involved, including twenty federal laboratories, seven federal agencies, several universities, industry trade groups, supplier companies, and independent entrepreneurs.

When it was announced, PNGV came under immediate attack from both ends of the political spectrum. It seems to the Nader-Claybrook-Ditlow group that any step away from regulations that command the manufacturers to accomplish arbitrary goals, under threat of disgrace and punishment for failure to meet them, is a sign of weakness and a concession to the enemy. A publication of Public Citizen, headed by Joan Claybrook, worried that the PNGV would be "a substitute for more realistic, near-term fuel-economy policies." It alleged that "President Clinton's retreat from his campaign promises to raise fuel economy standards is widely seen as an attempt to affirm his cozy relationship with the U.S. auto industry."[5]

On the other end of the political spectrum, some saw the PNGV as "industrial policy," with the government stepping into the private sector's preserve and "guiding" investment along paths chosen politically rather than through the market. Rush Limbaugh lampooned the project, saying, "Can you imagine Al Gore designing a car?" He added that it would "run on corn pellets from Archer Daniels Midland."[6] Others raised the specter of "corporate welfare," with big auto companies "feeding at the public trough." The *New York Times* headlined its story "Government Dream Car."

All the critics have been a little right and mostly wrong. Command-and-control regulation has not gone away by any means. CAFE remains in full force, but more stringent fuel economy rules, with all their unintended consequences, have not been enacted. While the government is sitting at the table where decisions are made about research directions, most of the input comes necessarily from the company engineers. And not much federal "feed" has flowed into the auto industry trough. Most of the investment in the goals of the program comes from the auto companies and their suppliers. Much of the government funding ($240 million in fiscal year 1997) is directed toward federal research laboratories and agencies. Most of the funds going to the auto companies is redirected to suppliers.

A Good Faith Effort

For their part, the auto companies have welcomed the opportunity to show that more command and control is not the way to go. They have pledged a "good faith effort" to meet the goals, and they appear to be living up to that pledge. For the government people, the most educational aspect is the opportunity to learn firsthand of the difficulty in meeting PNGV goals and to realize that no easy solutions are sitting on the shelf, with only the recalcitrance of the companies standing in the way of their introduction. This may be the most beneficial aspect of PNGV.

As problems are addressed, the PNGV experience should help to inhibit demagogues, within government and outside of it, from thinking that technology breakthroughs can simply be mandated. This value is lost on many conservative critics of the PNGV program. They do not understand that in the current climate, the choice is not "PNGV or nothing." "Nothing" should be quite acceptable in that case. The real choice is between PNGV and a major political battle over more stringent CAFE—with the outcome in doubt. This, for now, is the political reality. The PNGV may not be an ideal mechanism for addressing fuel-economy issues (the markets do that job most efficiently), but it is certainly preferable to more harmful regulation.

In addition to its value as an alternative to more CAFE, PNGV is making some progress. The program is reviewed periodically by a panel of the National Research Council (NRC), composed of experts from universities, research groups, and private companies. In the April 1997 report of the panel (its third), it listed several technical achievements, including a prototype fuel-processor for a fuel cell, an advanced lithium-ion battery cell, a more effective catalyst for nitrogen oxides (NO_x), advancements in ceramics for turbine engines, and the demonstration of a glass-fiber–reinforced, composite front-end structure.[7] The NRC panel also took note of the development of demonstration vehicles by the companies, some of which incorporated requirements related to PNGV.

In its discussion of "energy converters," the National Research Council found the technology for lightweight diesel engines to be the most advanced and recommended that PNGV focus on that engine. The compression-ignited direct-injection engine (CIDI) is one of the promising technologies, either as a single power source or teamed with an electric motor in a hybrid vehicle. True to form, professional activists immediately attacked the recommendation. A spokesperson for the Union for Concerned Scientists, always pessimistic, said the diesel would be "a significant step backward in air pollution."

In a PNGV symposium hosted by Vice President Al Gore on July 23, 1997, the vice president spoke about improvements in compression ignition direct injection engines. He said that "advanced diesels have the potential for fuel efficiency 40 percent better than current gasoline engines. . . . Since there is a direct relationship between fuel burned and carbon dioxide emissions," he said, "this would mean a 40 percent reduction in carbon dioxide emissions as well. . . . So we cannot remove diesels from consideration," he added, "but cannot use them without solving the emissions problem." Typically, Sierra Club spokesperson Daniel Becker reacted with vehemence, attacking the diesel and saying, "The Partnership for a New Generation of Vehicles is a scam."[8] Dealing with the realities of technology and manufacturing has its political penalties for Gore.

Other energy converters under review by PNGV include gas turbines, Stirling engines, and fuel cells. The fuel cell is by far the most intriguing. Used on U.S. space flights for decades, its only significant "waste" is drinkable water. It supplies electricity by combining hydrogen and oxygen electrochemically, without combustion, and it does so as long as its fuel system lasts. It consists of an electrolyte wrapped in two electrodes. Oxygen passes over one and hydrogen over the other, generating electricity, water vapor, and heat (exhaust). It operates on hydrogen as a fuel, but the lack of an infrastructure for the competitively priced and safe (remember the Hindenberg) production, storage, and distribution of hydrogen probably means another fuel will be converted into hydrogen on board the vehicle.

Chrysler has announced that it is working on a fuel cell that would use gasoline. Daimler-Benz has announced that it will work on a methanol-based fuel cell. (When converting other fuel to hydrogen, carbon dioxide and some other pollutants are emitted.) General Motors, Ford, and other companies also have fuel-cell projects underway. The fuel cell considered most promising is the proton-exchange membrane (PEM), having a thin coating of platinum catalyst on each side of its membrane, as the electrolyte. The NRC panel on PNGV, however, "is of the opinion that it is unlikely [that] dramatic reductions [in costs] can be obtained without significant technological developments and major breakthroughs."

Daimler-Benz (parent firm of Mercedes Benz) appears to be more optimistic. Reportedly it will spend $320 million to develop a methanol-powered fuel cell and will mass produce 100,000 fuel-cell vehicles by 2005.[9] This announcement immediately stirred the California air quality regulators to form a task force to look at fuel cells. It is to be hoped that California does not repeat the mistake of mandating technology untested in the market, as it did with the electric car. Such mandates inevitably inhibit companies from public discussions of any innovation, out of fear that it will be mandated. California should note the admonition of Ferdinand Panik, senior vice president at Daimler, who said that prior to mass production, "We have to reduce the cost by a factor of 100. That's really hard work."[10] He also said, "We have learned one lesson—environmental friendliness will not be paid for by the market."[11] (The low number of leases for the GM electric car has been cited as an example of the refusal of customers to pay any premium for a clean car.)[12] On this point, Robert Q. Riley said, "New energy-efficient vehicle types must have an intrinsic appeal of their own. Conservation and sacrifice are not marketable themes."[13]

The challenge in meeting PNGV goals is huge, as reflected in an April 1996 report from the PNGV secretariat entitled "Inventions Needed for PNGV." Two excerpts tell much of the story. First, the report states, "On the basis of realistically achievable thermal efficiencies of various heat engines, engine improvements alone may not achieve the fuel economy target. The thermal efficiency needed ranges from approximately 40 to 55 percent, which is about twice as efficient as today's engines. Even with advanced fuel cells, which have higher potential efficiencies than heat engines, other vehicle improvements are likely to be needed." The second major point is, "Even with the improved power converters and regenerative braking, reductions in vehicle mass on the order of 20 percent to 40 percent from today's baseline vehicles are required. These levels of mass reduction are beyond simple refinement of today's steel frame, steel body construction, and may involve the introduction of entirely new classes of structural materials."

The point that it may take a 20–40 percent reduction in vehicle mass, despite the addition of the best engine and other technologies, is a matter of serious safety concern.[14] This is why the PNGV list of necessary inventions stresses such priorities as low-cost carbon fibers for reinforcement of polymer composites or low-cost machining processes for advanced materials. Indicative of some progress, USCAR's Automotive Composites Consortium has designed a lightweight, composite front-end vehicle structure that has passed a 35-mph barrier crash test. While this was significant, USCAR cautioned that the development of structural composites for volume manufacturing was still in the early stages. The next stage of the project is to address the problems of manufacturing speed, quality, and cost, all major challenges for the project. If these problems can be overcome, composites may provide additional structural strength for vehicles. Nonetheless, all other things being equal, heavier, larger vehicles built with composites will always have a safety advantage over smaller, lighter vehicles built with the same materials.

Opportunities and Barriers Ahead

The most significant finding of the NRC peer review group was that there were serious barriers to the accomplishment of the PNGV goals. The report says, "Despite significant progress in a number of critical areas, there continues to be a wide gulf between the current status of system and subsystem developments and the performance and cost requirements necessary to meet major PNGV milestones. Some of the technical barriers to achieving PNGV objectives can probably be overcome with sufficient funding and management attention; others require inventions and very significant technical breakthroughs." This is sober news for those who may think that major breakthroughs in the reduction in fossil-fuel use are just around the corner.

The technical cooperation among the U.S. automakers under the umbrella of USCAR has produced significant progress, and the participation of federal labs and other outside organizations under PNGV, on balance, has helped in that progress. Whether government participation is essential is debatable. Most technical development would probably occur over time without government participation. It is probable, however, that as a result of the PNGV program, technological advances might come earlier than they otherwise would have. The likelihood of this benefit occurring depends on the ability of the program to avoid arbitrarily pushing the wrong technology, thus misusing talent and funds and delaying real progress. Joel Clark of MIT puts it well: "Aggressive goals can spur substantial improvements in automotive technology. But irresponsible cheerleading for preposterous targets can result in gross misapplication of R&D resources and unrealistic expectations."[15]

Progress also depends on the government's willingness not to force a diversion of talent, time, and funding to meet a new set of command-and-control regulations. In this regard, PNGV has been a success. No new standards have been adopted. There is no doubt that PNGV has been helpful in educating all parties about the challenges in achieving big fuel-economy gains without compromising the safety, performance, size, and utility of the vehicle. The NRC review is clear about the magnitude of all these challenges.

With the comparatively low price of gasoline, there is little demand for higher fuel economy, except from government officials (and, of course, professional activists). Perhaps the fact that the government is bringing heavy pressure to bear to improve fuel economy far beyond the level the customer is demanding in the marketplace is a sufficient justification for government participation in a program such as PNGV. The more serious issue is why the government should be making such demands. The original reason was to achieve "energy independence." CAFE failed to meet that goal. The new reason—global warming—needs close analysis.

PART TWO

Managing the Earth's Climate—
The Global Warming Issue

·6·

FILLING THE FEAR VACUUM

W hen the Berlin Wall fell and the Soviet Union shattered, there was euphoria in America. We had survived the hot wars and the cold war and emerged victorious. But it seems we cannot, for long, be without an overarching threat to our peace and tranquillity. If you do not believe that, listen to our vice president, Al Gore, who wrote, "We now know that their cumulative impact on the global environment is posing a mortal threat to the security of every nation that is more deadly than that of any military enemy we are ever again likely to confront."

Gore was not talking about the threat of terrorists or rogue dictators in possession of biological weapons or nuclear devices. He was talking about our automobiles and trucks. He was not talking about the lives and limbs lost in tragic traffic accidents. He was talking about what comes from the internal combustion engine that powers our vehicles; not the carbon monoxide, which can be fatal when inhaled in sufficiently high concentrations, but the carbon dioxide, heretofore always referred to as "harmless."

Even discounting Gore's rhetoric for its political content, he seems much too optimistic about military threats in the future and much too pessimistic about our cars and trucks. What in the history of the twentieth century would lead anyone to believe that the world has given up military action as an option in international affairs? And, while the motor vehicle creates problems as well as benefits, just how much of a threat does it represent?

The issue involved here is variously called global climate change, the greenhouse effect, or global warming. Several basic questions are involved: Is the global climate changing? To what extent does human activity adversely affect global climate? Do we have enough facts and are our theories good enough to justify an attempt to manage the Earth's climate? What should be done to deal with the global climate issue?

There is much at stake in the answers to these questions. The future of the automobile—and personal mobility—is one of many issues. People who are alarmed about the state of the world's climate assert that global warming is expanding the deserts, melting polar ice caps, raising sea levels, and intensifying hurricanes. They foresee food shortages, flooded coastlines, population migrations, increased pestilence, and a host of other calamities. Some people—not the scientists—even suggest that the heat-related deaths in Chicago in 1995 and the 1993 flooding in the Midwest are the early results of climate change.

In anticipation of global warming, active negotiations are underway to put legally binding international limits on the emissions of the gases that serve as a "greenhouse" around the Earth. When he announced this proposal at a United Nations meeting in Geneva in July 1996, Tim Wirth, U.S. undersecretary of state for global affairs, told a *New York Times* reporter, "This is a big deal." He is right.

Climate control issues are a big deal, for us and for future generations. They are being used to justify placing the sources of greenhouse gases produced by human activity, especially carbon dioxide, under federal government and even international control. An estimated 90 percent of the world's energy comes from carbon-based fuels, which, when burned, produce carbon dioxide.

Regulating carbon dioxide would mean more restrictive controls over everything from coal mining to natural gas transmission to the generation of electricity from oil, coal, or natural gas-fired plants. Home heating and cooling, cooking fuels, the operation of factories and shopping malls, railroads, airlines, and everything else that involves the production or use of carbon-based energy would come under direct or indirect regulation. The effect would be to ration the use of energy by country, by economic sector, and ultimately by families and individuals.

Cars and trucks—and how they are used—are directly involved. There is no other issue as potentially serious for the future of the automobile as global warming. No other issue is as threatening to personal mobility. When gasoline is burned, water vapor and carbon dioxide are produced in the combustion process.[1] Neither is toxic; both are "greenhouse gases" and, as such, contribute to the greenhouse effect. The greenhouse effect, in turn, is a critical factor in determining the Earth's climate and changes in it. Rationing energy to roll back greenhouse gases in an attempt to manage the global climate would be the most ambitious central planning scheme yet undertaken by humankind—and would inevitably affect the availability and use of gasoline.

Should We Be Afraid of the Greenhouse Effect?

Thank Providence for the greenhouse effect! It is what makes the Earth a livable place for humankind. Without the heat-trapping qualities of water vapor, carbon dioxide, and certain other gases found in the atmosphere, the Earth would be cold and without life, at least as we know it. Conversely, many scientists think that we may be getting too much of a good thing. They believe the Earth's atmosphere may be loading up with more greenhouse gases than are safe. They worry that these gases may be accumulating beyond the level needed to keep the global climate as it now is. The result, they fear, may be a level of global warming that seriously threatens to disrupt life on Earth.

Venus, with carbon dioxide estimated at more than 95 percent of its atmosphere, is said to have a surface temperature of up to 460° C. (It also is 30 million miles closer to the sun, on average, than is the Earth.) The surface temperature of Mars, conversely, may average about −16° C. Surprisingly, carbon dioxide also makes up about 95 percent of its atmosphere. (Why these two planets have extreme opposites in temperature while carbon dioxide levels are about the same is not fully understood, like so much else in this field.) Obviously, we do not want a Venusian or a Martian climate.[2] We want our greenhouse effect to keep on doing what it is doing, so it's a good idea to understand a little about it, especially since it will be a center of debate for the rest of our lives. Here is a thumbnail explanation.

The Earth receives radiation from the sun, which is "the source of energy which drives the climate."[3] (Much of it comes in the visible form of the electromagnetic spectrum, light, and some extends into the infrared and some into the ultraviolet.) About one-third of this solar radiation is reflected by the Earth back beyond the Earth's atmosphere into space. The rest is absorbed by the Earth's oceans, land surface, plant and animal life—and by the Earth's atmosphere. These are the elements of the climate system, defined by international agreement to be "the totality of the atmosphere, hydrosphere, biosphere, and geosphere and their interactions."

In simplified terms, the critical factors in determining the temperature of the Earth are first, the amount of radiation supplied by the sun, and second, the balance between this solar radiation absorbed by the Earth's climate system and the amount emitted back into space. The effect of the Earth's atmosphere on this balance is affected by certain contents of the atmosphere—the greenhouse gases—most of which are natural and some of which are anthropogenic; that is, they result from the influence of human beings on nature (such as burning fossil fuel).

The term *greenhouse* is appropriate because these gases are similar in effect to that of the glass roof of a greenhouse used to grow plants in climates too cool for them to survive in the open. The greenhouse gases serve the same function as do the glass roof panels. They trap heat from the sun that would otherwise be reflected back to space. The principal greenhouse gases are water vapor, carbon dioxide, methane, nitrous oxide, ozone, and chlorofluorocarbons. Water vapor is the most important greenhouse gas, with an atmospheric concentration varying from 1 to 3 percent. Carbon dioxide accounts for less than 0.04 percent.[4] All greenhouse gases, other than water vapor, make up only about 2 percent of the Earth's atmosphere, but without their heat-trapping capabilities, the average surface temperature of the Earth might be similar to that of Mars, ranging from −50°–−60° F.

Atmospheric concentration is not the only important measure of the effect of a greenhouse gas. Scientists have determined that each of these gases has a different global warming potential (GWP), based on several factors. For example, the reflective power (albedo) of each gas differs. Gases that reflect less radiation absorb or trap more of it. Highly reflective gases, however, may block some radiation from reaching the Earth and bounce it back beyond the Earth's atmosphere. Some gases may permit solar radiation to pass through and then, when this heat is reflected back from Earth, trap it or reflect a part of it back to the Earth's surface.

The wavelength of this radiation may also be important. It appears that, since each gas absorbs radiation in a specific set of wavelengths, a gas that is plentiful may have captured all the radiation possible in that specific wavelength. If so, an increase in concentration may have no additional greenhouse—or warming—effect. As in the case of many climate issues, however, there is disagreement about this possibility.

Another factor in calculating global warming potential is how long a gas stays in the atmosphere. Some gases may have a short life; others, such as perfluorocarbons, which may stay around for thousands of years, are assigned a GWP of between 6,000 and 12,500. (Fortunately, these emissions are very low in volume.) Scientists have chosen carbon dioxide as the "reference" gas by which to measure others, taking into consideration all known direct and some indirect effects. For these purposes, carbon dioxide is measured in carbon units.[5] Thus, for example, methane has been assigned a GWP of twenty-two times that of carbon dioxide. (These GWP numbers have changed over time and are still tentative, with a margin of error of plus or minus 30–40 percent.)

Water Vapor, Carbon Dioxide, and Other Complexities

One of the most complex greenhouse issues is the role of water vapor. The consensus among world scientists is that water vapor is by far the most important greenhouse gas, but how it relates in warming potential to the other gases is unknown. While it has been estimated that methane, for example, has a GWP twenty-two times that of carbon dioxide, no GWP has been determined for water vapor, the most abundant greenhouse gas. Insofar as water is concerned, the Earth, with its atmosphere, has been assumed to be a closed system; water may take many forms—liquid, gas, or ice—

and is present in the clouds and biosphere, but the total volume is presumed to remain the same. To be clear, this is an assumption, not a demonstrated fact. News reports of the discoveries of the German satellite CRISTA-SPAS say that measurements from one instrument aboard indicate much more water vapor in the upper atmosphere than traditional theory can explain, possibly lending credence to claims by University of Iowa scientist Louis Frank that the Earth's atmosphere is being bombarded by small water-depositing comets.[6]

Atmospheric concentration of water vapor varies widely over short time periods and in specific regions. It goes up as surface water evaporates and down when it rains or snows. But the global average concentration of water vapor—which is what affects climate—is not known. Climatologists assume that it is not changing. It is also assumed that the concentration of more water vapor in the atmosphere would not absorb any significant additional amount of solar radiation. As the U.S. government says, "According to currently available information, anthropogenic [human induced] water vapor emissions at the Earth's surface [for example, from auto exhaust] are unlikely to be an important element in either causing or ameliorating climate change."[7]

To ask climate activists about water vapor is considered by some to be an unfriendly act. As a general rule, policy advocates are annoyed (and even offended) by any suggestion that they examine more closely the basic data that underlie their proposals. Data are often messy—accompanied by many caveats and assumptions. Unfortunately, virtually everything we know about the effect of water vapor as a greenhouse gas is an assumption based on imprecise and limited data. The many unanswered questions about water vapor help explain why there are so many uncertainties about global warming projections.

Carbon dioxide appears to be the next most important greenhouse gas. Total natural and human-induced releases of carbon dioxide are estimated at 157.1 billion metric tons of carbon annually. Of this amount, an estimated 150 billion tons come from natural sources. (Some 90 billion tons come from the oceans, 30 billion tons from decay of vegetation, and 30 billion from plant and animal respiration.) An estimated 7.1 billion tons are human-induced. Some 154 billion tons are absorbed annually, leading to an estimated net increase of 3.1–3.5 billion tons.[8] These numbers are rough estimates and change as more information is obtained. They are developed by the Intergovernmental Panel on Climate Change (IPCC), which notes that they are "subject to considerable uncertainty."[9]

Another set of emissions—aerosols—has quite a different effect. Aerosols are made up of suspended particles and are sent into the atmosphere in the form of soil dust, smoke, and certain chemical reactions. Volcanoes are major sources. Aerosols can bounce solar radiation back into space, thus having a cooling effect, and they can affect the formation and lifetime of clouds, which can also reflect back solar radiation. As the IPCC scientists say, "There are many uncertainties associated with estimating the climatic influence of aerosols."[10]

To calculate the effect of greenhouse gases and other factors on global climate and how climate change may affect the Earth's ecosystems, researchers have developed general circulation models (GCMs). These climate models are the tools that researchers use to attempt to account for all relevant interactions of the Earth's oceans, atmosphere, and landmass, including its vegetation and animal life. It is no surprise that the reliability of these models is a center of intense debate.

Is the Climate Changing?

We can be certain about one fact: the Earth's climate *is* changing. It was never static and it never will be. We are well aware of short-term, regional changes in the weather—blizzards one year, an "unseasonably warm" winter the next. The weather is notoriously unreliable. But regional or year-to-year weather is not what scientists mean when they talk about global climate. That term refers to the average weather over the entire Earth and over an extended period, centuries or even millennia. Evidence of climate change occurs, for example, when the average temperature of the Earth rises or falls over a period long enough to discern trends as opposed to short-term variations.

The history of the Earth, to the best of our current knowledge, is one of dramatic and continual climate change. Scientists believe that for at least 3 million years, large sheets of ice—known as glaciers—have moved up and down the Earth, extending into the middle latitudes. This period included the Pleistocene Epoch, often referred to as the Great Ice Age, which, they say, began some 1.6 million years ago. Some researchers say there is evidence now that glaciers formed, advanced, and retreated over the Earth's surface as early as 10–13 million years ago. Even more recent is a study that suggests that 2.2 billion years ago, most of the Earth was frozen.[11]

The reasons for the cooling that caused the glaciers to advance or the warming that pushed them back are still a mystery. The last major advance of glacial ice is said to have ended an estimated 10,000 years ago, but scientists do not suggest that the Great Ice Age has ended. If ice sheets oscillated over the Earth's land masses for at least 3 million years and possibly for 10 million or more years, is there any reason to believe this pattern will not continue? Nothing has occurred that leads scientists to say that the Earth will not again see ice move down into what are now temperate zones, covering again all of Canada, Scandinavia, and much more of our inhabited world and crushing into rubble, as some commentators enjoy saying, cities like Chicago, Cincinnati, Milwaukee, and New York. The scientists say we are in an interglacial period, that is, between advancing glaciers. Not even politicians or journalists claim to know that ice will not again cover much of the planet.

Of course, these changes take time to occur. We will not wake up one morning and hear the crunch of advancing ice. These events occur over thousands of years, but anyone planning to regulate the world's climate should want to know whether the Earth is in a warming mode or we have passed the midpoint in our interglacial period and are in a long-term cooling period. Some imprecise temperature readings over the past few years—or decades—will not tell us the answer to that basic question. Without the answer, the would-be regulators could find themselves on the wrong side of the trend. In any event, climate regulators may find themselves in a situation similar to that of the legendary old king who was so powerful that he had his throne set on the seashore and commanded the tides to cease and desist. He learned his limits as the sea washed over him, his throne, and his authority. As it was with the king, it may be a function of human ego to believe we have the ability to change the direction of climatic trends.

It appears that not only do we have major glacial episodes spanning tens of thousands of years, but that within those episodes we may have short-term climate change every few thousand years. It may have been one of these short-term changes that brought about what some scholars call the Viking-Norman period, between 1000 and 1250, when an apparently worldwide warm-up permitted the Norsemen to explore the far North. In the tenth century A.D. a colony was established in Greenland and reached a population level of 5,000–6,500. Evidence is also accumulating that these intrepid explorers may have reached North America. Then came the Early Medieval cool period, from 1250 to 1500. The temperature dropped an estimated one degree Celsius worldwide. As growing seasons shortened, human life became insupportable on Greenland. By 1500, the colony had disappeared and the age of the Vikings came to an end.

Clearly, the geological record shows that "change is permanent" in climate, as in all else. To adapt an old saying about the weather, "If you don't like the climate, stick around for a few millennia and it will be different." Whether it will be warmer or cooler is anyone's guess. That should not, however, keep us from trying to educate ourselves about the issue.

Since climate change is a constant and the greenhouse effect is natural and necessary, the issue before us is neither of those. It is whether the climate is warming and, if so, whether the warming is the result of human activity. At another time it may be whether the climate is cooling, but today, the issue is global warming.

Truth by Negotiation

The underlying theory of the greenhouse effect, linking it to carbon dioxide, has been under scrutiny for one hundred years. In 1896, the year the Duryea brothers rolled out the first production automobiles, the Swedish chemist Svante Arrhenius published a paper on the subject, estimating that a doubling of carbon dioxide in the atmosphere might raise the Earth's temperature 5°–6° C. He believed the source of carbon dioxide was volcanic activity. On the whole he rather favored the idea of a slow warming, which certainly would have improved the living conditions and extended the growing season in his native land.[12]

One hundred years later, concern about the accumulation of carbon dioxide and its effect on the Earth's climate became an international issue. In an effort to arrive at the facts, the United Nations Environment Programme (UNEP) and the World Meteorological Organization (WMO) established the Intergovernmental Panel on Climate Change,[13] with an assignment to: "(i) assess the available scientific information on climate change, (ii) assess the environmental and socioeconomic impacts of climate change, and (iii) formulate response strategies."[14] In simple terms, the IPCC was commissioned by the UN to be the world's climate watchdog.

All member countries of the UN or WMO may participate as members of the IPCC. Some 2,000 scientists, government representatives, consultants, and others are involved in the IPCC assessments. The IPCC is not expected to conduct research and does not do so. Its assessments are arrived at by consensus, with government officials playing a significant role in the consensus-building. The conclusions, while presented in the language of science, are negotiated and therefore are political in nature. John Maddox, a former editor of the science journal *Nature,* made this point when he wrote, "As things are, IPCC should recognize that however robustly it resists 'those with various agendas,' consensus-building is inherently a political process whose practitioners are called 'spin-doctors,' in other trades."[15]

Global warming may be the most important scientific issue in history in which the "truth" is being established through international negotiation and consensus—with 2,000 participants of various levels of competence involved in the negotiations! For the general public, which, in a period of growing cynicism, clings to respect for researchers in white coats, this politicization of science must come as a disappointment. One more idol has fallen into the clutches of the political process.

Perhaps that is too harsh. There is obvious merit to the idea of an international approach. Having a secretariat where information can be collected and disseminated to all interested parties can be a good thing. Having conferences in which researchers from around the world discuss their ideas is meritorious. What is worrisome is the notion that scientific truth can be arrived at by negotiation. What is worse is the pressure brought to bear on the rest of the community to accept that so-called truth. This is less the handiwork of scientists (although some indulge) than it is of the political operators and professional activists who take up the so-called truth and use it to justify radical policies and to bludgeon dissenters into line.

We should have learned from the experiences of the Polish astronomer Copernicus and the Italian scientist Galileo. The truth, in their days, was the heritage of Ptolemy of Alexandria who, in the second century A.D., "proved" that the universe was Earth-centered, with the sun and all the heavenly bodies revolving around our globe. He developed his theory brilliantly to accommodate all planetary phenomena observable at that time. In effect, he built what today would be called a model of a geocentric universe that was so ingenious it was accepted as truth for more than 1,300 years.

The Ptolemaic system (or model) was displaced not for any failure to work. The problem was that with more data gathered from more extensive and accurate observations, the system became increasingly difficult to use in making accurate predictions.[16] In 1543, Copernicus challenged the truth of the day with his theory that the universe was heliocentric, or sun-centered. His model not only worked, it was more flexible and, as astronomers say, it was "aesthetically superior." But it was in conflict with the consensus. It fell to Galileo to take the case to Rome and, with his telescope, to demonstrate that Copernicus was right. For his efforts, he was eventually taken to court and, in 1633, found guilty and required to "abjure and curse" the errors of his ways.[17] Nonetheless, these two dissenters changed the scientific world, and their theory of the sun-centered universe has now been the "truth" for 450 years.

As this little history suggests, a problem in the physical sciences is the temptation to assert that a theory is truth because a formula computes or a model works. (In modern social sciences the flaw may be the reverse—the denial of all truths, leaving no social moorings.) In fairness to scientists of all disciplines, it is more often the nonscholars—special pleaders, opportunistic politicians, pseudo-scholars, and practitioners of "infotainment"— who promote extreme or distorted interpretations of scholarly works, and then demand conformity. It is worse yet if they have the power to enforce conformity.

You're Hot; You're Cold. In its January 2, 1989, issue, *Time* magazine declared the Planet of the Year to be the "Endangered Earth." In apocalyptic terms and with dramatic photographs, the magazine portrayed 1989 as the "year the earth spoke, like God warning Noah of the deluge." Citing droughts, heat waves, floods, and hurricanes, it talked of "the dreaded greenhouse effect" and reported that "everyone suddenly sensed that this gyrating globe, this precious repository of all the life that we know of, was in danger." It concluded that "our wasteful, careless ways must become a thing of the past. We must recycle more, procreate less, turn off lights, use mass transit, do a thousand things differently in our everyday lives."

In an issue containing nineteen pages of automobile and truck advertisements, *Time* told its readers that "cars and factories are spewing enough gases into the atmosphere to heat up the atmosphere in a greenhouse effect that could eventually produce disastrous climate changes." In its call to action, *Time* urged government to raise auto fuel-economy requirements from 27.5 mpg to "45 mpg by the year 2000."

Time did report that some scientists disagreed with the alarmist view, but the magazine's essay concluded, "The skeptics could be right, but it is far too risky to do nothing while awaiting absolute proof of disaster." Later in 1989, *Time* senior editor Charles Alexander said, "On this issue (the environment) we have crossed the boundary from news reporting to advocacy." (After receiving a multitude of complaints about this statement, *Time* responded that over the years it had undertaken to "add our own judgments on subjects that truly mattered," and that "we believe considered journalistic judgments are an important contribution to an informed society."[18] Apparently readers of articles in *Time* on the environment do not necessarily get the hard news but get the editors' judgments instead.)

By February 13, 1989, six different legislative proposals had been introduced in the U. S. Senate dealing with global warming. *Time*, of course, was not the origin of congressional concern. In 1989, Senator Timothy Wirth (D-Colo.), along with senators Al Gore (D-Tenn.) and John Chafee (R-R.I.), introduced a bill to "develop binding multilateral agreements" to reduce greenhouse gases by 20 percent from 1988 levels by the year 2000, a proposal so drastic in its potential effect on the national economy and individual standards of living that it went nowhere.[19]

Cooling Off

While *Time* magazine, in 1989, brought the global climate issue wide and dramatic public attention, it wasn't the first such journalistic effort. In the mid-1970s, the Earth was thought by some scientists to be cooling, with another ice age in the making. The April 28, 1975, issue of *Newsweek* reported that "there are ominous signs that the earth's weather patterns have begun to change dramatically and that these changes may portend a drastic decline in food production—with serious political implications for just about every nation on earth."

Citing shortened growing seasons, record "outbreak of tornadoes," and a survey by the National Oceanic and Atmospheric Administration, *Newsweek* concluded, "The central fact is that after three quarters of a century of extraordinarily mild conditions, the earth's climate seems to be cooling down." The magazine found "Climatologists are pessimistic that political leaders will take any positive action to compensate for the climatic change." *Newsweek* conceded that some solutions, such as "melting the Arctic ice cap by covering it with black soot" to retain the sun's heat, might create other problems, but the magazine concluded by saying, "The longer planners delay, the more difficult will they find it to cope with climatic change once the results become grim reality."

We should all be grateful that the "planners" do not always get their way. If they had in 1975, we probably would be spending millions today trying to scrape the soot off the ice cap; lawyers would be filling the court dockets with liability lawsuits over alleged damages from tampering with the weather, and congressional hearings would be underway with a special prosecutor not far behind.

This is no criticism of the scientists who said soot on the ice caps would help melt them. They were right. Societies need innovative people who can offer up all possible solutions to perceived problems. The difficulty comes in establishing whether there is a real problem and then in deciding whether a particular action makes sense. It is at this stage that planners and politicians can turn a scientist's work into a debacle.

Later the same year, but in more measured terms, the *Smithsonian* magazine published an article entitled "Climate Outlook: Variable and Possibly Cooler," by Henry Lansford of the National Center for Atmospheric Research.[20] "Most climatologists agree on one documented fact," Lansford wrote: "The Northern Hemisphere has been cooling off for the last quarter-century or so, especially in higher latitudes."

Mr. Lansford acknowledged that "we do not have certain knowledge that the climate is changing for the worse," but he quoted Stephen Schneider, then of the National Center for Atmospheric Research, as deeply concerned. Lansford wrote that "Schneider asks if we can afford to gamble that we will not have a series of years like 1972 and 1974, when droughts, floods, and early frosts drastically reduced crop yields." Schneider, he wrote, "advocates a food reserve policy that he calls the 'Genesis strategy,' after the Biblical book that tells how Joseph advised Pharaoh to store grain during seven years of plenty so there would be food for the people during the seven years of famine that followed."

In 1976, Lowell Ponte's book *The Cooling* detailed the "fact" that global cooling was taking place.[21] In his foreword, Senator Claiborne Pell (D-R.I.) said, "This book is as disquieting as *Silent Spring* in its analysis of environmental hazards that can affect our future."[22] Ponte wrote, "It is a cold fact: the global cooling presents humankind with the most important social political and adaptive challenge we have had to deal with for ten thousand years. . . . The cooling," he said, "has already killed hundreds of thousands of people in poor nations." This, because cooling was causing violent storms and flooding and other destructive phenomena. In support of this assertion, Ponte quoted a 1975 National Academy of Sciences study suggesting the possibility of huge, year-round snowfields in the United States and Europe. He cited Drs. S.I. Rasool and Stephen H. Schneider, then of the NASA Goddard Institute, as suggesting that the greenhouse threat from carbon dioxide is overrated and that even an eightfold increase over present levels might warm the Earth less than two degrees. Using a favorite putdown, Ponte responded, "A handful of scientists denied evidence that Earth's climate was cooling until the 1970s, when bizarre weather throughout the world forced them to reconsider their views."

Cooling was still on the scientific agenda in the September 1978 issue of the *Smithsonian* magazine to which British scientist Nigel Calder contributed a more measured assessment article entitled "Head South with All Deliberate Speed: Ice May Return in a Few Thousand Years." He made the point that glacial periods "have been *dominant* features of the Earth's climate during the last two million years or so." He wrote that "after climbing out of the freezer about 10,000 years ago, the Earth went through a 'climatic optimum' about 3000 to 4000 B.C. and then began its descent into the next glaciation." Today, the people concerned about warming dismiss the worriers of the 1970s as ill-informed and misguided. They do so, one imagines, secure in their own wisdom and confident about how they will be regarded in the decades ahead.

Calder was aware of the increase of carbon dioxide in the atmosphere through combustion of fossil fuel and the cutting of forests, and he suggested that "the excess carbon dioxide might reverse any recent cooling trend." Following up on this thought, he wrote, "One can imagine a future world government trying to regulate the Earth's heat budget by carefully timed releases of carbon dioxide to warm the atmosphere and particulates to cool it."

The concept Calder raised—world government trying to regulate the climate—may thrill those who still believe a collection of smart people in Washington, or in any central planning agency, can plan and implement the solution to almost any problem. To the rest of us, this should be a frightening specter. It conjures up pictures of vast, new government bureaucracies—the Department of Climate Control—and of a congressional Committee on Climate Affairs, perhaps with subcommittees on clouds, oceans, glaciation, and so on. Great debates would be held on whether the earth was in a long-term warming or cooling mode. Political parties would divide or splinter over the issue. It would become a litmus test for presidential candidates. Dozens of bills would be introduced in Congress. Professional activists would thrive on dire predictions of calamity (accompanied, of course, by requests for donations). Lawyers and lobbyists would prosper, with industries rushing to Washington to promote or protect their interests.

In short, the politics of the issue would quickly overwhelm the science as attempts to control the climate would extend government ever more deeply into how we conduct our businesses and our private lives.

Inevitably, this debate would have to be moved to the United Nations. (After all, China already contributes more than 10 percent of the world's carbon dioxide. With its fast-growing economy and with 75 percent of its energy coming from coal, that contribution will grow rapidly. Even Thailand produces 1.5 percent of human-induced greenhouse gases in the form of methane from its rice paddies.) Imagine, if you can, the kind of climate control actions that might come out of an international regulatory process. Calder did think about it, and in his *Smithsonian* article he cautioned, "If scientists tried to accelerate natural feedback processes, they might drastically overshoot the mark and perpetrate a disaster." If this sounds ominous, it is. It is all the more worrisome since action plans may be suggested by scientists but they are decided by governments, where short-term political considerations too often become paramount.

The UN Steps In

All this was forgotten in 1992, when representatives of 170 countries gathered in Rio de Janeiro for the United Nations Earth Summit to deal with global warming. After much drama, theater, rhetoric, negotiation, and denunciation—especially of the United States and President George Bush— a treaty was signed. As Gregg Easterbrook puts it, "Countries that ratified the greenhouse treaty—America among the first—agreed to submit to the authority of the United Nations for the purpose of regulating global-warming gases, surrendering any claim that greenhouse emissions are a matter of internal economic policy."[23] This treaty, officially known as the UN Framework Convention of Climate Change (UNFCCC) and popularly known as the Rio treaty, has as its objective the "stabilization of greenhouse gas concentrations in the atmosphere at a level that would prevent dangerous anthropogenic [human-induced] interference with the climate system." The UNFCCC asked the IPCC to provide scientific support for meeting its objective.

What brought President Bush his most vehement criticism was the U.S. refusal to accept, in the treaty, specific timetables and requirements for the reduction of greenhouse gases emitted by U.S. sources. The reason given by the Bush administration was the absence of adequate scientific knowledge to justify such drastic action. Knowing that President Bush's refusal made any action they took inoperative, much of the rest of the developed world proclaimed its dedication to rolling back emissions of carbon dioxide and other greenhouse gases to 1990 levels by the year 2000.

Senator Al Gore, in Rio to attend the conference, added his support for this pledge and his denunciation of President Bush.[24]

The goal of international cooperation in all global matters is not unjustified. If the global climate is being adversely affected by humankind, it is a problem that requires international attention. To be effective in regulating something like the emission of carbon dioxide, which becomes well-mixed in the atmosphere and disperses around the globe, all significant producing countries of the gas must agree on the action to be taken. Efforts by the United States alone to reduce carbon dioxide would have no appreciable effect, for example, if China and India, which together have 40 percent of the world's population and are rapidly increasing energy use, do not adopt and implement similar programs. The stress is on the word *implement;* history is replete with international agreements signed with great pomp and promise, only to prove inadequate or be ignored.[25]

People should be aware of the pitfalls of international agreements administered by international organizations, and above all they should demand that the problems be thoroughly understood before solutions are enacted. There is no shortage of world problems, but there is a shortage of resources and of will to commit them. These should be spent wisely. These caveats apply especially to climate issues, with their multitude of uncertainties, especially since the "solutions" can have such broad effect on human activity.

Vice President Gore Takes the Lead. In the same year the Rio treaty was signed, Senator Gore published his book *Earth in the Balance.*[26] Gore noted that "the collapse of communism deprived the [Western] alliance of its common enemy," and added that this "may create the ideal opportunity to choose a new grand purpose for working together." The new grand purpose, he proposed, should be a global Marshall plan, patterned after the post-Second World War plan by which the United States helped fund the rebuilding of war-torn Europe.

This new plan would be dedicated to addressing the environmental crisis and, he wrote, "will require the wealthy nations to allocate money for transferring environmentally helpful technologies to the Third World and to help impoverished nations achieve a stable population." He alluded to a requirement for "wealthy nations to make a transition themselves that will be in some ways more wrenching than that of the Third World." He proposed that these changes be brought about by the negotiation of "international agreements that establish global constraints on acceptable behavior [sic]" and that these agreements have "legally valid penalties for non-compliance."

Lamenting "humankind's assault on the earth," the senator wrote that global warming is "a strategic threat" and that "this increase in heat seriously threatens the global climate equilibrium that determines the pattern of winds, rainfall, surface temperatures, ocean currents, and sea level."

In January 1993, the capability of Mr. Gore to shape events took an upward turn as he was sworn in as vice president of the United States of America. On April 21, 1993, the first Earth Day after his election, President Bill Clinton rectified something Gore had considered was a grievous error made by President Bush. In a pivotal speech on the environment, Clinton proclaimed: "Today I reaffirm my personal, and announce our nation's commitment to reducing our emissions of greenhouse gases to their 1990 levels by the year 2000."

The underlying assumption of President Clinton's pledge was that the effects of these gases were well enough understood to warrant such a commitment and to justify the underlying costs and dislocations necessary to reach the goal. Clinton did not specify, however, what actions, when taken, would achieve this ambitious goal. Having moved away from the idea of increasing corporate average fuel economy (CAFE) standards during the 1992 presidential campaign, he did not raise the subject of motor vehicle fuel economy, although several of his White House associates favored much higher requirements.

With the defeat of more stringent CAFE standards in the Senate in 1992 and President Clinton's reluctance to raise the issue again, professional activists and their allies in the new administration began again to see the international agreement route as providing the best opportunity to implement new restrictions on cars, trucks, and industries.

People sharing this point of view were moved into key government jobs. Senator Tim Wirth became the undersecretary of state for global affairs. Rafe Pomerance, one of the most strident of the professional environmental activists, became his deputy assistant secretary of state for environment and development. Another experienced activist, Gustave Speth, former head of the World Resources Institute, was appointed as administrator, United Nations Development Program.

Rallying the troops against the forces of darkness, Vice President Gore, in a speech to a White House Conference on Climate Action on April 21, 1994, referred to the participants as "Paul Reveres of the environmental movement." (He added that "our enemy is more subtle than a British fleet. Climate change is the most serious problem that our civilization faces.") Gore had little patience for those who would disagree: "On one side are that vast preponderance of the serious scientists who have studied the evidence. And on the other hand, we have a tiny minority and a self-interested few saying, we just don't know; we don't believe there's any basis; we just dispute this. And all the while, the debate goes on, the gases continue to accumulate in the atmosphere!"

Despite his concern about the dangers of listening to the "self-interested few," Gore welcomed certain business groups to the debate. Not among those welcomed were "the self-interested cynics," whom, he says, "are seeking to cloud the underlying issue of the environment with disinformation."[27] Business interests that showed proper concern were treated differently. In his White House speech, Gore referred to a "study by the insurance giant, the Travelers Corporation," which predicts "a 30 percent annual rise in U.S. catastrophic losses from storms—just from a 0.9 degree Fahrenheit increase." He quoted the head of the Reinsurance Association of America as saying, "Global warming could bankrupt the industry." To help us understand the interest these insurance companies have in the issue, the vice president pointed out that "insurance companies set their rates in anticipation of future calamities." (He did not mention what happens to the funds thus accumulated if the calamities do not materialize.) This example clearly illustrates that one man's "self-interested few" may be another man's expert witnesses. It also shows that there are winners and losers among business interests in almost any public policy debate.

From Rio to Berlin to Geneva, and On to Kyoto

Moving from debate to action, nations from around the world met in Berlin in April 1995 for the first Conference of the Parties (COP) to the United Nations Framework Convention on Climate Change (UNFCCC). The mission was to review any progress made since meeting in Rio and to move forward on the environmental agenda. There was quick agreement that the commitments made at Rio were "not adequate" to stabilize concentrations of greenhouse gases. When it came to next steps, however, the consensus, after a week and a half of intense debate, was that they should keep on talking for two more years. The objective would be to try to set "quantified limitation and reduction objectives (for greenhouse gas emissions) within specified time-frames, such as 2005, 2010, and 2020."

Undersecretary Timothy Wirth, now heading the U.S. delegation, saw the opportunity to implement, through the UN, the legislative proposal that he and Senator Al Gore had advanced in the Senate in 1989, namely, to mandate greenhouse gas emissions reductions. At Berlin, he retained his fervor. "I don't think the question is any longer *if* we are experiencing, or are going to experience, climate change," he said. "The questions are: How much? How fast? And where?"[28] He was not able, however, to achieve his goal in Berlin. National and international realities required him to settle for more talk. Too many other countries were not ready to make the great leap.

Nonetheless, three important things did happen in Berlin: one ironic, one very serious, and another, quite predictable.

The ironic event occurred after the Berlin conference came to agreement on a concept known as "joint implementation," a provision that might permit advanced nations to get credit in meeting their greenhouse gas reduction quotas by helping developing nations to reduce their emissions.[29] Environmental activists monitoring the conference were especially offended by "joint implementation" and organized protests. These demonstrators, mostly American, wanted to hold the United States responsible for making all its cuts in the United States rather than by helping developing countries to cut back on theirs. They turned on their erstwhile hero Tim Wirth for agreeing to it. They demonstrated against the "Berlin Mandate" (as Wirth had suggested that the agreement be called) and interrupted his press conference by ripping up one of his old, militant speeches and showering him with the shredded paper. This was another lesson showing that zealots permit no deviations from their agenda and seem willing to consume any of their own who do. Those same activists protested the presence in Berlin of industrial representatives as observers. Calling them "carbon criminals," the activists chained themselves to buses outside their hotel in an effort to prevent the industry representatives from getting to events.

The most serious action came when the Berlin conference exempted developing countries (including China and India) from any real commitments to reduce greenhouse gases. This was a serious setback for the U.S. negotiators, and it placed in jeopardy the credibility of the entire approach. Without restrictions in fast-growing economies like China, the increase in emissions from those areas will overwhelm any cuts made by the United States and other developed nations that participate. Significantly, there is no indication that China and other developing countries are willing to stop their economic growth and the increase in the standard of living of their people in order to deal with presumed global warming. Zi Zhongyun of the Chinese Academy of Social Sciences has said that "like any other nation, China will come into conflict with forces that attempt to halt its unity and development."[30]

Presumably, President Clinton considers this to be an important issue. In an interview with Thomas L. Friedman in April 1996, the president told about his meeting with the president of China, Jiang Zemin, five months earlier.[31] He said Jiang Zemin had asked if he is "trying to contain China." Mr. Clinton said that he replied, "I don't want to contain you. It might surprise you to know what I think the greatest threat to our security you present is." Friedman reports that the president went on to say that he told Jiang Zemin the greatest threat is that the Chinese people "will want to get rich in exactly the same way we got rich. And unless we try to triple the automobile mileage and to reduce greenhouse gas emissions . . . we won't be breathing very well."[32]

The predictable occurrence in Berlin was the presence of business interests, many as nongovernmental observers (NGOs). As reported by the *Economist,* the meeting "saw the emergence of strong business pressure in favor of curbing greenhouse gases. . . . Insurance firms, for example, came to Berlin to give warning that they could be bankrupted if global warming led to a string of natural disasters."[33] (As Gore has instructed us, insurance companies will set their rates to collect the funds to anticipate calamity.) Other business interests at the conference included renewable-energy firms and those with solar energy interests. Natural gas representatives were present, as were people urging use of vegetable oil for engine fuel.[34] The *Washington Post* reported that at the Berlin conference, "Greenpeace . . . allied itself with the insurance industry to warn that weather run amok from global warming . . . could hurt consumers by causing higher insurance costs."[35]

Business and industry should be present at these meetings. The issues are too important to ignore. All sides should be represented to present the information only they may have about their businesses and products. The auto industry, oil companies, electric utilities, and all mining and manufacturing should be present, along with the insurance industry and those representing alternative energy sources. The broader and more comprehensive the debate, the better for informing the public—which is not permitted to attend the meetings.

The energy-producing and -using industries in the United States have organized a broad-based Global Climate Coalition as a coordinating and information center on this issue. Individual industry trade associations, such as the American Automobile Manufacturers Association and the American Petroleum Institute, as well as the National Association of Manufacturers, the U. S. Chamber of Commerce, and several others are working the issue, stressing the high cost and doubtful benefits of limits on carbon dioxide in the United States. The reinsurance industry is also busy working to show how costly extreme weather events can be. Thomas R. Karl, senior scientist at the National Climate Data Center in Asheville, North Carolina, organized a meeting of scientists and reinsurance industry representatives "to devise a plan of where we should go from here."[36] All of these interests should be involved in the process. The public will benefit, however, by understanding how this issue could affect each interest.

Despite its apparent lack of results in comparison with those of the Rio meeting, the Berlin Mandate adopted by the First Conference of Parties did lay down a path for arriving at more stringent regulation of carbon-based fuel use, at least by the United States and some other developed nations. A permanent Climate Convention Secretariat was established in Bonn; a bureaucracy for the management of the Earth's climate is now in its infancy. In Senate testimony on this issue, an AFL-CIO representative said, "In particular, we are concerned that the so-called Berlin Mandate requirement will have an adverse impact on the American economy but little or no effect on the problem of greenhouse gas concentrations in the atmosphere."[37]

The July 1996 climate summit in Geneva, at which Wirth pushed for legally binding cuts in carbon dioxide, was the next major step in nailing down that goal. In a House Commerce Committee hearing before the meeting, it became clear that the U.S. delegation was woefully underprepared. Ranking Committee Democrat John D. Dingell (D-Mich.) asked about the status of a long-promised administration analysis of the climate issue. The committee was told that it was about half done. Dingell asked the group, which included Rafe Pomerance of the State Department and others from EPA and the Departments of Commerce and Energy, how they could have developed a strategy for Geneva without an analysis of the issues. And how, he asked, could they protect U.S. interests without a strategy? The responses did not satisfy the subcommittee members. Subcommittee Chairman Dan Schaefer (R-Colo.) worried "that the United States will agree to further commitments which may . . . have serious negative economic consequences."[38] He and Dingell were justified in their concerns. "Serious consequences" are exactly what happened in Geneva when Secretary Wirth committed to legally binding caps and did so without commitments from developing countries representing more than half the world's population.

The treaty to bind the United States to cuts in carbon dioxide—which means cuts in energy use—is scheduled to come before the third Conference of Parties (COP-3) of the UNFCCC planned for Kyoto, Japan, in December 1997. This conference could set the course for the use of energy for personal mobility and for every other activity for generations ahead.

President Clinton Commits to Binding Limits—On the United States.
On June 26, 1997, under heavy pressure from professional activist groups and European politicians, President Clinton joined the Gore-Wirth call for cutbacks in greenhouse gases, which, in turn, means cutbacks in the use of carbon-based fuels such as gasoline. Speaking before the United Nations General Assembly, Clinton said "we will bring to the Kyoto conference a strong American commitment to realistic and binding limits that will significantly reduce our emissions of greenhouse gases."

Clinton's conversion came only four days after he was harshly criticized for failing to commit to cutbacks at the annual economic summit in Denver, Colorado, on June 22, 1997. The *Washington Post* headlined its June 23, 1997, report on his stance with "Discord on Pollution Strains United Front as Summit Concludes." French President Jacques Chirac told reporters, "We had a very difficult discussion with the Americans," and added, "The Americans are great polluters when it comes to carbon dioxide. The average American emits three times the amount of carbon dioxide as the average Frenchman."[39] British Prime Minister Tony Blair, commenting on the failure to agree at the summit, said, "We obviously want this to go further." Unmentioned at the conference was the fact that Germany's ability to cut carbon dioxide is almost entirely the result of closing or modernizing highly inefficient and grossly polluting plants in east Germany, and that Britain's cutbacks come largely from cuts in the subsidies for the mining of coal and switching to fuels producing less carbon dioxide. U.S. activists also attacked the president. Alan Meyer of the Union of Concerned Scientists said, "What we need is presidential leadership, not political platitudes."

Apologetic about the U.S. performance, President Clinton, echoing Chirac's criticism, told the United Nations, "Here in the United States, we must do better. We already produce more than 20 percent of [Earth's] greenhouse gases." To help assuage the guilt, the president pledged to give $1 billion to help developing nations to reduce greenhouse gas emissions. He also pledged to encourage or require private investment to meet environmental standards. To reduce fossil-fuel use in the United States he said he would work with business and communities to install "solar panels on one million more roofs around our nation by 2010."

The only other program mentioned by the president to cut back carbon dioxide was the Partnership for a New Generation of Vehicles (PNGV). Clinton told the UN, "Already we are working with our auto industry to produce cars by early in the next century that are three times as fuel efficient as today's vehicles." This reference underscores the heavy emphasis the Clinton-Gore administration is putting on the personal motor vehicle as a source of cutbacks in energy use. It also underscores how important it is that the administration understand the difficulties (outlined in Part One) that the PNGV program confronts.

In justification for draconian steps to curtail the use of energy that produces carbon dioxide, Clinton said, "The science is clear and compelling: we humans are changing the global climate." Unfortunately for Clinton's case, the science in *not* clear. What the scientists themselves say about the global climate is enlightening and compelling.

· 7 ·

THE SCIENCE OF CLIMATE CHANGE

T he single most important document produced by the Intergovernmental Panel on Climate Change (IPCC) to assist the UN Framework Convention of Climate Change (UNFCCC) is the *IPCC Second
Assessment, Climate Change 1995*. It is the contents of this document that
are cited as justifying immediate and drastic action to control the climate.

What the IPCC Actually Said

When it was still in draft form, the IPCC assessment became a source of
speculation and controversy. Predictably, environmentalists were quickly
out of the box to control the "sound bites." A headline in the *New York
Times* read: "Experts Confirm Human Role in Global Warming."[1] The article quoted someone at the Environmental Defense Fund as saying that the
scientific community "has discovered the smoking gun." When the IPCC
report was finally released officially, Tim Wirth said, "The science calls on
us to take urgent action."

It is always a good idea in any important debate to read the basic
documents. In contrast to the purple rhetoric used by activists, here is what
the IPCC actually said: "The balance of evidence, from changes in global
mean surface air temperature and from changes in geographical, seasonal
and vertical patterns of atmospheric temperature, suggests a discernible
human influence on global climate. There are uncertainties in key factors,
including the magnitude and patterns of long-term natural variability."[2]

To say, as the IPCC did, that "the evidence . . . suggests a discernible
human influence" is hardly a barn burner. Asserting that evidence suggests
that a condition exists is a far cry from stating it is a fact. It isn't even a basis
for saying there is a "solid body of evidence," and certainly it is not a "smoking gun."

Most important is the caution that the magnitude of natural variability is uncertain. This leaves the door wide open as to the relative importance of any human influence that may or may not be present. The statement was emphatically qualified: "There are many uncertainties, and many factors currently limit our ability to project and detect future climate change."

The IPCC pronouncement is exceedingly conservative and cautious, but even this carefully hedged statement was challenged, and there were charges of irregularities in the process by which it was put together. In a series of letters to the *Wall Street Journal* in June and July 1996, Frederick Seitz, former president of the U.S. National Academy of Sciences, and others charged that the IPCC document, as released in April 1996, was changed after it was approved by the members in Madrid in November. Omitted from the documents, Seitz wrote, was "the important statement that we cannot yet attribute the observed warming to the greenhouse effect." S. Fred Singer of the Science and Environmental Policy Project wrote that IPCC officials had been quoted as saying that changes were made "to ensure that it conformed to a 'policymakers' summary' of the full report." Singer asked the obvious question: "Should not a summary conform to the underlying scientific report rather than vice versa?"

Benjamin D. Santer of the Lawrence Livermore Laboratory in California was the lead author of chapter 8 in the IPCC report, which dealt with detection of climate change and attribution of causes. He was also the author of the changes to the key chapter that came under attack. He responded to Singer, saying that "all changes were made for scientific and not political purposes," and that "important scientific uncertainties have not been suppressed and are covered comprehensively in the published version of chapter 8." Charges came from each side that the other was subverting science. The controversy over these issues almost certainly will get more heated as the policy community moves closer to decisions on causes, effects, and remedial actions. The stakes are too great to expect otherwise.

On the surface, the issues at the core of the controversy over global warming appear to be straightforward. Beginning with Svante Arrhenius in 1896, scientists have worried about carbon dioxide accumulation in the atmosphere. The apparent consensus of the scientists, consultants, and others involved with the IPCC is that since about 1750, carbon dioxide concentrations have grown from an estimate of 280 parts per million by volume (ppmv) to almost 360 ppmv.[3] The IPCC consensus also is that global mean temperature, measured at the Earth's surface, has increased by between about 0.3° and 0.6° C. since the late nineteenth century. This change, according to the IPCC, "is *unlikely* to be *entirely* natural in origin [emphasis added]." This carefully drawn statement leaves open the question of how much, if any, effect human-induced greenhouse gases have on this change in surface temperature.

Patrick Michaels, a climatologist and professor at the University of

Virginia, raises a related point. "Virtually all the warming of the Northern Hemisphere," he says, "was prior to major post-war emissions of the greenhouse gases."[4] Fred Singer adds that when the IPCC "points to climate warming in the past 100 years, it doesn't reveal that the major temperature increase occurred around 1920, well before most of the carbon dioxide accumulated in the atmosphere."[5] Writing to *Science* magazine, he said that while the IPCC reports that the surface temperature has warmed by 0.3°–0.6° C. in the past 100 years, it "does not mention that there has been little warming if any in the last 50 years, during which time some 80 percent of greenhouse gases were added to the atmosphere."[6]

In a remarkable response to Singer and Michaels, *Consumer Reports,* in a lengthy article on global warming, said, "But perfect synchronization is an unrealistic expectation. Climate doesn't warm in lock-step with greenhouse emissions. It also responds to other, natural variations."[7] The magazine is right on both counts, but it is bizarre to suggest that warming that occurs *before* the greenhouse gas buildup could have been caused by those gases. Nature is wily, but to suggest that it warmed up in *anticipation* of the emission of more greenhouse gases is too much to swallow. (Number one in *Consumer Reports'* list of What-you-can-do-about-global-warming suggestions is: "Get out of your car. Walk, bike, carpool, take the train or bus." This is advice the magazine's own consumers obviously reject, as they eagerly buy the edition that suggests which car to buy!)

Two other factors about temperature are worth noting. Ground-based temperature readings show that most of the warming has occurred during the winter months and at night, and not during summer days, when elevated temperature could do the most harm. This finding is important in terms of the ultimate global effect of any warming. Even more important, however, are the results of a new method of temperature measurement. Historically, the Earth's temperature has been measured on land and at sea. Changing circumstances present problems with these measurements. Ocean circulation, for example, is not well understood, and deep waters may take centuries to move around the globe, affecting temperatures. On land, the cities and suburbs, which cover fields and forests with bricks, cement, asphalt, and other heat-retaining materials, change those areas into "heat islands" and raise temperature readings.

For the past several years, the Earth's temperature has also been taken by satellite. John R. Christy, a scientist with the Earth System Science Lab at the University of Alabama, has been tracking the satellite data and says, "There are large regional and globally averaged differences between the satellite temperatures (the temperature of the layer from the surface to 6 km altitude) and surface (scattered thermometers, mainly on land)." He concludes, "The satellite readings show no warming in the past eighteen years."[8] Eighteen years is much too short a measurement period to justify judgments, but it is not too short to raise questions about surface readings that need further exploration. Since the satellite readings clash with the politically correct position on global warming, we can expect them and their sponsors to come under criticism and even attack.[9]

To move from the past to the future and project "possible" temperature increases, the IPCC developed a range of scenarios of greenhouse gas and aerosol precursor emissions which, in turn, are in the IPCC's words "based on assumptions concerning population and economic growth, land-use, technological changes, energy availability and fuel mix during the period 1990 to 2100."[10] Taking the mid-range scenario, climate models used by the IPCC "project an increase in global mean surface temperature relative to 1990 of about 2° C. by 2100."

It is notable that the IPCC says, "This estimate [of about 2° C. by 2100] is approximately one-third lower than the 'best estimate' in 1990." In other words, the estimated temperature increase was reduced by one-third. We would expect that estimates made by Arrhenius in 1896 would be wrong, but this one-third drop in estimated warming came in only five years. The reason for the reduction is that scientists believe they have gained a better understanding of the role of aerosols in the atmosphere, one of the vast number of variables (some, no doubt, still unknown) that affect global climate. No reputable scientist would maintain that these estimates will not change again—in the negative or positive—in the next five years.

Do We Know Enough?

There are legitimate concerns about the state of the planet's climate. It would be foolish to ignore data that show potential warming. It would not be surprising if, over the next several decades, it could be demonstrated that the Earth's temperature has risen by a degree or two. But neither should it be surprising if it is shown that it has dropped a bit—or stayed the same. This is not to question the work or the integrity of the scientists. Much outstanding work has been done, but there is too much uncertainty about what has happened and is happening to the climate for hard judgments deeply affecting standards of living around the world. We do not want to take a course that, to use Nigel Calder's words, "might drastically overshoot the mark and perpetrate a disaster." We need to ask whether economic dislocation or living standard disruption is justified by what we know today.

The uncertainties are not trivial. They go to the heart of whether, by taking action, we will be hurting or helping. (Also, they affect who will be hurt and who will be helped, because inevitably, either action or inaction will affect different groups differently.)

Unfortunately, some journalists and politicians and many professional activists see catastrophe just ahead and are certain they know the cause. "Our aggravated assault on the atmosphere is one of our century's most damaging environmental legacies—and our love of cars has a lot to do with it." So wrote Gus Speth when he served as president of the World Resources Institute (before he went to the UN). According to the authors of the institute's 1990 booklet, *Driving Forces,* "Motor vehicles contribute to . . . the buildup of greenhouse gases—potentially the most serious of these [environmental] problems." Droughts, flooding, intense storms, and other calamities are projected. Worldwatch Institute advises that "the global economy is destroying the earth's ecosystems, the source of our wealth," and adds that it has a list of actions "that can bring us back from the brink of environmental destruction."[11] In his book on global warming, Senator Gore found that "human civilization is now the dominant cause of change in the global environment," and concluded that "research in lieu of action is unconscionable."

Scientists do not talk that way. Many who are on the front lines of the issue take pains to point out the uncertainties. Benjamin D. Santer, the author of the key chapter in the IPCC *Second Assessment,* is one of the most important. In July 1996, Santer and several colleagues published an article in the science journal *Nature* that further discussed the issues that are the basis for the IPCC findings. The article talks about increasing similarity in the patterns of observed temperature changes and those predicted by climate models, and it concludes, "It is likely that this trend is partially due to human activities, although many uncertainties remain, particularly relating to estimates of natural variability." It is largely on the basis of the kind of research reported in this article that the IPCC found that "the evidence suggests" there are human influences on global climate while also calling attention to the "many uncertainties."

This informative article in *Nature* does two important things. It is a serious reminder that the Earth's climate may be affected by the accumulation of carbon dioxide, some of which is anthropogenic. It is also a serious reminder of the many important questions that remain as to the causes of any climate change.[12] The article forthrightly lists "the main uncertainties in our work," which include "variations in solar output, . . . clouds, which directly affect global sensitivity, . . . [and] oceanic vertical mixing, which may affect interhemispheric asymmetry."

The most important uncertainty listed in the Santer et al. piece in *Nature* is that while the authors believe they have identified "a component of the observational record that shows a statistically significant similarity with model predictions" of human influences on temperature, "we have not quantified the relative magnitude of natural and human-induced climate effects." Unfortunately, activists, journalists, and some politicians ignore this vital caveat.

Uncertainty—From the Sun to the Deep Blue Sea

Perhaps the most intriguing uncertainty is the role of the sun. In 1991, two Danish geophysicists with the Danish Meteorological Institute reported that they had found a close correlation between changes in the intensity of solar radiation and fluctuations in the world's surface temperature.[13] In 1995, work by Darin Labitzke of the Free University of Berlin and Harry van Loon of the National Center for Atmospheric Research was reported in *Science* under the headline "A Fickle Sun Could Be Altering Earth's Climate after All." Science writer Richard A. Kerr, while skeptical, wrote, "But with the mysteries still lingering behind the warming of the past century and the chill of the seventeenth century's Little Ice Age, when solar activity hit rock bottom, there's plenty of incentive to get into the fickle field of sun-climate relations."[14]

In her testimony before the U.S. Senate, Sallie Baliunas, a scientist at the Harvard-Smithsonian Center for Astrophysics, said that the correlation of sunspot cycle length with surface temperatures of the Earth "is nearly perfect," going back to 1750. Baliunas testified that "a brighter sun may be the explanation for a substantial part of, and possibly most of, the 0.5° C. global warming observed in the last 100 years."[15]

It defies common sense for policy makers to ignore our lack of knowledge about the role of the sun as they address climate issues. It is like trying to regulate the heat in the house without knowing how the furnace works.

Once solar radiation reaches the Earth's atmosphere, there are uncertainties about what happens as it encounters greenhouse gases (natural as well as anthropogenic), aerosols, and clouds. The true measure of the climate change potential of any gas depends on what the scientists call "feedback." James Hansen, of NASA's Goddard Institute for Space Studies, has described climate feedbacks as "internal reactions of the climate system to (natural or anthropogenic) climate change. Positive feedbacks amplify the climate change and negative feedbacks diminish it."[16] In other words, feedback is the reaction of the climate system to a change in that system caused by a gas or other agent of change.

Questions about clouds and their feedback are perplexing and are shared by all sides of the global warming debate. Peter Pilewskie of NASA and Francisco P. J. Valero of the Atmospheric Research Laboratory, Scripps Institution of Oceanography, say the results of their climate-related studies imply that "the interaction between clouds and solar radiation is poorly understood."[17] James Hansen, who with his 1988 congressional testimony was instrumental in calling attention to possible global warming, says, "The models suggest that clouds are a potentially important feedback, but cloud modeling is so primitive that even the sign of the feedback is uncertain." Commenting on the IPCC activities in July 1996, the *Economist* reported that the panel "recognizes that there are many uncertainties in its climate equations. Clouds, for example, might either dampen or aggravate the greenhouse effect."

Robert Balling, Jr., director of the Office of Climatology at Arizona State University, writes that the complexities of the feedback from clouds "are not adequately handled in the [climate] models, and relatively small adjustments in the representation of these feedbacks can have a profound impact on the calculated climate response."[18] Robert Cass, modeler and cloud specialist at State University of New York, Stony Brook, says, "It's not clear to me that we have clouds right by any stretch of the imagination.[19] We are sure clouds affect the climate, but we do not know how and to what degree."[20] So modelers make assumptions, and the results are the basis for policy decisions.

Oceans, which cover over 70 percent of the Earth's surface, are a larger mystery yet. Even Jessica Mathews, an advocate of immediate and drastic action to regulate the climate, says, "We know more about the surface of the moon than about Earth's deep oceans."[21] Francis Bretherton, director of the Space Science and Engineering Center at the University of Wisconsin-Madison, has added scientific corroboration of our lack of information about oceans. "In fact," he said, "we know much less about the dynamics of oceans than we do about the dynamics of the atmosphere." Understanding ocean circulation is a particular problem. While an atmospheric model could be evaluated after running through only a few annual cycles, Bretherton says "the intrinsic time scale in the ocean is measured in centuries, because that is how long it takes the ocean to respond to changes in external conditions."[22]

Taro Takahashi, a marine geochemist and associate director of the Lamont-Doherty Geological Observatory of Columbia University, along with associates Pieter P. Tans and Inez Fung add to the complexity with a study reported in *Oceanus*.[23] Their paper states, "The oceans and land biosphere are two major reservoirs exchanging carbon dioxide with the atmosphere at a significant rate." According to government estimates, oceans release around 90 billion metric tons of carbon dioxide a year.[24] Plant decay and plant and animal respiration produce another 60 billion tons, and human sources add around 7 billion tons, for a total of around 157 billion tons. [25]

As the Takahashi paper notes, studies show that the rate of accumulation of carbon dioxide in the atmosphere is only about half the rate of the estimated human-induced emissions of that gas. An unsolved question is, What happens to the rest of these emissions? Earlier studies showed that oceans were the most important sinks (traps) for carbon dioxide. The study by Takahashi et al. suggests that the northern forests may actually may be a more important sink. (The authors note that a survey of New England areas has shown that forests have been recovering from the deforestation that occurred during pioneer days.) Oceanographer Takahashi and his colleagues recommend "increased forest productivity via advanced ecosystem management" and "reduced deforestation activities." As good scientists, the authors are cautious: "Presently, too little information is available to substantiate or refute our conclusion." Another ocean-related issue is the estimated rise in sea level, presumably as a result of melting glaciers and thermal expansion of the oceans.

Former U.S. secretary of energy James D. Watkins writes that "understanding the natural variability of ocean processes to distinguish it from human-generated variability was neither given high priority nor was it a sought-after outcome of the [Rio de Janeiro] convention. Consequently, five years later, little has changed . . . there is little new knowledge . . . and unenlightened rhetoric has been elevated."[26] R. S. Nerem of the NASA-Goddard Space Flight Center, after studying global mean sea level variations, found that "a longer time series is necessary before climate change signals can be unequivocally detected."[27] These are some of the unsolved mysteries of the oceans. There are many more.

Unfortunately, the public has not been informed about these gaps in the science, nor has it been given to understand that even if humankind, with its power plants, factories, cars, and stoves, is affecting the climate, the scientists do not know how serious that effect may be. Is this a solid foundation for a vast new regulatory program? Shouldn't the public be told about this black hole in our knowledge?

Who Will Tell the People?

Jessica Mathews addresses the issue of an uninformed public in an honest if disturbing admission. She says, "Environmentalists agonize over the resulting dilemma: They fear that greater public awareness of what we don't know might encourage inaction rather than be understood as the reason for greater precaution in human activities that could be changing who knows what."[28] In this dilemma, Mathews reflects the suspicion about the competence of the general public shared by all central government guardians of the public interest, who believe only they are sufficiently enlightened to decide upon such matters. Public involvement would only confuse the issues and delay the action they deem necessary.[29]

Gregg Easterbrook, author of *A Moment on Earth*, said, "Lately Gore and the distinguished biologist Paul Ehrlich have ventured into dangerous territory by suggesting that journalists quietly self-censor environmental evidence that is not alarming, because such reports, in Gore's words, 'undermine the effort to build a solid base of public support for the difficult actions we must soon take.'" In other words, trusting the people is too big a risk. Better to leave these important issues to the self-styled experts.

The most forthright discussion of this problem came from Stephen

Schneider of the National Center for Atmospheric Research, who said scientists are in a bind because they are ethically bound to tell "the whole truth . . . , which means that we must include all the doubts, caveats, ifs, and buts." Nonetheless, he says, to get the action they think is necessary, "We have to get some broad-based support, to capture the public's imagination. That, of course, entails getting loads of media coverage. So we have to offer up scary scenarios, make simplified, dramatic statements." He concludes, "Each of us has to decide what the right balance is between being effective and being honest. I hope that means being both."[30] Former congressman Paul G. Rogers had it wrong in an editorial in *Science* when he wrote, "Too many members of the [scientific] research community remain quite removed from advocacy; the new politics in Washington demand new politics in science." Sorry, Messrs. Schneider and Rogers; one cannot be a true scientist and a spin artist at the same time. If the science is convincing, the truth will out.

The manipulation of the public by "scary scenarios" and half-truths is something the public cynically has come to expect from many of its aspiring political leaders, media personalities, and private-sector organizations promoting their own self-interest. Unless scientists want to be viewed with the same cynicism as these groups, they should stick to the whole truth, with all the ifs and buts. The facts will emerge, and when the public has them, they make pretty good decisions. Scientists who stick to the facts and do not become political may miss some of the spotlight and fame their less careful colleagues receive, but they will be honoring the scientific method to which they are ethically bound. Patrick J. Michaels of the University of Virginia said it well: "Exaggeration of environmental threats in the name of good intentions will have the unintended effect of harming science, a resource surely as valuable and vulnerable as any endangered species."

Modeling the Climate

With all the uncertainties about global climate change, it is no wonder that climate models do not give us all the answers we need. The effort to build a model to predict climate change is a fairly recent undertaking, and one thing is clear: no one is yet satisfied with the results. In science writer Richard A. Kerr's words, "These computer simulations of how solar energy and Earth's ocean and atmosphere interact can't even get today's climate entirely right. And when they're asked to prognosticate, the results are even worse."[31]

The modelers' lot is not an easy one. They must understand the incredibly complex nature of all the factors and systems that make the Earth and its atmosphere "work," and must then convert these factors into a mathematical formulation that can tell a computer how to predict the effect of changes in the variables. Models are built up in essentially two ways. One approach is to start with basic principles, such as the laws of physics, then add in some observed conditions, and then see what the computer produces. The other approach is to collect as much "real world" data as possible and then build a model that fits the data. Many models end up as a combination of both approaches.

Scientists are generally very frank about the state of the modeling art. Francis Bretherton has said, "Every experienced modeler is acutely aware of the possibilities for producing numerical garbage—and the more complex the model, the messier the garbage."[32]

In most models of climate and weather, atmospheric physics and conditions are covered more comprehensively than oceans, land, or living things. Their accuracy, however, depends on how well they take all factors into account, especially the relationship between the atmosphere and the ocean. One of the problems in knowing how to account for the effect of the oceans is the difficulty in understanding the processes by which the oceans take up carbon dioxide. Taro Takahashi of Columbia University's Lamont-Doherty Geological Observatory has said that these "processes are known to be highly variable in time and space, and are neither thoroughly documented nor completely understood."[33] According to Francis Bretherton, "Oceanographers have not had the benefit of the weather services of the world taking measurements for them over the last 100 years. In fact, we know much less about the dynamics of oceans than we do about the dynamics of the atmosphere." Additionally, the ocean reacts to changes in conditions over very long periods. "We are really in a bind with ocean circulation," says Bretherton, adding, "We have to run the model far longer, because the ocean time scale is measured in centuries."

Another key in building a climate model is to factor in the flow of carbon dioxide correctly to and from the atmosphere, through photosynthesis and respiration. For example, the growth of vegetation is dependent to a large degree on the moisture of the soil, but the soil's moisture also depends on the vegetation. Correctly modeling this feedback is similar to the problem of understanding the feedback from clouds and water vapor mentioned earlier. Berrien Moore III, director of the University of New Hampshire's Institute for the Study of Earth, Oceans, and Space, captured the difficulty when he said, "So, not only are we dealing with partial differentials with multiple variables, but the variables themselves are functions of other multivariables—they're tightly coupled. There are feedback loops all over the place."[34]

In April 1993, the Office of Technology Assessment of the U.S. Congress held a workshop on "Climate Treaties and Models." Participants in the workshop included experts in modeling, environmental policy, international negotiations, and law. They came from universities, laboratories, policy institutions, and government. The report of the workshop claimed, "Perhaps the strongest conclusion of the workshop concerned the long-time horizon of the problem, and the weakness of our present analytic and institutional tools in the face of an issue so enduring. Participants returned repeatedly to the difficulty of understanding an issue evolving over centuries."

The workshop participants were concerned about the difficulty of communicating model results, with their complexities and subtleties, to decision makers. On this, the report said, "Such facts can easily be lost in the noise of a political environment." That point is demonstrated repeatedly by the alarmist message of activists and some politicians. The misuse of the IPCC conclusion is a prime example. The report also observed, about moderate changes to a few parameters, that "Each change lying within the uncertainty may change a policy target from trivially easy to impossible." While it may be beneficial to lower carbon dioxide emissions when considering only that action, it may be less desirable if the full effects of the actions necessary to make the reduction are understood.

A key variable in any model must be the estimate of human population growth. The IPCC uses a mid-range emission scenario, known as IS93a, in its model-runs, which project a surface temperature increase of 2° C. by the year 2100. This scenario assumes world population will be at 11.3 billion by 2100. Ben Wattenberg of the American Enterprise Institute has examined the demographic data involved in such projections and finds them flawed. "Never before in history," he writes, "have birth rates and fertility rates fallen so low, for so long, in so many places all around the world." He reports that many demographers believe "that global population will top off at about 8 billion or 9 billion toward the middle of the coming century ... and then decline."[35] This would have a significant effect on the projections of greenhouse gases released into the atmosphere by human activity.

Thomas R. Karl, of the National Climate Data Center, summarized the dilemma for modelers and for policy makers. "The primary difficulty," he said, " relates to uncertainties about the sensitivity of the climate system. Imprecise measurements of past rates of observed climate change, and inadequate data regarding the timing and magnitude of many climatic forcings preclude precise answers. As a result, it is impossible to completely dismiss extreme positions."[36] In these circumstances, we should not be surprised if we have global warming or global cooling. The only surprise would be to have no change at all.

Robert Repetto of the World Resources Institute added a dimension to the problems of models in his testimony before a Senate subcommittee. "These models," he said, "are complicated and hard to understand but nonetheless are gross simplifications of the real world; what modelers leave out influences their predictions as strongly as what they put in." Repetto was talking about economic models used to predict the costs of stabilizing or reducing greenhouse gases. His group studied predictions from sixteen models and, as reported by the *Washington Post,* "found they could get either very optimistic or pessimistic economic projections by fiddling with eight of the assumptions that underlie the competing economic models."[37]

Building reliable models on which to base policies affecting the Earth's climate, national economies, and all of our lives is a monumental task. Given the complexities and the unknowns—and perhaps the unknowables—anyone responsible for climate policy and "counteraction" measures should look closely at the models, disagreeable as that task may be, before making decisions. It is also reasonable to require that these models be explainable to anyone about to lose his or her job, property, or standard of living because of policies or actions based on the assumptions contained therein.

· 8 ·

JUST IN CASE—
SHOULD WE TAKE
PRECAUTIONARY
MEASURES?

What if it turns out that global warming is a real threat? Shouldn't we be taking precautionary measures now—just in case? The easier course is to go with the crowd and say Yes. As we know, the climate *will* change—it always has—and some who say the globe is warming dangerously have no shame about claiming any kind of change in the weather as a signal they are right. No matter what happens, the villain is global warming. In January 1996, Washington, D.C., was locked in a blizzard. In the *Washington Post*, Jessica Mathews wrote, "Hard as it may be to believe, blizzards like this one are part of what the experts tell us to expect of a warming climate."[1]

The "No-Regrets" Approach

In response to questions about taking precautionary measures, many scientists, concerned about potential climate change but conscious of the vast uncertainties surrounding the predictions of severe global warming, have advocated what have come to be called "no-regrets" measures to reduce greenhouse gases. These are considered to be measures that are worth doing anyway, because they presumably make sense for reasons aside from any benefits from global warming mitigation.

The great difficulty comes in identifying specific measures. One person's no-regrets measure may very well cost another person his or her livelihood. One measure suggested by the Intergovernmental Panel on Climate Change is the reduction of energy use through a tax based on the amount of carbon in the fuel. Such a tax would hit the coal industry the hardest, since coal has the highest carbon content per unit of energy. Any level of tax on coal that is high enough to induce conservation could also induce coal users to switch to oil or natural gas. Mines could be closed, throwing people out of work, thus harming families and communities. Manufacturers using coal would have increased costs, either for the now-taxed coal or for higher priced oil or natural gas. Jobs would be endangered and lives disrupted.

An even more frequently urged "no-regrets" conservation measure is a higher tax on gasoline. While the Europeans, Japanese, and others have accepted high motor fuel taxes (some have the equivalent of $2 to $3 of taxes a gallon), Americans, who travel much more, expect low-priced gasoline (around the price of bottled water). Congressmen who have been around long enough to vote on a gasoline tax hike know that a vote in favor risks their defeat in the next election. President Clinton, in his first term as governor of Arkansas, put through a gasoline tax increase and was subsequently turned out of office. (The gas tax was not the only reason, but it was a factor.) As dependent as they are on their motor vehicles, Americans do not see increased operating expenses as something over which they have "no regrets." This is especially so with lower income groups, who spend a larger portion of their income on gasoline.[2] One of the arguments most often heard in opposition to higher gasoline taxes is their regressivity.

In 1992, the automobile industry informally suggested that if there was a demonstrated need, the implementation of a "greenhouse fee" measured either by the carbon content of a fuel or by BTUs (the British thermal unit is the common measure of energy in a fuel) would be the most effective way to cut fuel use. While a BTU tax is not based on carbon content, it turns out to have a similar general effect on carbon-based fuel, but by covering noncarbon energy sources it avoids further distortion of the market.

President Clinton proposed a BTU tax in his State of the Union speech on February 18, 1993. He said, "Unlike a carbon tax, it's not too hard on the coal states; unlike a gas tax, it's not too tough on people who drive a long way to work; unlike an ad valorem tax, it doesn't increase just when the price of an energy source goes up. And it is environmentally responsible; it will help us in the future as well as in the present with the deficit." Despite all these political pluses, the president's proposal came under immediate and strong attack by virtually all sectors except the auto industry, which preferred the tax to more CAFE. The professional environmentalists who had given lip service to the idea ran for cover. Some did not want to offend their grassroots support. Others worried that such a tax would be viewed as a substitute for command-and-control regulatory programs that they favored.

Congress looked for less volatile ways to address the perceived problems, and as usual, some members proposed greater regulation of motor vehicle fuel use. It is easier to pretend that energy conservation can be accomplished by regulating a handful of vehicle manufacturers than it is to call on the general public for some sacrifice. In view of safety consider-ations and the poor record of CAFE, however, they did not prevail.

The point is that an energy tax, sometimes called a greenhouse tax or fee, may be the most efficient method of government intervention to reduce carbon dioxide emissions; but any move in that direction would result in a large number of opponents loudly warning that any politicians who imple-ment such a tax would have plenty of regrets. Many of these same constitu-ents are catching on to the fact that they pay for regulation, too, in dollars and in less performance and utility—and most important, in reduced safety.

In contrast to CAFE or higher taxes, the Partnership for a New Gen-eration of Vehicles featured by President Clinton in his June 26, 1997, speech to the UN on global warming may have fewer economic and political re-grets than other alternatives affecting personal mobility.

The Tree-Growing Option

Another no-regrets measure suggested by the IPCC as offering "large po-tential, modest costs, low risk, and other benefits" involves forestry. There are two approaches: the first is more tree planting and the second is less tree cutting. The value of forests in taking up and holding carbon dioxide is well illustrated by what has happened in the United States. While for de-cades we have been told that our forests are being decimated, that is no longer true. In the colonial period, forests covered about 850 million acres, mostly west of the Mississippi, in what are now the contiguous forty-eight states. In the early decades of America's growth, much of this acreage was cleared and converted to pasture and cropland. Much was also cut to provide firewood, a major source of energy, and for lumber for homes and other buildings. By 1920, the forests had been reduced to 567 million acres. This, it turns out, was the low point; since then, America has been reforesting.

Notably, the reforestation of America has been more the result of eco-nomic development than of conservation programs. A large part of New England, not ideal for agriculture in the first place, was abandoned for such purposes when land opened up in the West. From 1920 to 1945, some 30 million acres were no longer cultivated as cropland in the East, while about the same acreage was added in the West.[3] In New England, much of the former cropland has returned to growing trees. The western lands newly opened up for crops (in large part because of advances in irrigation) had not been tree-covered. The result was the beginning of the return of much of eastern America to tree coverage. Today, forests cover about one-third of the country—more than 737 million acres.[4]

Two other developments helped the process of reforestation—first, the use of coal and oil for heat and power, and second, the spread of the automobile. Use of oil and coal meant that Americans did not need to denude the land of trees for fuel, as has happened in too many countries where the poor use wood to make charcoal or, more directly, for heat and cooking. For its part, the motor vehicle replaced the farm horse, whose presence peaked in 1910 at around 20 million. In 1960, the last year the Department of Agriculture kept a count, the number of farm horses had declined to under 4 million, thus freeing up millions of acres that had been used to supply horse feed.[5]

By 1985, the average annual tree planting in the United States exceeded 2.6 million, much of it, of course, replacing timber cut by lumber and paper companies.[6] It is an irony that the trees most effective in pulling carbon dioxide out of the atmosphere are the young, growing ones and not the old-growth forests that receive so much attention from the professional environmentalists. Every tree (and green plant) is a solar-powered system that takes carbon dioxide from the atmosphere, separates the carbon atoms from the oxygen atoms, releases the oxygen to the atmosphere, and uses the carbon to make roots, trunks, branches, and leaves. This process—photosynthesis—begins to slow as trees age; they begin to release carbon and ultimately become net carbon emitters as they begin to decay. As a result of this natural process, well-managed commercial forests where trees are harvested before they become net emitters of carbon, and where the land is replanted, are the most helpful in reducing carbon dioxide concentrations.[7]

For all these reasons, the forests of the United States are major factors in containing carbon. While it had been assumed that most forests eventually give off as much carbon as they have sequestered in their life cycles, estimates are that in 1992, U.S. forests and the wood products they produced sequestered around 111 million metric tons more carbon than they released. They were net reducers of greenhouse gases—not just maintainers of the balance. The root systems sequestered another 127 million metric tons in forest soils.

A report from the Forest Service of the U.S. Department of Agriculture states, "Between 1952 and 1992, carbon storage on forestland in the coterminous United States increased by 11.3 billion metric tons, an average of 281 million metric tons per year, an amount that offset about one-quarter of U.S. emissions of carbon for the period."[8] This annual sequestration of carbon by forestlands exceeds the annual emissions of all gasoline-powered motor vehicles in the United States, estimated at 270 million metric tons of carbon in 1993.

According to the Department of Energy, it has been estimated that, excluding Alaska, "the U.S. forest ecosystems contained 54.6 billion metric tons of carbon in 1992—the equivalent of nearly 40 years of U.S. carbon emissions from fossil fuel consumption."[9] As a "sink" for carbon, the forests of the world are obviously critical. After a lengthy study of the matter, a prominent oceanographer and team concluded, "In contrast with earlier estimates, the major sink for industrial[10] carbon dioxide released into the atmosphere appears to be not the oceans, but the northern forests!"[11] A wrap-up of other research into these matters appeared in *Science* under the headline "Resurgent Forests Can Be Greenhouse Gas Sponges."[12]

Planting more trees is clearly a no-regrets measure. Stopping the cutting of trees is not. Much attention is focused on the slash-and-burn agricultural practices in developing countries. Logging the rainforests of South America and elsewhere is the subject of much anguish and finger-pointing. In both cases, the livelihoods of a multitude of very poor people are at stake. It is indeed sad to see the barren hills and mountains of much of Latin America, where subsistence farmers have cut or burned the existing plant cover, planted crops in the thin topsoil, depleted its nutrients, and moved on to repeat the process elsewhere. Merely forbidding this technique is neither humane nor effective. Desperate people will either be forced to continue illegally or will join the throngs moving into the cities, which too often are unprepared and unable to offer the opportunity for decent housing and other elements that give life dignity.

Instead of promoting costly, energy-rationing programs that would make life more difficult in developed countries, it makes better sense to use those resources for tree planting. There are many model programs to learn from. In Honduras, one of the most poverty-stricken countries of the Americas, the Zamorano school teaches students from many countries agricultural techniques that increase production while conserving the land. Logging companies around the world know how to replant what they cut. Incentives to do so could be built into the granting of logging rights in public lands. Also, since young trees are the ones that sequester the most carbon dioxide, the emphasis should be on reforestation, not deforestation.

For the record, tree planting is very popular with the IPCC, which has found that the importance of such forestry measures "is due to their expected large storage potential [of carbon dioxide] and relatively modest costs. The enhancement of forest sinks is also one of the lowest-risk options and offers substantial positive side effects in the environmental and sometimes also in the socioeconomic sphere."[13]

As environmentalism has become "professionalized" and "institutionalized," its professionals, to maintain their institutions, have increasingly limited their serious demands on their members and supporters to requests for money. Their mailings, often with appealing pictures of wildlife, generally say that calamity is at hand but that a donation will help them forestall it. The rest of the actions requested of their members are generally letters to government officials condemning polluters and supporting regulations.

Environmentalist organizations could do more work encouraging people to plant trees and spend less time in heaping blame on others.

What about Nuclear Energy?

Nuclear energy is not a no-regrets measure. There are many costs, and even more worries involved. It is not, however, an alternative power source to be discarded or ignored. If electricity is to be the fuel for a significant number of vehicles in the future, more generating capacity will become important. Since the dire predictions of the 1970s about the impending depletion of the world's oil, not much has been said about eventually declining reserves.[14] There turned out to be much more oil than central planners had thought existed. Looking ahead, if governments do not intervene with price controls or obstacles to new energy sources, oil will not run out but will just become too expensive to burn in a car or use for other purposes. As it becomes more expensive, new energy sources will emerge—unless governments stand in the way. While the U.S. taxpayers have a huge investment in the development of nuclear energy, the government today is the single most important impediment to its expansion.

Today, nuclear energy is still a good long-term bet to provide cheap and clean energy—if the roadblocks can be overcome. Notably, the IPCC, in its 1995 assessment, boldly lists nuclear-generated electricity as an alternative energy supply. "Nuclear energy could replace baseload fossil fuel electricity generation in many parts of the world," the IPCC noted, adding, "if generally acceptable responses can be found to concerns such as reactor safety, radioactive-waste transport and disposal, and nuclear proliferation." Clearly the *if* is a very large one, but the potential benefit is also large. There are no emissions of particulates, oxides of nitrogen, hydrocarbons, or any other pollutant. In contrast, electric utilities in the United States produced the equivalent of 493.8 million metric tons of carbon in 1995.[15] Nonetheless, under the most optimistic scenario for nuclear energy, the fossil-fuel industries have little to fear from that competition.

While both oil and coal take regular knocks from the environmental extremists, no industry is as hog-tied as the "nukes." By 1996, there were 110 licensed plants in the United States with a generating capability of more than 101 million kilowatts, which represented about 20 percent of total electricity consumed. Nuclear energy supplied more than half the electricity in South Carolina, Maine, New Jersey, Connecticut, Illinois, and Vermont. The future, however, is not bright.

No U.S. electric utility has ordered a new nuclear reactor since 1973. The construction of both nuclear and nonnuclear generating plants in the 1970s and 1980s resulted in extra capacity, and many utilities have simply not needed more. Slow growth in demand, effective conservation measures, and failure of the price of oil to reach predicted levels were also factors. Additionally, the industry is highly regulated; dozens of permits must be obtained, some from various federal offices, including the EPA, and others from state agencies.[16] These requirements stretch out the average construction time to something more than ten years, and these delays run up the costs.

Another factor is the adamant emotional opposition to all things nuclear. The Tennessee Valley Authority knows about that. In 1995, when it powered up its Watts Bar nuclear plant in Tennessee, Greenpeace, Earth First, and other professional activist groups stepped up opposition that had already helped draw out construction time to twenty-three years. A member of We the People, Inc., described as a "national organization of nuclear whistleblowers" by the *Washington Post*, raised the familiar cry, "This is another Three Mile Island waiting to happen."[17]

Activists express complete faith that technology will overcome any problem that regulations may cause for the motor vehicle; for example, they affirm with great conviction that technology will render air bags safe for everyone, and other technology will permit high fuel-economy requirements. When it comes to dealing with the problems of nuclear safety, however, they deny any possibility that technology has made or can make the industry safe.

Concern about global warming has at least reopened the subject of nuclear energy. In his book *Earth in the Balance,* Al Gore recommended that research and development "should continue vigorously." He also wrote that when he began his own efforts to spread the word about global warming, "Even the major environmental groups resisted the issue. . . . A few of them were overly sensitive to an admittedly difficult political problem: if global warming were taken seriously and the world began searching for substitutes for coal and oil, nuclear power might receive a big boost."

Today, Japan has forty-nine nuclear power reactors, with four new ones under construction and plans for forty more. France, which already produces most of its electricity with nuclear plants, is building four new ones.[18] The People's Republic of China has three operating plants and three more on order. With substantial uranium resources and facilities to produce nuclear reactor fuels, China has been negotiating with the French and others for help with more reactors. Reactors are under construction in Brazil, Argentina, India, Ukraine, and the United Kingdom. South Korea has eleven in operation and plans for nineteen more.

According to Philip H. Abelson, writing in *Science*, there were eighty U.S. universities with nuclear engineering departments in 1978; today there are thirty-five. Abelson says, "Without the stimulus provided by the building of competitive advanced plants, U.S. capabilities in nuclear technology will gradually become second class."[19] A friend, wise in the ways of the world, has commented that he fears that one day the countries without nuclear power will be dominated by those that have it. The current U.S. path will take us to second-class capability. One benefit from the concern about global warming could be to stimulate the development of safe nuclear energy generation and waste disposal. Professional activists who stand in the way are no help to the environment they claim to champion.

Isn't There Something Else We Can Do?

With all these uncertainties in mind, should governments now attempt to manage the climate? If so, how? Here is one way. An important oceanic function is the seasonal switch of oceans from sources of carbon dioxide to absorbers of carbon dioxide. In the winter, chilled surface waters become more dense than the deep waters. This causes the deep, carbon dioxide–rich waters to rise to the surface and release the gas. In spring and summer, more sunlight stimulates rapid growth of phytoplankton, which takes up carbon dioxide. The proliferation of these microscopic plants turns the ocean into a carbon dioxide trap.

An experiment in the South Pacific by Kenneth Coale and Ken Johnson in May 1995 demonstrated that by dumping iron into the ocean, phytoplankton mass increased thirtyfold. (Writing about this in the *Smithsonian*, James Trefil speculates about what happens when phytoplankton die. He says, "At the moment . . . there seems to be a reasonable chance that iron fertilization could pull large amounts of carbon from the atmosphere and store it on the ocean floor.") This has led to the suggestion of fertilizing the oceans with iron to increase phytoplankton and thereby mitigate global warming. This may even be a cost-effective measure; oceanographer John Martin reportedly said, "With half a shipload of iron, I could give you an ice age."[20]

Unfortunately, this thought recalls the notion, when scientists thought the climate was cooling, of spreading soot on the ice caps to retain heat and melt them. It turned out that although it was feasible, this was a solution to a problem that did not exist. That may be the case with iron fertilization as well. Also, there would almost certainly be consequences that have not been anticipated in fertilizing the ocean. Kenneth Coale says, "There are a lot of things I'd want to think about before we did anything like that." (But he adds, "It could well be that we will need iron fertilization as a last-ditch method of averting global warming.")[21]

Then the thoughtful Coale said, "Wouldn't it be easier to try carpooling first?" Maybe so—but it would be smart to see what carpooling and other efforts to cut back on America's personal mobility would accomplish.

Your Car and Global Warming

Americans enjoy the highest level of personal mobility in the world. On average, they travel more—about 10,000 miles annually per person—than the citizens of any other country in the world, nearly twice the distance of the citizens of the richest European nations.[22] This means, on average, Americans use more energy to get around in their cars and trucks—five times as much as the average Japanese, and almost three times as much as the average citizen of France, Britain, or Germany. This also means these personal vehicles produce a lot of carbon dioxide.

While industrial activity, with 462.9 million metric tons of carbon equivalent, is the major human-linked source of carbon dioxide emissions in the United States, the transportation sector of the economy, with 457.2 million metric tons, is close. Of this amount, it is estimated that motor gasoline consumption in 1995 accounted for some 280.7 million metric tons.[23] Total U.S. carbon dioxide emissions in 1995, from human-related activity, amounted to 1,442 million metric tons of carbon. Total worldwide carbon dioxide emissions produced by human activity were estimated at 7,100 million metric tons. Total worldwide emissions from all sources were estimated at 157 billion tons (carbon equivalent).

Using these government estimates, if all cars, vans, sport-utilities, and light pickup trucks—all vehicles fueled by motor gasoline—were removed from the roads in America, worldwide human-induced carbon dioxide (equivalent) would be reduced by only 4 percent. (This assumes that no replacement transportation system would produce carbon dioxide—a highly unlikely possibility.) Eliminating all U.S. gasoline-powered vehicles would reduce total worldwide carbon dioxide emissions by eighteen one-hundredths of 1 percent (0.18 percent), hardly a significant step in rolling back carbon dioxide. (The reader should note well that all these numbers are estimates, and that scientists change their estimates as new data become available. For example, the estimate of total world emissions of carbon dioxide from all sources dropped by ten billion metric tons between 1995 and 1996 as a result of a recalculation by IPCC groups, starkly illustrating the very large swings in estimates that are critical to understanding the issue.)

These numbers do not tell the whole story. They deal only with the effect of the U.S. car and light-truck fleet on emissions of carbon dioxide, one of many greenhouse gases—and not the most important one. According to the *Climate Action Report*, water vapor has the largest heat-trapping capability of all greenhouse gases.[24] In order to establish the motor vehicle contribution to global warming, it would be necessary to establish the global warming potential for all the gases. While a GWP exists for methane, nitrous oxide, and other gases, no GWP has been established for water vapor, the most important greenhouse gas. There are estimates of the concentration of gases in the atmosphere that indicate there is 2,500 times as much water vapor as carbon dioxide. This does not necessarily mean that water vapor is that much more powerful as a greenhouse gas. That has not been determined. But it does suggest that the effect of the personal vehicle fleet of the United States on global warming is even less than the eighteen one-hundredths of 1 percent cited above.

In turn, this means that programs that would require further reduction in size and weight of motor vehicles to increase fuel economy would have no real effect on the global climate but *would* further erode the safety provided by larger, heavier vehicles. Proposals to tighten the corporate average fuel economy (CAFE) law to 40 or more miles per gallon have no serious bearing on the greenhouse effect, but they do have a direct bearing on the safety of vehicle occupants. Similarly, a proposal by former CIA director John Deutch to impose a carbon tax—which would amount to a 2.5 cents-a-gallon gasoline tax—would have no appreciable effect on worldwide carbon dioxide emissions. It would, however, transfer around $2–$3 billion from taxpayers to the government.[25]

Despite the lack of any real greenhouse gas savings from cuts in U.S. car and light truck carbon dioxide emissions, the Clinton-Gore administration has put much effort into finding ways to do it. In 1994, White House staff set up a committee officially called the Policy Dialogue Advisory Committee to Develop Options for Reducing Greenhouse Gas Emissions from Personal Motor Vehicles. Since the usual acronym approach—PDACDORGGEPMV—obviously would not serve, the committee was dubbed Car Talk. The purpose of the White House was to find ways to roll back carbon dioxide emissions to 1990 levels by a specific future year. The government officials involved insisted that there be no debate about the science of global warming. Accepting Vice President Gore's dictum that global warming catastrophe is at hand was the price of admission to the table.

With the help of a facilitator, the oil companies, auto companies, and the UAW sat down with Joan Claybrook, president of Public Citizen, and Clarence Ditlow, director of the Center for Auto Safety (both seasoned associates of Ralph Nader), John DeCicco, associate of the American Council for an Energy-Efficient Economy, and Dan Becker of the Sierra Club. These four had worked hard for the passage of a bill to raise CAFE to 40 mpg. At the beginning of the meetings, White House staff threatened action on greenhouse emissions from automobiles "immediately after the process is completed . . . with or without consensus" of the participants—not exactly the most cooperative stance to take.

A variety of policy options were examined: no-drive days; no-drive zones; parking changes and limits; employer trip-reduction programs; road-building limits; zoning and other land-use controls; controls of vehicle speed and power; fuel composition standards; caps on carbon dioxide emissions; mandatory sales of alternative fuel vehicles; and of course, stricter fuel-economy requirements. The activists proposed 45 mpg standards for cars and 34 mpg for light trucks. The auto manufacturers reaffirmed their commitment to the Partnership for a New Generation of Vehicles, never popular with the activists who prefer command-and-control regulations.

The talks continued for a year. The major accomplishment was to confirm that the activists have no interest in compromise, and the auto manufacturers would not agree to CAFE-type rules that would further compromise their ability to provide their customers what they want to buy. Car Talk came to an end, and the administration began to concentrate on two other strategies: an effort to bring the private sector around to its policy positions through the President's Council on Sustainable Development and, more seriously, the effort to regulate motor vehicles and other carbon-based fuel users by negotiating an international limit on greenhouse gases.

The Council on Sustainable Development was a more sophisticated approach than Car Talk, with a vision statement no one could fault: "Our vision is of a life-sustaining Earth. We are committed to the achievement of a dignified, peaceful, and equitable existence" and so forth. It also presented a "We believe" statement artfully worded in nonthreatening, but not always benign, language: for example: "Even in the face of a scientific uncertainty, society should take reasonable actions to avert risks where the potential harm to human health or the environment is thought to be serious or irreparable."

The members of the council came roughly one-third from the government, one-third from the corporate world, and one-third from the activist community, including from the NRDC and the Sierra Club, two famous litigants against the EPA for being too soft.

The upshot of this effort was a beautifully printed report entitled "Sustainable America: A New Consensus." Increased CAFE or any direct attack on the automobile similar to those in the Car Talks was avoided, but recommendations that led to them were part of the "consensus." For example, one action would be to "shift tax policies and reform subsidies to improve . . . equity in the transportation sector significantly." This is aimed at taking more of the taxes that highway users pay and diverting them to build subways, bike paths, and so forth—which would mean more road congestion. Another calls for "transportation efficiency: decrease in the rates of freight and personal transportation [read: cars'] emissions of greenhouse gases and other pollutants." This can be interpreted as laying the groundwork for more CAFE (and new air quality standards, as well). Another calls for "progress toward stabilizing the number of vehicle miles traveled per person." This could be the basis not only for more CAFE but also for no-drive days and any other anti–personal mobility rules. In a more arcane approach, the consensus says that "the federal government should give communities credit toward attainment of national ambient air quality standards under the Clean Air Act when they use community design to lower traffic by adopting zoning codes, building codes, and other changes that encourage more efficient land-use patterns to reduce pollution from motor vehicles and energy use." This action would be a powerful invitation to states to engage in a comprehensive central government planning effort to get people out of their cars.

The IPCC has looked at options such as these and said, "The use of motor vehicles might be reduced by changing land-use patterns and lifestyles to reduce the need for goods transport and travel; restrictions on the use of motor vehicles; and fiscal or other measures to discourage motor vehicle use and to encourage the use of nonmotorized transport. *No confidence can be placed in estimates for the ultimate potential mitigation through these measures* [emphasis added]."[26] This forthright statement reinforces the notion that the reasons for proposed limits on the use of the automobile are not always apparent or justified by analysis.

Also relevant are the rough estimates by the IPCC of total worldwide carbon dioxide emissions and uptake. As reviewed earlier, the estimate is that a total of 157 billion metric tons of carbon are emitted annually, and about 153.5 billion metric tons are taken up again by natural processes, leaving a net increase of around 3.6 billion. Since about 7 billion tons come from human activity, mostly from fossil fuel consumption, simple arithmetic leads to the question of what would happen if this anthropogenic carbon dioxide were cut back by more than 3.5 billion tons. This would mean a reduction in worldwide carbon dioxide. Would it mean a serious cooling spell? Perhaps, then, the regulators would be looking for ways to generate more carbon dioxide.

What other single action would cut back as much carbon dioxide as the elimination of all passenger motor vehicles? Cutting out all electricity produced with coal, oil, or natural gas hardly seems practical. Unfortunately, rolling back greenhouse gases would require a multitude of actions with massive cuts in energy use to make a slight dent in the atmospheric concentration of carbon dioxide. As the report of the President's Council on Sustainable Development says, "Since the world depends on fossil fuels . . . for 90 percent of its energy, the implications of global warming could be profound. If the risks of warming are judged to be too great, then nothing less than a drastic reduction in the burning of coal, oil, and natural gas would be necessary." The IPCC makes clear what it would take to stabilize concentrations. Today, carbon dioxide concentrations are estimated at 360 parts per million by volume (ppmv) of air. To hold levels at 750 to 1,000 ppmv during the next century, the IPCC says, "the global annual average emissions would need to be less than 50 percent above current levels on a per capita basis."[27] Such reductions would affect virtually every human activity; the effect on standards of living would be incalculable, and the political repercussions would be swift.

A Rollback? The Costs and the Benefits

Despite all the uncertainties about climate change, the professional activists and their political allies argue that the consequences of global warming would be so horrendous that we should take action now to reduce the amount of greenhouse gases being emitted into the air. They ask, "Doesn't common sense suggest that we ought to be doing something?"

The answer seems clear enough until we consider exactly what actions we ought to be taking. Do we limit the use of coal or oil by electric utilities, which are the largest U.S. producers of carbon dioxide? Do we ban the use of automobiles one or two days a week, or raise the gasoline tax by a dollar or two a gallon? Do we eliminate the subsidy of certain fuels? Do we ban wood-burning fireplaces, or require people to live near their work, or work near their home? When any specific actions are mentioned, all those adversely affected immediately object and start talking about the costs—and it makes good sense to worry about the costs.

Estimates of the costs of stabilizing the emission of carbon dioxide vary considerably. The hard fact is that no one knows what the costs or the benefits are. The problems of modeling the economic effects of proposed reductions of greenhouse gases are of the same magnitude as those of modeling the climate, described earlier. Just as in those models, the results reflect the assumptions made by the modelers, and those assumptions vary widely in quality.

Acknowledging the tentative and controversial nature of attempts to model the costs of curtailing carbon dioxide, the *Economic Report of the President,* transmitted to the U.S. Congress by the Bush administration in 1990, said, "A recent estimate based on energy-output balance relationships suggests that global carbon dioxide stabilization could cut world economic growth in half, even after accounting for substitution toward cleaner energy." The *Report* also said, "One recent study placed the cost of gradually reducing U.S. carbon dioxide emissions by 20 percent between now and 2100 to range from $800 billion, under optimistic scenarios of available fuel substitutes and increasing energy efficiency, to $3.6 trillion, under pessimistic scenarios."

Climate activists say that reference to models that come up with these estimates is "unconscionable" and suggest that there are considerable potential benefits from the actions taken to cut greenhouse gas emissions. Some assert that there would be net economic gains rather than losses by stabilizing carbon dioxide. Others believe that high cost estimates are too pessimistic about decreasing costs of renewable energy sources such as solar radiation and wind.[28]

W. David Montgomery, an energy economist and vice president of Charles River Associates, a leading economic research group, conducted a study released on December 11, 1991, which found that carbon dioxide stabilization "would produce annual losses of 1.7 percent of the Gross National Product (GNP) in 2020, increasing to 2.4 percent in 2100."[29] Montgomery's report concluded that "the economic benefits associated with ameliorating global climate change might not appear until the end of the next century and could amount to no more than 0.5 percent of GNP."

In President Clinton's 1995 *Economic Report of the President,* no estimates of either the costs or the benefits, in monetary terms, of carbon dioxide stabilization are included. Several administration objectives are cited, including cost-effectiveness—so that greenhouse gas control policies are achieved at minimum cost—and flexibility—to allow policy makers "to benefit from new information about climate change hazards and technologies, and to adjust behavior and policies to differing near-term economic development objectives." The *Report* for 1997 is even less specific. It simply says, "All nations benefit from efforts to reduce emissions of greenhouse gases that may lead to global warming." There is no further explanation of the benefits and no mention of the costs, but it does say that the United States is working toward "an international agreement in Kyoto in December 1997 to limit these [greenhouse] emissions." The absence of cost estimates suggests that not much progress in modeling has been made since the 1990 *Report.*

The IPCC wrapped up the problem succinctly, saying,

> Estimates of the cost of greenhouse gas emission reduction depend critically upon assumptions about the levels of energy efficiency improvements in the baseline scenario (that is, in the absence of climate policy) and upon a wide range of factors such as consumption patterns, resource and technology availability, the desired level and timing of abatement, and the choice of policy instruments. *Policy makers should not place too much confidence in the specific numerical results from any one analysis.*[30] [Emphasis added.]

The president's 1997 proposed global change research program makes the same point, saying that research will

> enable us to improve estimates of the potential economic effects of options for anticipating and responding to global changes. Economic estimates for reducing the impact of human activities on the environment (e.g., by reducing greenhouse gas and aero-

sol emissions through improvements in energy efficiency or development of alternative sources of energy) range from large costs to large benefits. This research will contribute to making these estimates more precise.[31]

The Office of Technology Assessment of the U.S. Congress put it even more clearly: "Costs of controlling emissions are highly dependent on assumed rates and determinants of technological innovation, and this process is not adequately understood or modeled at present."[32] Robert Repetto and Duncan Austin, authors of the World Resources Institute study mentioned earlier, found that the predictions for sixteen economic models of the effect of curbs on carbon burning varied from a loss of 8 percent of total U.S. economic output to a 5 percent gain. The headline on a news account of this report read, appropriately, "Studies on Costs of Global Warming Don't Clear the Air."[33]

For those who say "Damn the costs, full speed ahead; we can't afford the risks of delay," the IPCC again offers a good insight into what those risks may be. In the Second Assessment, the panel says, "Some studies suggest that the cost of delay is small; others emphasize that the costs could include imposition of risks on all parties (particularly the most vulnerable), greater utilization of limited atmospheric capacity, and potential deferral of desirable technical development. No consensus is reflected in the literature." The U.S. Congress Office of Technology Assessment took a stand. "Delaying the implementation of emission controls for 10 to 20 years will have little effect on atmospheric concentrations." [34]

In April 1997, *Inside E.P.A.* reported that the U. S. Department of Energy had received a draft study, led by the Argonne National Laboratory, that concluded that "rising energy prices driven by new climate commitments could have a crushing effect on six U.S. industries: paper and allied products; iron and steel manufacturing; petroleum refining; aluminum production; chemical manufacturing; and cement manufacturing." For example, according to *Inside E.P.A.*, these economic changes "would cause all of the U.S. capacity [for aluminum production] to be noncompetitive by 2010."

In July 1997, the White House released the Argonne National Laboratory study, which confirmed the estimated "significant reductions" in output and employment in these six industries. The study predicted that 20–30 percent of the nation's chemical industry would move to developing nations that would not be required to reduce greenhouse gases.[35] The administration spokesperson said the study was based on "outdated" scenarios.

The White House also released the long-awaited study of the interagency team headed by the Commerce Department. Janet Yellen, head of President Clinton's Council of Economic Advisers, explained it to Congress by first acknowledging "the uncertainties associated with estimating both the costs and the benefits." One reason is, "Many unanswered questions exist about the biophysical systems, potential thresholds, and economic impacts."[36] Yellen forthrightly announced "one clear conclusion: the effort to develop a model or set of models that can give us a definitive answer as to the impacts of a given climate change policy is futile." Costs will depend on a number of "ifs," including "if the Federal Reserve Board pursues a monetary policy oriented toward keeping the economy at full employment," and "if technological change occurs at a rapid rate."

Yellen cited scenarios including "revenue recycling." These would have the federal government realizing increases in revenue, presumably from taxes on energy. She said, "If these are used to reduce distortionary taxes that diminish incentives to invest, save or work" or go "into deficit reduction," they could give economic growth "a long-term boost." Commenting on this general concept (which asserts that "green" taxes have a "double dividend"), the *Economist* makes the point that raising prices through taxes on, say, petroleum would cut "consumers' demand for the product—this is, after all, precisely the purpose of the taxes—and hence the industries' demand for labour. Higher prices, in turn, leave people with less to spend on other things, costing jobs elsewhere, at least in the short term."[37] A free lunch is still hard to come by.

Economists need to pursue the elusive costs and benefits, but their task is no easier than that of the climate modelers. Also, hard as it may be for economists and scientists to accept, they are not the decision makers in these matters. It is the politicians who will make the decisions. Stephen Schneider understood the role of the politician when he wrote, "Of course, whether to act is not a scientific judgment, but a value-laden political choice that cannot be resolved by scientific methods."[38] There are many outstanding men and women in politics, but there are others who, too often, use data as the drunk uses a lamp post—more for support than illumination.

The state of the art of cost-benefit analysis of climate issues is such that the advocates for almost any position, including the extremes, can find a lamp post on which to lean.

Warm or Cold—Which Is Better?

The history of the Earth's climate provided by Al Gore in his book *Earth in the Balance* offers another perspective on how fearful we should be of global warming. According to Gore, in the period 8000 to 7000 B.C., "when favorable climate conditions prevailed as glaciers were melting," civilization got its start in Mesopotamia, where "the oldest known city," Jericho, is found. Around 1600 B.C., a cold period, perhaps brought on by the eruption of the volcano Santorini, near Crete, "most likely contributed to the sudden disappearance not long afterward of the Minoan civilization."

Around 300 B.C., the climate began to warm, according to Gore, and Alexander the Great spread the Greek civilization throughout the Mediterranean. But later, "a prolonged freezing in Central Asia" drove the inhabitants south and west and contributed to the fall of Rome. The Little Ice Age (1550–1850), he wrote, drove one-tenth of the Scots to Ireland, "setting in motion the enormous problems and seemingly insoluble violence that continue to this day." Gore goes on, "After the warming epoch, temperatures dropped again at the beginning of the fourteenth century, causing major problems in Europe and Asia." Among the problems were the Great Famine of 1315–1317 and the Black Death. In 1788–1789, one of the coldest Mays in history resulted in "disastrous crop failures in France" and was one of the causes of the French Revolution. Gore found that the cold of the early 1800s brought snow to New England in June and food riots to Europe in 1816, which caused the "near-collapse of society throughout the British Isles and Europe."

This list of global climate change problems could almost lead one to believe that this chapter of Gore's book was written at the time when we were concerned with cooling, not warming. It is strange that, included in this excitable treatise on global warming, almost all the historical examples of climate change disasters are on the cooling side of the ledger. Thomas Gale Moore, senior fellow at the Hoover Institution at Stanford University, took this thesis to its logical conclusion in a 1994 paper entitled "Why Global Warming Would Be Good for You." "An examination of the record of the last twelve millennia," he wrote, "reveals that mankind prospered during the warm periods and suffered during the cold ones." His conclusion: "Global change is inevitable; warmer is better."[39] The people of North America who leave the cold north for the more comfortable climates of Arizona, Florida, New Mexico, and other southern states merely confirm the obvious—given a choice, people would rather be warm than cold.

What about the Effect on the Food Supply?

Senator Gore sounded the alarm about food in his book, saying, "Changing climate patterns due to global warming . . . will also pose problems for food production." The Worldwatch Institute cited "a rise in the anxiety level of government officials responsible for maintaining adequate food supplies."[40] Warnings of famine or at least food shortages are commonly made by those advocating immediate action to cut back carbon dioxide emissions. This was also a major theme of Lowell Ponte's book about the dangers of global cooling. Perhaps the government might form a commission to look into the feasibility of food contingency plans that could accommodate either a warming or a cooling. Stephen Schneider proposed a similar plan in the 1970s.

At least such planning would have a chance of being 50 percent right. Planning for just one eventually has a chance of being 100 percent wrong.

What is virtually unreported and is not mentioned by the activists is this finding by the IPCC: "Existing studies show that on the whole, global agricultural production could be maintained relative to baseline production in the face of climate change projected under doubled equivalent CO_2 equilibrium conditions." In other words, even if carbon dioxide concentrations in the atmosphere doubled (from the preindustrial concentration of 280 ppmv), there should be no food shortage. Production may shift and, under some scenarios, certain regions would suffer while others would prosper, but total production would be maintained. This point is reflected deep in a 1996 document outlining White House proposals for global change research. It states, "On the whole, the effects of climate change over the next century on total global food production may be small to moderate in comparison to the effects of population change and demands for improved nutrition."[41] A key factor in this finding is that it takes into consideration "the beneficial effects of CO_2 fertilization."[42] Research shows many crops thrive with higher levels of carbon dioxide concentration.

Environmental activists, like most human beings, have a weakness for picking and choosing among facts and findings to make the best case in support of their interests or biases. In this context, it is understandable that they ignore the IPCC finding and the comment in the president's research budget about food supplies. What the authors of the IPCC and the White House documents have done is to overcome what some observers have called the "dumb farmer" approach to the analysis. Early studies assumed that as climate changes (which it inevitably does), farmers would continue to plant the same crops, in the same fields, using the same techniques. History shows that farmers are not so dumb. They make sensible adaptations to changing conditions. The IPCC finding and the White House commentary deserve more public attention. Since they run contrary to the sensational charges of activists about runaway effects of global warming, they are largely ignored.

History also shows that the ability of science and the market economy to work wonders in food supply is one of the least celebrated events of our time. Rice production is a perfect example. In 1960, the International Rice Research Institute was established by the Rockefeller and Ford foundations. In a few years it introduced a new hybrid rice called IR8. It matured in much less time and allowed farmers to harvest two or three crops a year. It produced twice as much rice as did the seeds from which it was derived. This and other new rice varieties succeeded in doubling world rice production—creating a true "green revolution." Again, these success stories are not what the professional activists like to call to our attention.

· 9 ·

WHERE DO WE GO
FROM HERE?

E conomists debate the potential costs of attempting to regulate the
Earth's climate and the potential costs of not attempting to do so.
Politicians debate whether the risks justify the costs of government
regulatory action, and if so, which actions are politically safe for them to
promote. Driving the debate are professional activists and their political
allies, skilled at spreading fear among the citizenry and mobilizing a fair
number of them. Caught in the middle, although many do not yet realize it,
are businesses, industries, farmers, miners, and anyone dependent on the
use of energy, including especially individual users of cars and trucks—in
other words, just about everyone. The immediate question is: Should we
sign on to legally binding international agreements to limit the emission of
carbon dioxide? This is exactly what the Conference of Parties of the UN
Framework Convention on Climate Change is planning to consider in Kyoto,
Japan, in 1997.

Vice President Gore, visiting Japan in March 1997, spoke to an audi-
ence that included three former Japanese prime ministers (and a vice president of the Sierra Club). Brushing aside the multitude of uncertainties and
qualifications of the Intergovernmental Panel on Climate Change and other
scientists, he said "The scientific community confirmed that human activities are altering the planet's climate systems." He went on to "pledge the
commitment of the United States to work closely with Japan to ensure that
this meeting succeeds in producing a meaningful agreement." According to
Gore, "The developed world must agree to realistic and achievable legally
binding targets for greenhouse gas emissions."[1]

Is the Kyoto Action Plan Justified?

To address this issue, four basic questions were posed at the beginning of
Part Two. Is the global climate changing? To what extent does human ac-

tivity adversely affect global climate? Do we have enough facts, and are our theories good enough to justify remedial action? If so, what should be done to deal with climate change?

As we know, the climate is changing and always will be, but we do not yet know how much it has changed in the past few hundred years, or in which direction it will change in the next few hundred. We have good evidence that the atmospheric concentration of carbon dioxide has increased in recent years, and that human sources (such as burning fossil fuel) contribute to this concentration. But we do not know the importance or magnitude of this contribution—this, according to the IPCC.

We do not adequately understand the roles of water vapor, clouds, and the oceans. We therefore do not have adequate knowledge of the interrelationships among the Earth, its oceans, and its atmosphere. There are huge gaps in our knowledge of how the sun works and how it affects climate. In sum, we do not have the facts necessary to attempt to model the global climate, much less manipulate it. Any action plans based on current models do not inspire confidence and cannot justify disruptive actions. Neither do we know whether global warming, on balance, would be harmful or helpful; in any event, we can have little confidence that any remedial action we might take would be effective, especially considering the likelihood of unintended consequences.

In January 1997, five distinguished economists called for action on global warming. They assumed the science was clear enough to judge the costs of cutbacks in carbon-based fuel use, but their main point was that greenhouse gases should be controlled by market-based mechanisms. It is tempting to see the effort to manage the global climate as an opportunity to experiment with global economics, but it is premature, at best. While the IPCC scientists say that "the balance of evidence *suggests* a discernible human influence on global climate," the economists say, "A review of the evidence *has found* a discernible human influence." The IPCC scientists caution that they are unable to quantify the magnitude of any human effect because of "uncertainties in key factors." The economists, however, are ready not only to quantify the effects but to tell us how much they will cost. One of the leaders of these economists, William Nordhaus of Yale University, scoffed at "the idea of waiting around until everything is resolved."[2] The problem is, *nothing is resolved.*

The deep concerns of the private sector over the international negotiations on global warming were expressed in an unprecedented letter dated July 8, 1996, to President Clinton, signed by the chief executive officers of 120 major U.S. corporations.[3] They told the president they were "deeply concerned that such negotiations may lead to premature agreements that will severely disadvantage the U.S. economy and U.S. competitiveness simply to meet an arbitrary deadline." They called attention to the "great uncertainty about the extent, timing and effects" of climate change and the problems with climate models, as well as the exemption of developing nations, which are or will be major emitters of greenhouse gases.

The president responded on September 17, 1996, saying, "Vice President Gore and I are dedicated to promoting both sustainable economic growth and responsible stewardship of the environment." He said there would be consultations with the business community, but he made clear that his administration believes the process should go forward, adding, "We will at some later point in the negotiations be able to support a specific target and timetable."

The CEOs responded with another letter, dated December 9, 1996, saying that their concerns continued and that "a premature policy decision that could cost the equivalent of our annual economic growth for a decade warrants careful review and analysis." They added, "Given the long-term nature of this issue, there is time to reduce scientific uncertainties and refine the climate models. . . . It is imperative that we take time to do this right."

While the business and industrial community may not make much of a dent in the rush toward Kyoto, perhaps labor unions can get more attention. Cecil Roberts, president of the United Mine Workers, says of the UN global climate negotiations: "The economic stakes for American workers and consumers are enormous." Concerned that the proposed, legally binding caps on carbon dioxide will not cover China, India, Korea, Mexico, and other large producers, Roberts says, "The result is no benefit to the global environment, but a great deal of harm to American workers and low- and middle-income consumers."[4]

In February 1997, the AFL-CIO Executive Council released a statement making the same point about exempting China, India, and other developing countries, but it also pointed out that "carbon taxes, or equivalent carbon emission trading programs, will raise significantly electricity and other energy prices to consumers. These taxes are highly regressive and will be most harmful to citizens who live on fixed incomes or work at poverty-level wages." On June 19, 1997, Richard Trumka, secretary treasurer of the AFL-CIO, testifying before a Senate subcommittee, said, "The current approach in the UN negotiations is fatally flawed." At the same hearing, the representative of the American Farm Bureau Federation expressed the concern of America's farmers and said, "The administration should withdraw support for legally binding and enforceable caps on greenhouse gases."

In a three-page advertisement, some 1,300 businesses, farm groups, labor unions, associations, and other organizations urged President Clinton not to "rush into an unwise and unfair" global climate agreement.[5] The signatories ranged from the Alabama AFL-CIO to the Wyoming Mining

Association, and they included such disparate groups as the Olive Growers Council of California and the Police Department of Holdrege, Nebraska. Another opposing ad became a First Amendment issue when Ted Turner's CNN refused to continue running it after proponents complained. The sponsoring group called the CNN action "censorship,"[6] and Steve Yokich, head of the United Auto Workers, called it "un-American."

As part of its effort to rally support, the White House called in 110 weathercasters from America's eighty most populous television markets to be briefed by Vice President Gore and government scientists. White House press secretary Mike McCurry later commented artlessly that the weathercasters "appreciated being treated as something other than airheads," adding that "some of them are actually going to go out and report stories."

Another initiative was a White House Conference on Climate Change, hosted on October 6, 1997, by President Clinton's alma mater, Georgetown University.[7] The role of the automobile was discussed in the context of the Partnership for the Next Generation of Vehicles. The president said, "The leaders of the Big Three auto companies and the UAW came in to see us . . . and said they're going to meet" their PNGV goal. He added, "The real problem is, once they develop a prototype, How quickly can it be mass-produced and how will people buy it, and will they buy it at present fuel prices?" Later he underscored the lead time and marketing problems by saying, "Sooner or later, we're going to have the partnership. . . . The question is always, though, who will buy this stuff." The PNGV process appears to have had some educational benefit about what can be expected from the automobile and its customers.

On the basic issue, however, the president said, "Although we do not know everything, what we do know is more than enough to warrant responsible action." He failed to define "responsible action," but he alluded to a key controversy by saying all nations, including the developing ones, must participate "in a way that is fair to all." What is "fair" will be a burning issue in the effort to obtain Senate ratification of any treaty signed at Kyoto. The president lamented that "popular democracies are better organized to take advantage of opportunities or deal with immediate crises than they are to do the responsible thing . . . far enough in advance." Later he added with seeming regret, "You still have to have 51 percent in order to develop any kind of political consensus for doing anything." To which we should all say, "Hallelujah."

When the president did not reveal his plan for Kyoto at this conference, the Japanese made waves with the announcement of their position on October 6, 1997. In contrast to the proposal of the European Union (EU) for a 15 percent reduction below 1990 levels of greenhouse gas emissions by 2010, the Japanese urged the goal of a 5 percent reduction by 2012.[8] For themselves, however, they said that their past efforts to improve fuel efficiency were so effective that it would be unfair to hold Japan to their own suggested 5 percent level. Japan (and some others), they said, should be held to no more than a 2.5 percent reduction, and even this should be adjustable.[9] Professional activists were appalled; the Sierra Club, the National Wildlife Federation, the Environmental Defense Fund, and fourteen other organizations advised President Clinton that they would be "compelled to oppose such a treaty." Also, according to *Washington Post* writer Fred Hiatt, "They wrote that any ceiling on how much cost the United States was willing to bear would totally ruin a treaty." A remarkable but unsurprising attitude by this all-or-nothing group.[10]

But these groups have influence. The president on October 22, 1997, announced his plan, saying that the United States "simply must be prepared to commit to realistic and binding goals" at Kyoto. His proposal calls for the United States to cut greenhouse gas emissions back to 1990 levels between 2008 and 2012, and to cut below those levels in a five-year period thereafter. He called for a "joint implementation" system that would give a firm in one country (the United States) credit for reducing emissions in another country. And he said that key developing nations must "meaningfully participate in this effort." This plan came under immediate attack by the environmentalists and the Europeans. "It is simply not good enough," said the spokesman for the European Union. Much of the American media called it "modest" and "a fair start."

In judging how modest President Clinton's plan is, it is important to know why the United States did not meet the president's promise of 1993 to set a course that would cut back the gases to 1990 levels by 2000. (Current projections indicate that the United States will show a 13 percent emissions increase by that date.) This was foiled, as the *Washington Post* said, by "cheap fuel and a relatively rapid economic growth."[11] Anyone, including the president or vice president, who suggests that the goal of the plan can be reached without high fuel prices and cutbacks in economic growth is simply not credible.

As to the "meaningful participation" of developing countries, on the day of the president's announcement, the representative of Tanzania, speaking for the group of seventy-seven developing nations and China at the Bonn meeting of the ad hoc group on the Berlin Mandate, said that there are to be "no new commitments" for these countries. He went on to say that the developed countries must reduce greenhouse gases to 1990 levels by 2000 and must make further reductions in future years. Then, because cuts in these gases by developed countries might have "social, environmental, and economic impacts on developing country parties, . . . a Compensation Fund shall be established," to compensate them for any losses they may experience.

Congressman Dingell summed up well by saying that "the practical consequence is that we may be slouching toward Kyoto with only the barest appreciation of what we are doing and how it will affect us." It seems clear, however, that if a treaty is signed in Kyoto, the United States will bear the brunt of any energy use cuts. The EU countries would do no more than they are now doing, for other reasons. Japan would find a way out. The developing nations fully intend to grow—not to cut back. But in America, we can count on the professional activists to sue our government to ensure that the treaty is met.

Even if the Clinton-Gore administration will not listen to American industry, labor, farmers, or congressional leaders of both parties, the president should listen to the scientists before leading America into this great leap forward toward more central government control. The scientists all agree on one thing—the need for more research. No responsible scientist would say that we know all we need to know about the global climate. Even those who personally believe that preventive actions should immediately be taken are quick to point out the scientific uncertainties that must be cleared up.

Unfortunately, too many journalists and politicians do not show the same restraint or objectivity. But some journals do get the word out, and Congress has not yet leapt off the parapet, thanks to some very sturdy members, including Representatives John D. Dingell (D-Mich.) and Dan Schaefer (R-Colo.) and Senators Robert Byrd (D-W.Va.) and Chuck Hagel (R-Neb.), who care about jobs and the economy.[12]

The availability of affordable energy is central to all human activity. The operation of our economy and the way we live are dependent on it. Turning over to governments the power to regulate—on an international scale—the use of carbon-based energy, which accounts for 90 percent of the world's energy supply, would be giving the regulators control over the most sensitive and vital factor in our material lives. No persuasive case has been made for taking this drastic step.

Get On with the Research!

Research to clear up the uncertainties about global warming has had bipartisan support, as it should. The U.S. Global Change Research Program (USGCRP) was established by President Ronald Reagan and was included in President Bush's FY 1990 budget proposal. President Clinton's subcommittee on Global Change Research laid out a plan calling for a budget of $1.7 billion to begin to answer the outstanding questions. The program recognizes the need "to address the uncertainties about changes, both natural and human-induced, in the Earth system." It also proposes "to monitor, understand, and predict global change" and "to provide a sound scientific basis for national and international decision making on global change issues." On one specific, the USGCRP document says, "Reducing uncertainty about the magnitude of feedbacks is thus essential to providing more accurate predictions of how climate will change in response to alternative emissions scenarios for greenhouse gases, and to developing the capability to provide more accurate estimates of the regional patterns of climate change." Surely it is sensible to address this kind of question before we launch into the unknown to solve problems we are not sure of, with "solutions" that will almost surely have unintended consequences.

How much should be spent on research is difficult to determine, but if government enthusiasts insist on more and more regulation, Congress owes the country adequate research to ensure the greatest benefit—or at a minimum, the least harm—from such programs. Conversely, serious scientists with serious projects ought to receive adequate funding, and they should not be tempted into covering up uncertainties or resorting to "scary scenarios" to attract adequate support. It is of concern, however, that research dollars directed to space programs may be redirected to the study of the Earth's environment. America and the world cannot afford to pull back from programs aimed at understanding our universe and beyond, any more than we can afford to look at only one country or one region in our attempts to understand the Earth. We must not become an inward-looking people. Humankind has always reached out to understand and experience the new—and must continue to do so. The answers to our future needs are as much there as in our small corner of the universe.

Conclusion

As with most issues of public importance, the public debate over global warming is plagued with emotion and name-calling. Forecasts of cataclysmic disaster—the stock-in-trade of the professional activists—are common. Those who see things differently or want more facts are labeled as unconscionable procrastinators or special-interest pleaders.

The public is concerned, but also confused. People are unconvinced by the arguments of either side. In their lifetimes, so many Americans hear the voices of doom and gloom so often they tend to tune out. They do not want the globe desecrated, but neither do they want more government control over their lives. Very specifically, by what they do, they show how much they value their right to mobility. A principal American rite of passage is getting a driver's license—and the keys to the car. The freedom and opportunity provided by the motor vehicle are important to our concept of a high standard of living. Since the 1960s, however, the professional activists have led a drum-fire against the car, and old-fashioned guilt has crept into the minds of many Americans about the "profligate" way we travel. But the limits of that guilt are apparent when anything really gets between us and our cars. Politicians who take advantage of busy people by "scare-the-hell-out-of-them" tactics are abusing their positions of trust. They contribute heavily to the distrust people have of governments and the people who run them. Instead of using scare tactics, they should help the scientists get on with needed research.

It would also make sense for all of us, as tenants of this globe, to take personal responsibility for passing it along in good shape. Since the strongest impulse of humankind seems to be to perpetuate the species, maintaining our habitat should come naturally. This doesn't mean rejecting the benefits of the modern world or embracing every proposal advanced in the name of the environment. It does mean going beyond sole reliance on market forces or government action, and exercising a personal discipline about the way we live, with some thought toward simplifying our lives and moderating our consumption of the Earth's resources. By doing so, we might also conserve some of our personal resources, including especially our physical and mental health. Let's not only plant some trees but take some time to walk among them.

PART THREE

Clean Air and Your Car

· 10 ·

BAD NEWS, GOOD NEWS

If all goes according to plan, the number of Americans living with officially designated dirty air will increase by nearly 65 percent early in the decade beginning in the year 2000. This will happen, but not because the air is getting dirtier. It is actually getting much cleaner. It will happen because the Environmental Protection Agency, according to a plan endorsed by Vice President Gore and approved by President Clinton, will have changed the rules. With the stroke of a regulator's pen, the air millions of people are breathing will change from healthy to unhealthy. States, counties, and cities that worked diligently to comply with the Clean Air Act will find the finishing line moved far down the track, with a need to expend billions of dollars more in their attempt to finish the race.

Areas that are now in compliance will suddenly be on the bad air list.[1] Thousands of professional activists, government regulators, businesses that profit from pollution controls, and many others who make their living from the politics of air pollution will be quite happy. Millions of citizens of affected areas will be paying billions, either in taxes or in higher prices for goods, services, and transportation, to bring their areas into compliance. The jobs of many will be at risk. Even with the new standards, there is no guarantee that the EPA will not tighten the rules again in the future. That is the bad news.

The Good News

The air in America is cleaner than it has been for decades. In fact, today it is about 30 percent cleaner than it was twenty-five years ago—and it will get cleaner in future years, even without new government regulations, as older cars are replaced with new, cleaner ones and emissions from stationary sources are further reduced—under current law.

Although the numbers of vehicles and the miles they travel have increased dramatically in recent decades, the atmospheric concentrations of pollutants from motor vehicles and other sources of combustion have been cut significantly. Since 1985, the atmospheric concentration of carbon monoxide has been reduced by 37 percent. Lead has decreased by 78 percent, and is down 98 percent below the 1970 level. Oxides of nitrogen concentrations have been cut by 14 percent since 1985, and 1995 was the fourth year in a row that all monitoring locations in the United States, including Los Angeles, met the federal air quality standard for this pollutant. Ozone declined by 6 percent.[2] Concentrations of particulate matter over the 1988–1994 period were down 20 percent. Sulfur dioxide concentrations were brought down 25 percent during the 1985–1994 period.[3] We have spent untold billions of dollars to clean up the air—and it *is* cleaner.

But how many Americans know and understand this good news? Not many. The *Washington Post* of December 18, 1996, carried the news under the headline "EPA Reports Improvement in Air Quality," citing a news conference by EPA administrator Carol M. Browner. But the article was brief and buried on page 8, with the underwear ads. Even then, one-third of the story dealt with the EPA's claim that much more needs to be done, and in her remarks the administrator did not stress the great progress in environmental protection but emphasized rather that economic growth could occur at the same time as the environment was improved. "Over twenty-five years, the gross domestic product increased 99 percent, while emissions of the nation's six major pollutants declined by 29 percent," Administrator Browner said.[4]

She could have added that "emissions for all criteria pollutants except nitrogen oxides [for which air quality standards are being met] decreased between 1970 and 1995," and that this occurred while "population increased 28 percent [and] VMT [vehicle miles traveled] increased 116 percent."[5]

There is another major piece of good news not given much play: "Between 1986 and 1995, the total number of days with PSI values greater than 100 decreased 54 percent in Los Angeles, 35 percent in Riverside, and 59 percent in the remaining major cities across the United States."[6] The Pollutant Standards Index (PSI), according to EPA, "integrates information on criteria pollutant concentrations across an entire monitoring network into a single number that represents the worst daily air quality experienced in an urban area." These data show that even Los Angeles and Riverside, with the worst air pollution problems in the United States, are making great progress.

Why We Keep Getting Bad News

One reason most Americans do not know the good news about the environment is the natural reluctance of the media to give much time or space to good news. That simply is not what gets the attention of the readers, viewers, or listeners. After all, the communications media is a highly competitive business, and it seems we are willing to pay more for bad news than for good. Shame on us.

Then there are the professional environmental groups—dozens of them. They live on the bad news. If the news were good, how would they raise their money? None of them sends out fundraising letters saying, "Look how much cleaner the air is." Their solicitations, and they come in the mail by the dozens, proclaim that disaster is at hand and only a healthy contribution might enable the soliciting organization to fend off the evil doers. Good news might have their constituents thinking about giving their money to some other worthy cause, or even keeping it for personal use. Good news could put them out of business, or at least cause a serious "downsizing." So they deny it or ignore it and concentrate on bad news, accurate or not.[7] Shame on them.

There is another reason why we do not get to celebrate the fact that our air is much cleaner. Some government regulators see good news as a threat. Once a year the EPA is required to report to Congress on the progress made in cleaning up the air. Most government agencies trumpet any improvements in their areas of responsibility (whether they had anything to do with them or not). This is not the case with environmental agencies. Like the professional activists, they seem to feel their future is better ensured by the bad news than by the good. The record would seem to support that view. The EPA did not exist until 1970, when it was established (with staff from other agencies) by President Richard Nixon. By 1980, it had a staff of 10,945. By 1990, there were 17,170 regulators under the EPA roof. The EPA budget went from just under $1.3 billion in 1970 to over $5.1 billion in 1990. The proposed budget for 1998 is $7.6 billion, and it calls for 18,283 employees. This steady growth of staff, power, and consequence is facilitated by bad news about the state of the environment and fear for its future. Budget requests are accompanied by dire predictions about the state of the environment.

The reluctance to celebrate the good news is not a cynical tactic by all or even most of those involved. Most government officials are as objective as conditions permit. Contrary to the way they are popularly portrayed, government employees are, in the majority, hard-working, dedicated professionals trying their best to carry out the policies and processes adopted by the Congress and the president.[8] They may disagree with these policies, but our republican form of representative government would collapse if career government employees were permitted to pick and choose which policies to implement.

Of course, there are many officials, career as well as appointed, who believe passionately in enacting the most stringent environmental protection possible. The nature of environmental protection work encourages those in the field to assume a certain moral superiority, even zealousness. Their mission is to stop polluters. Since all industries, and most other economic activities, create pollution of one kind or another, environmental officials look upon them not as productive, job-providing pillars of the economy, but as polluters, engaged in doing exactly what the officials are dedicated to stop. In these circumstances, a difficult relationship is to be expected between government and industry.

Whatever their motivation, many regulators also believe that their ability to accomplish their mission may be impaired if the public is exposed to too much good news about how much cleaner the air is today. This is a special concern as the EPA undertakes to craft and enforce new and exceedingly strict national ambient air quality standards (NAAQS) for ozone and particulate matter (PM). By changing the classification from clean to dirty for the air millions of people are now breathing, these standards will result in a flood of new regulations for motor vehicles and virtually every economic activity in the nation. And it is all because, despite the good news, Administrator Browner says there are "too many Americans at risk."

Dealing with Threats

The national security establishment knows how this works. When the threats from the Soviet Union were obvious, budgets went up. When the news turned good, with the dissolution of the USSR, the Pentagon's budget went down. EPA and environmental activists do not want to travel down that path. The zealous will concentrate on the risks, however small, and ignore the good news.

Professional environmentalists have learned well from also observing other techniques used by national security advocates. For decades, "national security" was invoked as justification for all manner of military, intelligence, and security projects and programs, most quite essential but some of dubious merit or carried too far. Today, many of the champions of "environmental protection" are following the same pattern. Like national security, the environment poses real problems that must be met, but environmentalism can also become the "last refuge of the scoundrel"[9]—or at least of the opportunist. It is invoked by extremists with the same threatening rigor as was national security by demagogues of past years.[10] Skeptics are vigorously denounced and their morals and motives questioned. Echoing past excesses, the secretary of the interior, Bruce Babbitt, has labeled two entire industries as "un-American" for questioning new environmental regulatory proposals.[11]

Both these national interests—defense and the environment—are deeply important, but there must be ways to ensure that real needs are met without impugning the character of anyone who questions a proposal and without stampeding the country into silly or harmful actions that waste resources needed for other good works. Environmental extremists should not be permitted to undermine legitimate environmental concerns, as some security extremists did in their field, with irresponsible charges that spawned public fear, confusion, and controversy.

Despite the similarities in the way zealots in both these fields operate, there is a significant difference in their villains. In national security, the other superpower of the time was the clear enemy and its authoritarian ideology was anathema. For the environmental zealot, humankind is the villain, and the Biblical exhortation to subdue the Earth and to have dominion over its creatures for the betterment of the human population is an abomination. For those who need such motivation, the environmental "crisis" provides that overarching threat that justifies moral certainty and single-minded commitment to the defeat of the enemy and his creed.

Perhaps the most articulate advocate of this point of view—certainly the most strategically situated—is Vice President Al Gore. In his book *Earth in the Balance* he wrote, "We must make the rescue of the environment the central organizing principle for civilization." He talked about the "epic battle to right the balance of our earth," the need to arouse the world to the "urgent danger" and to an understanding of the "crisis." He has pinpointed the villain: "The struggle to save the global environment is in one way much more difficult than the struggle to vanquish Hitler, for this time the war is with ourselves. We are the enemy."[12]

Funding the "War with Ourselves"

The war with ourselves to protect the environment differs radically from the effort to protect national security. The national defense budgets are established by annual appropriations that must come from taxes levied by Congress. In contrast, the billions of dollars spent on environmental protection are not tax dollars, at least in the traditional sense. ("No new taxes!" is still a potent political concept.)

Concerned about voter backlash, politicians have slowed the process of authorizing new programs that require them to levy taxes. Instead, they pass laws requiring someone else to spend the money to achieve the legislated goal. The sponsoring legislators can then claim the credit for any good in the program but avoid the blame for "tax-and-spend" policies. The most common way to do this is through regulation. Congress passes a law authorizing or ordering the EPA to reduce a pollutant. The EPA promulgates a regulation that commands private companies to cut their plant or product emissions by a set amount. The companies do so and then pass the cost of the control technologies on to the customer. The customer does not have a chance to say whether he wants to buy the technology or not. In fact, the customer does not usually know that he has bought anything. For example, the design of dozens of components of the automobile is determined by the requirements of EPA regulations.[13] This does not come free. The customer has paid for a government program, and the money he paid was "appropriated" from him by the government through regulation, but he doesn't know it; certainly he doesn't know how much it cost him or what, exactly, he got for his money. What he does know is that prices keep going up. He may also hear politicians taking credit for bringing the polluters to heel.

This process may give politicians some protection from the tax-and-spend charge, but in a democratic system it undermines accountability. When Congress actually appropriates money for a program, voters can find out how much is being spent to get the promised benefits and can react at the polls. When Congress, through regulations, requires private companies, organizations, and individuals to spend money to meet those regulations, it sets no limits on total expenditures. In practice, it turns over to government agencies the power to draft the regulations, which in substance are laws, and gives the same officials the power to promulgate, interpret, and enforce the laws and to apply the punishment for infractions.

Nobody knows how much additional spending is "commanded" by the government through regulation. Some valiant efforts have been made to calculate the cost, including studies by Professor Thomas D. Hopkins at the Rochester Institute of Technology. In 1995, he estimated that the cost of all government regulation was around $600 billion annually. If this amount is added to traditional government spending, which was around $1.5 trillion in 1995, the share of gross domestic product (GDP) commanded by the government goes from about 22 percent to 30 percent.[14] Because these costs are required by government, they have the attributes of taxes—except for accountability. Americans want cleaner air and will pay to get it, but the current system does not let them know how much they are paying for progress or whether each expenditure makes sense.

Hundreds of billions of dollars have been spent in this way—dollars that could have been spent instead on education, crime prevention, medical research, and other good things. With expenditures of that magnitude, if the air were not getting better, a grand jury should be looking into the program. Surely the American people have reached the point that environmental warriors can trust them enough to permit a celebration of the good news about cleaner air. They have paid dearly for it, whether they know it or not.

Worse yet, the EPA is still working on the problems of the 1960s. The billions budgeted for air pollution control are being spent to bring certain vehicle and plant emissions to within a few percentage points of zero, as compared with precontrolled levels. Instead of redirecting these resources to other priorities, the EPA wants to continue to tighten down on the same emissions, whether that makes sense or not. Auto-emission control is an example of overkill. By any measure, the reduction of pollutants is a success.

The Car's Contribution to the Cleanup. Ultimately, the success in cleaning up the air is a credit to the doers, not the talkers. The automotive scientists and engineers from the auto companies, independent suppliers, and other sources have analyzed the problems, researched the solutions, invented the technology, and improved it over time. These talented men and women do the real work of cleaning up the air. The professional activists, environmental politicians, and zealous regulators get the publicity—sometimes by saying that the car people are dragging their feet.[15] The fact is, success in cleaning up the car is the single largest contribution to cleaner air.

As the auto companies like to point out, cars today are so clean that a round-trip drive between Washington, D.C., and New York City in a new car would produce fewer pollutants than would mowing your lawn with a gas-powered mower. Also, a new car driven about 60 miles would give off fewer smog-forming emissions than would a 1965 model parked in the driveway all day with the engine off. That is the result of the new technology now controlling hydrocarbon emissions caused by gasoline evaporation from the fuel systems of cars and light trucks, a process that occurs even when they are parked with their engines turned off.

The most dramatic breakthrough in emissions control was the development of the catalytic converter, now found on virtually every car and light truck sold in America. This device takes on the toughest cleanup job—engine exhaust. Despite great improvement in the combustion process of the engine, a small amount of the fuel is not oxidized (burned) in the cylinder and is expelled in the form of volatile organic compounds (VOCs).[16] Additionally, some of the carbon in the fuel is only partially oxidized and becomes carbon monoxide (CO). A third pollutant is formed when a very small amount of the nitrogen present in the air in the cylinder is oxidized at very high temperatures to become nitric oxide, a small portion of which is converted to oxides of nitrogen (NO_x).

These three gases are expelled and flow into a device called a three-way converter, where they interact with the catalyst materials: platinum, palladium, and rhodium. A combination of the first two is an excellent catalyst for oxidizing CO, which converts to carbon dioxide (CO_2). This combination also converts VOCs into water (H_2O) and carbon dioxide (CO_2). To control NO_x, a mixture of platinum and palladium with rhodium (all of the platinum family) provides the catalyst that reduces NO_x to elemental nitrogen (N_2). This can take place only if the supply of oxygen is great enough to oxidize the CO and VOCs, but not so great as to inhibit the decomposition of the NO_x into N_2. To accomplish this, the air-fuel mixture entering the engine must be delicately balanced at the chemically correct or stoichiometric point, which means that just the correct amount of oxygen is present to burn all the fuel. Maintaining the right mixture requires an oxygen sensor that measures the oxygen in the exhaust before it reaches the converter. This sensor transmits a signal to the electronic control unit that directs the fuel system to adjust the air-fuel ratio to keep it close to stoichiometric composition.

To work properly, the converter must be hot. During the first few seconds the vehicle is operated, little conversion can take place. As exhaust gases pour into the device, however, it soon reaches between 700° and 1,400° F. The most rapid possible heating of the catalyst is an important way to reduce emissions.

An added problem was the secure procurement of the catalytic materials, the main sources of which are South Africa and Russia. Rhodium is found in nature only in combination with platinum, and in very small quantities. Since a larger proportion of rhodium is needed than occurs in nature, an excess of platinum must be mined and refined to obtain enough of the material for a three-way catalyst. (This makes rhodium a very expensive metal.) The mixture of platinum, palladium, and rhodium is spread over the ceramic honeycomb within the converter, which contains around 500,000 square feet of surface.

The three-way catalyst, along with other control technologies, has been a great success in removing automotive pollutants from the atmosphere. In the 1960s, before motor vehicle emissions were controlled, cars emitted 87.0 grams per mile of carbon monoxide, 10 grams per mile of hydrocarbons (HC), and 3.6 grams of oxides of nitrogen. New exhaust standards were phased in beginning in 1994 and were applied to all light-duty vehicles in 1996. They set CO at 3.4 grams, HC at 0.25 grams, and NO_x at 0.4 grams. As a result, CO from new cars has been reduced by 96 percent. HC have been cut by 97.5 percent, and NO_x is down by 89 percent.[17]

The news is even better. The actual reductions of new-car emissions are greater since, to ensure compliance with the standards, vehicles are designed to produce fewer emissions than required—a margin of safety. The result of these reductions is a dramatic shift in the role of auto emissions as causes of ozone. In 1994, the American Automobile Association (AAA) commissioned a study that concluded that in the ten cities examined, "Automobiles and light trucks are no longer the primary or even secondary cause of summertime ozone 'smog.'"[18] As the AAA study reports, "Clearly, automobile and light truck emissions reductions have outpaced reductions in emissions from other sources." This is not what you hear from the professional activists who are loath to give up their favorite demon, the car.

The Costs of Control

These reductions in pollutants did not come free. The U.S. General Accounting Office estimated that between 1970 and 1991, U.S. government and industry spent close to $1 trillion dollars on pollution control of all kinds.[19] (By comparison, total federal government spending in 1970 was less than $200 billion. It did not reach a trillion until 1990.) The U.S. General Accounting Office has estimated (conservatively) the cost of air pollution abatement to have been $113 billion in 1992 alone. The GAO has also pointed out that this cost "represents resources lost to the economy through regulation," and that "costs stemming from environmental regulation represent the amount of economic resources that are not available to be spent on other economic activities."[20]

Estimating the cost of pollution controls is very difficult. Actual costs change. As manufacturers learn how to make simpler, more efficient controls, costs may be reduced. As new rules come into force, costs increase to cover the new technologies needed to meet the rules. Government data indicate that between 1987 and 1993, the motor vehicle industry spent more than $100 billion on pollution abatement and control.[21] Patrick Bedard, using data from the U.S. Bureau of Labor Statistics (in 1993 dollars), estimated the cost of emission-control equipment added to a new car through the 1994 model year to be around $2,010.[22] Industry sources have recently estimated these costs to be around $1,500, as a result of engineering and manufacturing improvements that cut costs. At this rate, if sales in one model year reach 15 million vehicles, the total costs for that year of controls now in the car would be more than $22.5 billion. Beyond that, requirements on the books at the federal or state level will raise costs substantially (and in California, could double the cost) as they are implemented.

It is the customer, of course, who ends up paying these additional costs. If new national ambient air quality standards announced by the Clinton administration in 1997 are implemented, it is likely that more stringent auto-emission standards will be proposed, adding significantly more cost. Car buyers do not know this, and professional activists do not want them to.[23] If the public really understood what it cost them, there might be more critical public judgments about additional controls. People might become more interested in what they are getting for their money and what they are giving up to get it.

Unfortunately, no one really knows the costs of current controls, and certainly not the costs of future controls. Neither does anyone know the value of the benefits of regulation. All numbers are based on estimates and assumptions that are constantly challenged and changed.

· 11 ·

THE
GOVERNMENT'S
ROLE

T he costs of government regulation are important, but calling attention to them should not imply that the government has no proper
role in cleaning up the environment. Contrary to public myth, the
auto industry actually supported the enactment of legislation to involve the
federal government in the control of auto emissions. Thirty years ago, at
hearings held by the U.S. Congress on proposed legislation to control pollution, the president of the Automobile Manufacturers Association, Thomas C. Mann, flanked by the engineering vice presidents of Chrysler, Ford,
General Motors, and American Motors (since gone out of business), testified before Senator Ed Muskie, sponsor of the Clean Air Act. [1]

"Government standards," Mann said in 1967, "are desirable in this
area [air pollution] which is so intimately related to the public welfare."[2]
He went on to point out how competitive the industry was, and how car
buyers understandably want to buy the lowest-cost vehicles that meet their
needs. He added that consumers were reluctant to pay more for cars equipped
with emission-control devices. Some consumers were skeptical because
they did not see any immediate and direct personal benefit from these expenditures; some were dubious, believing that if they bought the devices
while others did not, the air would be contaminated anyway and they would
have wasted their money. In these circumstances, Mann said, a car company that adds to the cost of its product by installing emission controls will
lose sales to competitors who do not.

"Reasonable and practicable government emission standards, by putting consumer and competitor alike on an equal footing, facilitate the ability of the industry to cope with the problem of reducing emissions of
objectionable gases from its product. We therefore consider them desirable," Mann concluded. In other words, all competitors would be required
to add emission controls, and all consumers would have no choice but to
buy them.

Pandora's Box

At the time, some critics, inside the industry and out, believed that Mann was opening the fabled Pandora's box by endorsing government action to curb pollution. The result, they were certain, would be irrational and excessive regulation. Why would an industry take a big step down the slippery slope of more central government regulation? Where would it end?

Mann was correct, but so were the critics. He was correct because people did not shop for a car on the basis of how many grams-per-mile of hydrocarbons or other pollutants it might emit. Customers did not hold up on their car purchases until they verified that they came equipped with catalytic converters.

The marketplace did not address this lack of consumer interest in emission controls. If auto emissions were to be reduced, something other than pure market forces must be brought into play. Manufacturers might have worked together to control emissions, but unfortunately, antitrust law prevented manufacturers from agreeing among themselves to pollution reduction programs. Government involvement became inevitable.[3]

The critics were also correct. Pandora's box was opened, and out flew a new flock of special interests—a federal bureaucracy, several state bureaucracies, a burgeoning number of environmental advocacy groups living on grants and contributions from a well-meaning constituency, and finally, a growing number of businesses (and private-sector bureaucracies) benefiting from more stringent environmental regulations.[4] This new set of special interests, with the help of the media, seized the public relations high ground as the champions of clean air, leaving industry in the dust—or smog, as it were. For legitimate reasons, government intervention was invited (it would have happened anyway). But this was the first step on the slippery slope. From the government's perspective and that of the professional activists, there was no natural stopping place. The requirements continue to get increasingly stringent.

Except possibly for the airplane, there is no more thoroughly regulated manufactured product on the market than the automobile. The federal and state laws, rules, and regulations covering the car fill thousands of pages. Hundreds of federal government officials as well as legislators and their staffs are involved in administering, overseeing, and updating the old rules, as well as researching, devising, advocating, and enacting new ones. Hundreds more state and regional agencies have their own requirements. Many professional activist groups make their living criticizing the car and its makers. Some would like "the bridge to the next century" to be for pedestrians and bicycles only. Many would like to see a modern-day Red Flag law enacted that would end the use of the motor vehicle as we know it.[5] (At least they would like to get *other* people out of their cars.) They share the

Duke of Wellington's aversion to anything that might "encourage the common people to move about needlessly."

This wave of regulatory controls by the federal government was facilitated by a changed public attitude and by the recognition of some real, car-related problems. First, the almost frenzied desire to own a car had been largely satisfied in America (at least among adults). Having been exposed, at the turn of the twentieth century, to the marvels of a new mode of personal mobility and the opportunities it brings, Americans invested this mode—the car—with an importance and priority that, as the Lynds reported, sometimes went beyond reason (much as some teenagers do today).[6] As the twenty-first century approaches, 20 percent of American households have three or more vehicles. The daily average number of vehicle trips made per household is between four and five. Americans today assume that they will always have the use of a car, van, or truck. They may hope that government will come up with plans to keep others off the road, but they do not imagine their government will get between them and the use of their own cars.

As people began to take their "right" to a car for granted, however, they also became much more sensitive to the fact that cars can bring problems as well as utility and pleasure. Something economists call "externalities" began to attract increasing attention.

Externalities Explained

Externalities, simply stated, are side effects or unintended consequences that are created by an activity or transaction but are not accounted for in the price of that activity. These externalities can result in costs (or benefits) that are paid for by neither the buyer nor the seller but are suffered (or enjoyed) by others not party to the transaction. (In the literature about externalities, most attention is focused on their costs rather than on their benefits. These costs are not dealt with through internal processes by those who incur them, but are "externalized," by being passed on to others.) When externalities adversely affect the so-called public interest, there are strong incentives for seeking government intervention to address them. This is what Thomas C. Mann, the head of the auto manufacturers association, was talking about when he testified before a congressional committee in favor of government involvement to deal with automotive emissions. These emissions are a classic example of externalities.

Externalities are often explained as failures of the market properly to address the full consequences of a transaction. Advocates of virtually every intervention by the government into the private sector claim it is needed as a correction of "market failure." Sometimes they are right. In "the good old days," when people used the streets for sewers, the resulting stench and pestilence were the externalities. Neighbors and the entire community suffered. By and large, private companies were not rising to the challenge of getting the citizenry to agree to pay to have sewers built. It fell to government of one form or another to take over the task of dealing with these externalities. Perhaps if a private-sector company had undertaken the task, it ultimately might have done a more efficient job than did the government. But the private sector, for whatever reason, did not rise to the occasion.[7]

The sewage problem is a reasonable example of a market failure. In this instance, a demonstrable public health need existed and the private sector did not address it. The issue was not whether the government should have a role in addressing serious public health and safety problems that are the side effects or externalities of an activity, and are not being addressed by the market. The challenge is to determine when and how—and how much—government intervention makes sense.

The reaction in the 1860s to the first self-propelled road vehicle—the steam car—provides an early example of one way to address externalities. The "public interest" disturbed by those first cars was the orderly life of the landed gentry, concerned that their horses would be startled by these noisy machines, and annoyed by the noise and dust they caused.

These externalities were unintended, but they were real to the affronted gentry who perceived no benefit to themselves from the vehicle and received no compensation for their concerns. In this case, the frightened horse, the dust, and the noise were the costs, and neither the seller of the steam car nor the buyer compensated the horse's owner, or anyone else who might have been affected by the dust and noise. Using their political influence, these early "public-interest activists"—along with the economic interests opposed to steam power on the roads, notably the horse and wagon carriers and, later, the railroads—succeeded in driving steam power off the road.[8]

While the country squire may have believed that he and his peers were harmed by the steam car, the general community would have benefited from the vehicle by gaining an additional method of transport and communication, along with the economic stimulation those activities provide. Of course, the benefits from such developments are about as difficult to quantify as are the costs of noise, dust, or startled horses.

Of course, the horse itself was associated with some rather significant externalities. In New York City in 1900, horses left some 1,000 tons of manure and 70,000 gallons of urine on the streets each day. An average of twenty horse carcasses were also left each day for the city to remove. An analysis of typical road mud in London in 1886 found that it was 30 percent abraded stone, 10 percent abraded iron (from horseshoes and wheels), and 60 percent organic matter and manure. A London doctor wrote that "the amount of irritation to the nose, throat and eyes in London from dried horse manure was something awful." [9]

Using the Sky as a Dump

Air pollution is a classic externality. Since the dawn of history, humankind has used the sky as a dump. When the cave man captured the use of fire, he gave no thought to the effect of smoke on the ecology. What concern his successors felt, until recent times, was largely directed at how to get the smoke out of the cave or hut or factory and into the "open air." Since no one owned the open air, there were no restrictions or fees for the privilege of using it as a dump for the smoke.[10] Smoke was looked on as a natural occurrence, even though, on cold winter mornings, the smoke from fireplaces and wood stoves in log cabins could cast a pall over the valleys of frontier America and could wrap London in a "fog."

What has been called the worst air pollution disaster in history occurred in London in 1952. Powered largely by coal, British industry was benefiting from the postwar economic recovery. Smokestack controls were nonexistent. Apartments were heated by coal-fired boilers. Fireplaces were common. Often the quantity of soot was ten times that of the levels found in the United States. In a foggy December in 1952, a temperature inversion held the air over London in a stagnant, polluted mass for most of the month. In that time, at least 4,000 "excess deaths" (that is, more deaths than are "normally" expected in the period concerned) were attributed to respiratory ailments. More than 80 percent of the deaths reportedly occurred among people with known heart and respiratory disease. The specific causes of death were undetermined. Subsequently, it was suggested that sulfur dioxide and soot may have been the causes. Recently, there has been some speculation that the sudden onset of cold weather and an influenza virus may also have played a role.[11]

The London disaster was preceded by two other events with excess deaths occurring during a period of heavy air pollution. During a five-day fog in December 1930, sixty-three people died in the Meuse Valley of Belgium. Most of those who died were older persons known to have diseases of the heart or lungs. Even less is known about the specific causes in this event, but sulfur dioxide is suspected. In October 1948, twenty people died in Donora, Pennsylvania, during a week of air stagnation. Again, the majority were older persons with previous heart or respiratory disease.

There is no conclusive evidence establishing a cause of death in these incidents. It is likely that there was a combination of causes, and since many of the deaths occurred among persons with significant existing health problems, it is also difficult to judge their normal life expectancy. How long those people would have lived in the purest of air is unknown. The number of deaths attributed to these events was also the result of statistical analysis—comparing death rates in those periods with the expected death rate. There are inevitably problems with such analyses. For example, many of the deaths may have come about in the weeks following the episode, but were hastened by environmental factors.

Although there are many uncertainties about causes and effects, it seems reasonable to assume that the heavy air pollution in these three cases contributed significantly to the illnesses and excess deaths. As a result, changes were made in coal-burning techniques, and many industries and residences switched to oil or natural gas. These changes did not eliminate all emissions of soot and other pollutants, but no similar events have occurred, despite predictions to the contrary.[12] In a 1968 book, Paul Ehrlich presents a scenario in which a 1979 killer smog in Los Angeles wipes out 90,000 people.[13] Fortunately, even predictably, the doomsday seers have proved to be wrong.

When to Intervene. Not all externalities justify government intervention. If you happen to sit on the bus next to someone using a fragrance that stops up your nasal passages or aggravates your asthma, it may be an annoyance but it hardly justifies government regulation of that person's personal odor. (The exception, it seems, is the city of San Francisco, which is becoming involved in such matters.) It is not always easy to distinguish between those externalities that justify government intervention and those that do not. We also need some way to recognize the most effective means of intervention, and the point where intervention should stop. Recent history gives us a starting place in finding the answer.

There is broad agreement that the worst pollution problems in the industrial world have occurred in those countries where the government was entirely in charge. The air quality in East Germany, Poland, and other countries under Communist rule was abominable. From the disaster at Chernobyl to the leaking natural gas pipelines throughout the country, central government control failed to protect either the citizenry or the environment of the Soviet Union. "The Vistula River in Poland," according to Vice President Gore, "has so many poisonous and corrosive pollutants gurgling toward Gdansk that much of its water cannot even be used to cool factory machinery."[14] Even in the United States, some of the worst toxic waste sites are government facilities, and the government so far has been a failure in developing technical—and political—ways of disposing of accumulating nuclear waste.

There is another very good reason to be skeptical of government control. History shows that every new regulation creates new pressures for ways to avoid or to exploit it. (Complex tax laws, for example, have spawned a growing number of practitioners skilled in finding legal loopholes.) The more stringent the regulation, the greater the incentive for finding a way around it. Unfortunately, the more a society is regulated, the more opportunity there is for official corruption.

We like to think that most corruption takes place in other countries, but it takes very little research to find that Lord Acton's famous admonition, "Power tends to corrupt, and absolute power corrupts absolutely," applies also in the United States.[15] Even when there is no personal enrichment, more power in the hands of the government means that the value of public office increases accordingly. The high cost of election campaigns in the United States—and the willingness of groups and individuals to contribute huge sums to candidates—is one example of how valuable the goodwill of the Congress and the presidency itself have become. [16]

Government interventions, whether they are taxes, market-based systems such as emission-trading programs, or command-and-control rules, are all political at their core. In each instance, the government will set the limits on the side effects and write the rules to achieve those limits; and all government decisions are political. In all societies around the world, rules beget permits and permits beget opportunities for corruption. Even when acting in the most altruistic and objective manner, government planners do not have the information that free-market prices provide automatically in setting economic priorities and policies. With this background, it would be wise to begin consideration of ways to meet any perceived public need by acknowledging that private solutions are preferable to government involvement.[17]

The markets are the most efficient and effective economic decision-making mechanism known to humankind. They have unsurpassed success in creating wealth and material well-being. One of their major advantages is that they "regulate" automatically, without the arbitrariness of the political process. If a product fails to be competitive in meeting consumer expectations, it faces the most stringent of all regulation—rejection. Personal connections, political influence, or under-the-table payments cannot save it. Another virtue of the markets is that they can work without being understood. It is not necessary for the buyers and sellers to understand all the intricate forces, actions, and decisions that make the market succeed. In contrast, government intervention, especially if unintended consequences are to be minimized, must be thoroughly understood; rules must be carefully drawn and responsibilities must be specifically assigned, and even then the intervention rarely achieves its objectives.

But unfortunately, free markets cannot do every job or solve every problem. This may sound like apostasy to some purists, since there is always the potential for abuse by the government. Thomas Jefferson said if it were left to him "to decide whether we should have a government without newspapers, or newspapers without a government, I should not hesitate a moment to prefer the latter." Presented with similar absolutes, it may well be better to have a free market with no government than a government with no free market. (Notably, political freedom cannot long survive without economic freedom, and vice versa.) Fortunately neither Jefferson nor we, today, have had to choose between these extremes.

While abstinence from intervention is the preferable starting assumption, there is still an appropriate role for government. The challenge is to involve the government *only* when it is appropriate.[18] This is difficult given our present condition, in which legislators and regulators see in every problem the opportunity to forge a new government program or to revise and extend an old one. As a result, the challenge is not to find areas suitable for intervention; it is to devise tests that help limit government intervention only to those areas where it does more good than harm. What we need is to ensure that once we take the first step on the slippery slope of government intervention, we don't find ourselves caught up in an avalanche of new, burdensome regulations.

Judging from practice, it makes sense as a basic rule for government to intervene when it can be demonstrated that a health or safety problem affects the public at large (or a significant segment of the public); that the problem is not being addressed by the market; and that the cost of the govenment's intervention is justified by the benefits. If the public health and safety problem is caused by something that is not bought and sold—for example, sewage—then the government has reason to take the initiative to protect the public interest. (It seems likely, in contrast, that startled horses and occasional dust did not justify the government rules that ran the steam car off the road in England.)

Are People Concerned?

Like so many things in life, ozone can be good or bad, depending on where and when it occurs. In the stratosphere (a layer of the atmosphere nine to thirty-one miles above the Earth), ozone filters out harmful rays from the sun, including ultraviolet B. Exposure to ultraviolet B has been linked by scientists to skin cancer and cataracts.[19] Protecting the stratospheric ozone is a major environmental goal.

The bad ozone, commonly called smog, is close to ground level and is the result of a combination of emissions from many sources, including cars, airplanes, trucks, factories, electric power plants, dry cleaners, bakeries, restaurants, paint, gasoline-powered lawn mowers, backyard grills, and more.[20] All combustion of carbon-based fuel can contribute to ozone formation, as does painting your house or cleaning your clothes with solvents.

Every public opinion poll that raises the question confirms that people do not like air pollution. That is no surprise. Liking air pollution would be similar to liking sewage or garbage. Pollsters repeatedly ask Americans if they consider themselves to be environmentalists and repeatedly get positive answers. Again, no surprise. (A poll in 1994 reported only 2 percent of the people as "unsympathetic" toward environmental concerns—and it is hard to imagine what those few people are like.)

Americans want a clean and healthful environment. But they do send some conflicting signals about just how concerned they are. In January 1995, a Gallup poll asked Americans to identify the "most important problem." Only 1 percent listed the environment.[21] In 1994, a Roper Starch Worldwide Inc. survey showed only 12 percent of the people listing "pollution of air and water" as one of their top two or three concerns. Crime was listed by 51 percent, drug abuse by 32 percent, "the way the courts are run" by 29 percent; twelve other categories were ahead of pollution of air and water.[22] Polls also show that people believe that the national pollution problem is worse than pollution in their own area or community. (This reflects a pattern found in asking about most problems. People think crime is worse nationally than in their community. They also think that while Congress as a whole is incompetent, their own member of Congress is above average.) The signals about public attitudes are not steady.

The California Experience. Even in California, the signals are no clearer than the air during an inversion. California is a pioneer in dealing with air pollution. It implemented the first laws requiring exhaust-emission controls on autos in 1965. Los Angeles and the Riverside-San Bernardino areas have the worst ozone problem in America. With many more smog days than the rest of the country, California has a unique problem and has the legal authority to deal with it.

While Southern Californians lead in complaints about their air quality, the seriousness of their concern about health effects is clouded not by what they say but by what they do.[23] In 1950, when Professor Arie J. Haagen-Smit at the California Institute of Technology was investigating the causes of and establishing measurement methods for Los Angeles smog, Californians numbered 10.5 million, with 4.8 million in the smog belt of Los Angeles, Orange, Riverside, and San Bernardino counties. By 1970, when it was well confirmed that autos, factories, and other human-related activities were the major sources of the smog problem, California's population had nearly doubled and stood at 20 million, with 9.6 million in the smog belt.

In 1980, the state population had grown to 23.7 million, with 11.5 million in the four-county smog belt. In 1990, the population reached nearly 30 million, with 14.5 million in the smog belt. In 1994, with a state population of 31.4 million, 15.3 million were breathing the infamous Los Angeles area smog. Air quality may have been one of the reasons some people left the area, but those departures were overwhelmed by the number of people moving in. Despite all the complaints, air quality alerts, and health warnings, people did not leave the area in any significant numbers; instead, they poured in. While the population of the United States grew by 71 percent between 1950 and 1994, the population of the Los Angeles area smog belt grew by 219 percent.

Of course, people did not like the quality of the air during much of the time. On smog alert days, some were uncomfortable, and those with respiratory problems were more than just uncomfortable.[24] Yet the population grew, albeit at a slower rate, since some people left as a result of the so-called peace dividend that came after the collapse of the USSR and, for California, meant the loss of high-paying defense jobs. Contributing to the departure of still others were the increasingly stringent controls on emissions.

A case in point was the effect of emission controls on the furniture-making business. In 1987, the South Coast Air Quality Management District in Southern California set standards requiring severe reductions in the use of lacquer, varnish, and other finishing products. The timing and levels of reductions were too stringent for the industry to meet. Production costs went up and quality and productivity declined. As a result, that industry and the jobs it provided were reduced by about 50 percent through business failures and relocations to other, less regulated areas, including Mexico.

Another example of the tenuousness of the public's commitment to pollution reduction is the rejection of serious vehicle inspection and maintenance programs around the country. Maryland is an example. In 1996, the Sierra Club and other environmental activists sued the Environmental Protection Agency, alleging that Maryland was not meeting the national ambient air quality standards (NAAQS). The EPA reacted by threatening to withhold highways funds and to take other measures against the state unless it implemented a plan to meet the standards. Governor Parris Glendening (D-Md.) announced that he would put an inspection and maintenance plan into effect, requiring the testing of all automobiles on a dynamometer (similar to a treadmill) to ensure that they meet emission standards. In February 1997, hundreds of protestors showed up at the State House with signs saying, "Not in my tailpipe, Parris," and "Say no to dyno."[25] This is typical of resistance around the country to serious testing of private vehicles, with complaints that lines at test centers are too long and the cost of bringing failed vehicles into compliance too high.

These complaints also call into question opinion polls that report the public is willing to pay a significant amount to achieve cleaner air. Judging by the actions of the public, which speak with more authority than do the polls, people want cleaner air but won't leave town to get it, and they become hostile when the regulators require something that directly costs them time and money.

The Clean Air Act and Its Two Kinds of Standards

In 1965, California led the world in enacting a law requiring emission controls on cars. In 1970, the federal government followed suit with the Clean

Air Act, one of the most complex regulatory laws in history. Under this act, there are two sets of standards that affect cars and trucks, one indirectly and one directly. The first set consists of the national ambient air quality standards, which establish the legally permissible concentrations of pollutants in the air around us. They are intended to "protect the public health with an adequate margin of safety." For example, in April 1997, the NAAQS for ozone was 0.12 parts per million (ppm) of air. This level cannot be exceeded in an air district for an average of more than one hour in three days over a three-year period. If ozone concentrations in a designated area exceed these levels, the district is legally out of compliance and is designated as being in nonattainment. To enforce the NAAQS, the EPA requires each state to file a state implementation plan outlining how it will achieve or maintain compliance.

There are six pollutants for which NAAQS are set and for which "criteria documents" are prepared by the EPA, summarizing available scientific knowledge. The six criteria pollutants are: ozone, sulfur dioxide, nitrogen dioxide, carbon monoxide, particulate matter (PM10), and lead.[26] Lead from vehicles is no longer a problem. No change in the NAAQS for carbon monoxide is being considered. Federal regulation of carbon monoxide is indicative of the confusion about air pollution health effects. The Occupational Health and Safety Administration permissible exposure limit is 50 ppm of CO in the workplace. The Consumer Product Safety Commission recommends no more than 15 ppm for indoor areas. The EPA, however, has set a limit of 9 ppm for outdoor air!

The second set of standards limits the emission of specific pollutants by source. For example, ozone results from the photochemical reaction of volatile organic compounds (VOCs) and nitrogen oxides (NO_x).[27] When these pollutants, in the proper mixture, are "baked" over time by sunlight, ozone is formed. To control ozone, the EPA sets emission standards for all human-induced sources of VOCs and NO_x. For the motor vehicle, this means setting standards that limit tailpipe and evaporative emissions of VOCs (primarily hydrocarbons) and NO_x. These requirements, at least in theory, are set at a level that will contribute to the attainment of the NAAQS. When the latter standards become more stringent, they provide the basis for the proposal of more stringent automotive-emission and other standards.

Targeting the Car

When the Clean Air Act of 1970 was enacted, health effects of various pollutants were not well understood. It was not clear what levels of concentrations were dangerous. The lack of this knowledge did not inhibit Congress or the EPA from regulating. Auto-emission standards became the preserve of Congress and were determined through the legislative, and therefore political, process. While these emission standards were supposed to be designed to help meet the NAAQS, the first NAAQS were not established until after the act, with its emission standards for autos, had already been passed. There was no broad constituency for insisting on thoroughly diagnosing the malady before prescribing the cure. Motor vehicles were an obvious target for stringent regulation; they were major emission sources, and the manufacturers were minor participants in public policy formation.[28]

As Congress and the administration worked on proposed emission standards, the auto industry was invited to comment on what was feasible. Its view did not prevail. Whatever regulatory requirements the industry suggested as feasible immediately became unacceptable to the advocacy community. (This pattern prevailed over the years. Efforts by the industry to be "positive" in its response to regulatory proposals were simply taken as a starting point in the next negotiations. As the advocates continuously raised the ante in this clean-air poker game, industry was continuously on the defensive, appearing negative.)

This was the "hold-their-feet-to-the-fire" approach to regulation. Environmental politicians, urged on by the activists, tightened the proposed standards to the point where industry's cries of agony were convincing enough to lead the regulators to let up for a time. The emission reduction numbers legislated by Congress were not based on science; they were arrived at through a painful, inevitably political, process. The result was a set of highly ambitious, ultimately unrealistic requirements.

The auto companies, already reeling from bad press in the safety field, were quickly labeled as polluting demons, as well as unsafe at any speed.[29] These characterizations, plus the continuing demands for new, politically determined engineering requirements, set the stage for very sour relationships between the industry and the Washington, D.C., establishment. The technological requirements of the new standards seriously challenged industry engineers, who often could give no assurance that the standards could be met. Engineering solutions might (and some did) compromise the performance of the vehicle. Worse yet, designs could fail with serious consequences.

Faced with proposed legislation and regulations containing tough standards—almost always set beyond levels and timetables that industry engineers said they might be able to meet—auto company people generally reacted by saying, in effect, "We don't know how to do that," or "We need more time." Either way, political advocates and professional activists, who had no responsibility for inventing, developing, manufacturing, or selling these controls, were quick to call the industry people foot-dragging, unconscionable polluters.

Since industry was a major source of emissions, many environmental regulators viewed industry representatives and executives much as police officers view criminal lawbreakers. As polluters, they were often treated with disdain, as ignorant, arrogant malefactors. Of course, industry executives were not blameless. Accustomed to running their businesses without the "help" of government, they were resistant to any interference from "bureaucrats," whom they treated with their own form of disdain for the latter's lack of business experience and limited engineering background. Regrettably, industry officials often failed to respect the duty of the government to enforce the laws, while government officials tended not to recognize technological limitations and to ignore the need of industry to meet consumer demands. The result was much "hate and discontent" on both sides—and less real progress than might otherwise have been achieved.

More important was the lack, in the regulatory process, of an effective voice for the consumer. While the industry was directly affected by regulation, it was the consumer who would pay the costs and live with any deterioration in utility or performance of the vehicle. Consumers are sympathetic to the need to clean up the environment, but consumers do not have a seat at the bargaining table, where decisions are made about costs and benefits. They have no way of knowing whether they are getting a bargain in resulting regulation. The consumer's interest is especially at risk when company officials become too accepting of regulation, whether it is good for the consumer or not. This can happen when bureaucracies grow within companies for the purpose of managing regulations and become resistant to any change. It can also happen when companies support regulation to satisfy and maintain good relations with the regulators, even though the consumer is getting a bad deal. And it can happen when companies have a stake in a technology that is used only to meet a regulatory requirement that may not be in the consumer's interest.

Presumably the government would be the surrogate for the consumer. That is the way it is supposed to work. Unfortunately, government officials, elected or regulatory, often have their own agenda. They may become cheerleaders for a proposal and "forget" to give the citizenry all the information available if it is contrary to their point of view. These are some of the many traps for the parties to the regulatory process.

The Optimism Trap. While many industry people are perceived as too negative, there are some who might be too positive. Auto companies have had difficulty in managing two different kinds of approaches needed within a company to address regulatory issues. Inside the company, it is essential to have "gung-ho" engineers and managers who can cheer the troops on, giving them confidence that they can do what needs to be done. This motivational leadership is helpful, even essential, inside the company. Often, however, the reach of the enthusiasts exceeds their grasp. Some projects simply do not work out, and the engineers must go on to the next challenge with equal enthusiasm.

Outside the organization, this "can do" attitude is often misunderstood or even exploited. It stimulates some politicians and regulators, who find it advantageous to be "aggressive" with corporations, to advocate unrealistic or premature regulations. They seize on optimistic comments from the corporate enthusiasts to justify mandating technology prematurely, or they show their "toughness" by demanding even more.[30]

Some foreign manufacturers often help to confuse the issues by predicting a new technological breakthrough in emission control. That is no sin, and everybody does it; but the announcements by foreign car makers were often hailed by the media as evidence of their superiority over U.S. manufacturers. Ultimately, it was U.S. technology, the catalytic converter, that proved to be most effective and efficient in controlling exhaust emissions. It was adopted by all car makers.

"The Industry Whines but Always Meets the Standard." Critics are still ridiculing auto industry engineers. In a discussion of proposed new standards on February 10, 1997, EPA chief Carol Browner said that auto engineers reacted to early standards by saying, "No, no. We could never do that." But, she said, they then developed the catalytic converter and met the standard. This reflects the principal argument used by proponents of more stringent auto standards to justify their confidence that automotive engineers can meet just about any standard the advocates want to suggest. The common myth perpetuated by Browner and others, and by the media in general, is that when standards are set, the industry whines a lot but then, when forced, goes ahead, does the job, and meets the standard. This is the major "technology" argument of the activists and politicians. Any time a question is raised about the technological feasibility of a standard, the advocates invoke this myth.[31] Vice President Gore used it again when he and Browner announced new air quality standards on July 16, 1997. He asked, "Can we do it?" and answered, "You bet we can. We've done it before."

Browner and other critics conveniently ignore the fact that in 1977, nearly 5.4 million vehicles were recalled for failure to meet federal emission standards. That is not exactly "meeting the standards." For each year during the 1980s, between 1 million and nearly 5 million vehicles were recalled. The total recalled since emission standards were first put in place is more than 50 million vehicles.[32] Recall is the EPA's primary enforcement tool. No company wants a recall that means its engineers must dedicate time and resources to improve systems often built to meet timetables and standards required by laws and regulations that do not permit adequate field testing. Recalls also mean millions of owners driving to their dealerships to get corrective work done. This costs the owners time on the road (resulting in more emissions and exposure to accidents), and it costs the manufacturers large sums and some damage to their reputations, while often accomplishing little, if any, net improvement in air quality.

A recall is generally viewed by the media, the government, and the public as a manufacturer's failure to do the job correctly. It would often be equally correct to interpret a recall as a demonstration that the standard is premature in stringency or deadline—the government's failure. The engineers, who had said they weren't sure how to meet the standards or had asked for more time, could have pointed at the recalls and said: "I told you so." But they could take no comfort in that.

The phenomenon of millions of recalls of vehicles failing the emission tests demonstrates that the industry does not always meet the standard when forced to do so. Another conclusive demonstration is the fact that, in past years, the EPA and Congress have found it necessary to relax the air quality and emission requirements on several notable occasions.

When the Government Backed Off

In 1976, it became clear that the industry had not yet been able to develop the technology necessary to meet the emission standards set for 1978 model vehicles. There was promising work underway on a device, the catalytic converter, that would "catch" the emissions—hydrocarbons, nitrogen oxides, and carbon monoxide—in the exhaust from the engine and "reduce" most of them to water vapor and carbon dioxide. But there were bugs to work out, and durability was a question mark. After delving deeply into the auto industry's capabilities, the EPA became convinced that the standards could not be met and postponed the deadlines, first in 1973 and then in 1974. It had no authority to postpone further. As a result, the industry felt it had no choice but to ask Congress for a change in the Clean Air Act.

The process of getting any environmental legislation passed is a bruising, bloody, massive undertaking. The act, which covers stationary as well as mobile sources, is so comprehensive and the regulations so pervasive that virtually all industries—in fact, every economic activity, as well as a multitude of political and advocacy groups—are vitally interested in how the legislation is written. Any attempt to change it brings out legions of lawyers and lobbyists and presents lawmakers with painful choices. Professional activists immediately brand as "antienvironment" any legislator willing to change standards in any way that appears favorable to industry. He or she becomes eligible for the "dirty dozen" list and is likely to become a target in the next election.[33]

In 1976, Jerry Ford was in the White House. The Congress was Democratic and poised to add more environmental regulation, not less. Senator Ed Muskie, sponsor of the first Clean Air Act, was the Senate leader on environmental issues, had presidential ambitions, and was hostile to the industry's request.

In the summer of 1976, Senator Muskie developed a 400-page bill that generally tightened restrictions on pollutants from factories, utilities, and other sources, as well as motor vehicles. Lobbying for the bill were Clarence Ditlow of Ralph Nader's Public Interest Research Group (PIRG), Rafe Pomerance of Friends of the Earth, Barbara Reid Alexander of the Sierra Club, and many other paid and unpaid activists. They worked under the umbrella of the National Clean Air Coalition, formed specifically to organize and help finance the fight for passage of the Muskie bill.

The broad bill, approved in the subcommittee that Senator Muskie chaired, included a slight relaxation of the auto standards and deadlines. The sponsors hoped to attract the industry's support or at least to neutralize its opposition. The marginal relief was too slight to give the engineers confidence they could meet the standards. In the full committee, over Senator Muskie's objection, the bill was amended to extend the auto standards deadlines to 1981. This was an improvement for the industry but it still did not meet their needs, especially since it did not address the car companies' inability to meet the proposed nitrogen oxides requirement. The environmentalists, however, were outraged at the Senate action giving companies some leeway. Alexander, working under Sierra Club auspices, held Muskie responsible because he had "lost control of his committee." She told the press, "For the Senator known as 'Mr. Clean' in the nation, Senator Muskie has performed miserably."[34]

In the House of Representatives, Henry Waxman, the Democratic congressman from the Hollywood-Beverly Hills district in California, was adamantly opposed to relief for the auto industry.[35] (California's politicians have always been anxious to have national standards set at levels to meet the unique needs of the Los Angeles, San Bernardino, Riverside area. In that way, the costs of regulation would be the same nationwide, avoiding a price differential between California cars and cars sold in the other forty-nine states.) Representative John D. Dingell (D-Mich.), author of earlier environmental protection laws, was concerned about the effects on jobs of a possible postponement of 1978 models and led the fight for relaxation of the standards. Dingell had good reason to understand the implications of legislation affecting the auto industry. His district included the headquarters of Ford Motor Company, and thousands of his constituents work for General Motors, Chrysler, and Ford. His amendment to provide relief succeeded on the floor of the House. When the bill was considered in conference between the House and the Senate, however, Senator Muskie prevailed. The auto industry was then faced with the choice of endorsing the bill with its slight relaxation or opposing it and taking a chance that Congress would give the needed relief the next year. The industry felt it had no real choice.

It did not have the technology to meet the nitrogen oxide standard, and it announced its opposition to the Muskie bill.

An angry Senator Muskie denounced "Detroit's attitude" and warned, "If they think they can come back . . . next year and get a quick fix . . . to make them legal, they better take a lot of long careful thoughts about it." The president of General Motors, Elliott "Pete" Estes, somewhat carried away with the situation, said in an interview, "They can close the plants. They can get someone in jail—maybe me. But we're going to make [1978] cars to 1977 standards."

A Reality Check. As it turned out, Senator Muskie did not take into consideration two important factors. First, the industry was not "crying wolf." The fact that the technology was not yet available was widely recognized by people outside the industry, including the National Academy of Sciences, which was monitoring the issue. It would have been irresponsible for the industry to promise otherwise and then be unable to get certification from the EPA for the production of the 1978 models. Congress was swimming in new waters, with some senior members under the misapprehension that if they passed a law requiring a technological achievement by a certain date, it would be done. They assumed that if industry failed to do it, it could only be a matter of recalcitrance and arrogance. (Many members of Congress—which has only a handful of people with scientific or industrial backgrounds—still tend to think the world works this way. There are notable exceptions.)

The second fact forgotten by supporters of the Muskie bill was that jobs were truly at stake. The United Auto Workers (UAW), after a careful review of the situation, concluded that its members would suffer if adequate relief were not approved. UAW president Leonard Woodcock, with strong Democratic credentials and not known for giving political support to the industry, became actively engaged in fighting the bill.[36] The auto dealers association, concerned that 1978 models would be delayed, also joined the fight against the Muskie bill.[37]

On October 1, 1976, the Muskie bill died on the floor of the Senate on a procedural vote. Senator Muskie said that, as a result, the automakers would be required to meet stricter rules for 1978 models than he had proposed.[38] This came just five weeks before the election of a new Congress and a new president, Jimmy Carter.

When the new Congress, still under Democratic control, convened in 1977, the effort was begun to pass various amendments to the Clean Air Act, including relief for the auto industry that was tooled to begin producing the 1978 models in August 1977. If relief could not be achieved by then, the new models could not be certified by the EPA, and the plants would be shut down. On July 29, 1977, John J. Ricardo, chairman of Chrysler

Corporation, told the press, "It is inconceivable to me that we won't have a bill from Congress to ensure an orderly production process."[39]

The prospect of closing down the biggest industry in America got the attention of the new Carter administration. It made contingency plans to keep the plants open by allowing production, but reportedly would have assessed a penalty for each car produced. Fortunately, with the leadership of Representative Dingell, Congress acted in time on legislation relaxing the requirements. President Carter signed the bill, the auto-emission standards were changed, and the new cars rolled off the assembly line.

The changes in the law were substantial. Before the 1977 amendments, the Clean Air Act would have required emissions of hydrocarbons (organic compounds) and carbon monoxide to be reduced to 3.4 and 0.41 grams per mile (gpm) respectively by 1975. Nitrogen oxides were to be cut by 95 percent, to 0.4 gpm by 1976. As noted earlier, when the industry demonstrated that the technology was not available to meet these requirements, the EPA, as permitted by the act, had delayed implementation until 1978. In its 1977 amendments, Congress changed the nitrogen oxide standard to 2.0 gpm through 1980 and 1.0 gpm for 1981 and thereafter. The 0.4 gpm requirement was designated as a "research goal."

The professional activists, of course, complained long and loudly about a sellout and a gutting of environmental protection. An interest in keeping the economy together and themselves in office, however, gave the politicians courage enough to do what had to be done. This legislative brinkmanship helped neither the public interest nor the reputations of all concerned. The auto companies, already favorite targets, once again were characterized as polluters without consciences or, at best, as incompetent. The relationship between these companies and the politicians and activists who put them in this corner deteriorated even further. The public, confused by the complexities of the issues, saw the fight as additional evidence that the nation was on the wrong track in solving its problems. This event contributed to what Meg Greenfield of the *Washington Post* has since described as "a pervasive credibility problem [which] dogs all sides in the environmental debate."[40]

A Little More History

A little more history is useful. In January 1979 the country was in another fight, this time over the national ambient air quality standard for ozone, which had been set in 1971 by EPA at .08 parts per million by volume of air. Of the 105 major urban areas in the United States, only Honolulu and Spokane could meet the standard. States and cities across the country were concerned about the expected costs of compliance. The industrial community petitioned the EPA for a change to .16 ppm or higher. Environmentalists, of course, argued for a tightening of the existing requirement. An auto industry spokesperson estimated that a .10 ppm standard would cost the national economy up to $19 billion in one year. The EPA estimated the cost at $6.9–$9.5 billion. In the Carter White House, the Regulatory Analysis Review Group, which came under the direction of economist Charles Schultze, estimated that the costs of a .10 ppm standard could be up to $24.3 billion a year—assuming that the selected technology would work. Even though the law required the consideration of health effects only—not costs—concerns about the economy were overwhelming. The rate of inflation, driven in part by skyrocketing oil prices, was at the highest it had been in the post-World War II period. White House economic advisers Alfred Kahn and Charles Schultze were persuasive and, after great debate and controversy, the EPA relaxed the NAAQS from .08 ppm to .12 ppm (the level it is in 1997).[41]

The lesson here, and the point of this history, is that the auto engineers are not always able to toe the line drawn by the political "engineers," and there are times when the government must back off. In any event, it is not sensible to regulate solely on the basis of what is possible. Regulations should reflect a common-sense approach to what needs to be done—not what can be done, needed or not. Despite this history, the Clinton-Gore administration, pressed by EPA administrator Browner, is preparing for a return to the .08 ppm standard.

Finally, there is a vast difference in the way government regulators, as opposed to auto company managers, view what can be done in emission control and other regulatory areas. Zero-emission (electric-powered) cars are presently on the road. The problem is to produce vehicles with these attributes that will still meet the needs of the consumer—at a price he or she can afford to pay. It does no good to force the production of cars that consumers will not or cannot buy. Regulation that adds cost, limits utility, and degrades performance puts the car makers in conflict with their customers. The critical role of the auto engineer today is to attempt to reconcile what the government demands with what the consumer will buy. This is accorded little importance or value by professional advocates and by too many regulators who are able to escape public scrutiny for their role in the conflict, and whatever goes wrong becomes the manufacturers' fault.

· 12 ·

HOW FAR SHOULD REGULATION GO?

Common sense leads to the conclusion that breathing polluted air does not enhance human health. The automobile industry, largely through the work of the General Motors Research Laboratories, concluded in the 1960s that auto emissions were a major source of precursors to ozone and should be reduced. (Health-effect studies indicated that high levels of ozone were at least undesirable. In the 1970s, industry scientists believed that a level of .16 parts per million [ppm] of ozone would protect public health with an adequate margin of safety.) This was the basis for the industry's early support for vehicle pollution–control devices, and because customers were not demanding such controls on the cars they bought, the industry also supported government actions to require such controls.

Once it is agreed that pollution has adverse health effects, the challenge is to determine what level of control is necessary to meet public health needs. Once the government has the authority to regulate emissions, how does society decide what level is acceptable, and how does it protect itself from zealous regulators who would go beyond that level?

Numbers and Common Sense

It is entirely appropriate to approach this tough problem by attempting to add up and compare the dollar value people attribute to the benefits they might achieve by lowering emissions with all the costs that might result in the attempt to do so. Analysts will acknowledge, however, that it is virtually impossible to get a consensus on the value of a view of the mountains or the absence of a sneeze or cough. It is also hard and ethically worrisome to attempt to calculate the worth of an extra few days or weeks of life for an elderly, terminally ill person (for whom appropriate care unhesitatingly should be provided and whose dignity should be honored). It is also diffi-

153

cult to establish how much it costs to invent, improve, manufacture, and maintain a new control technology, especially as it evolves with time. Even more difficult is the attempt to identify and evaluate other benefits that may have been gained from the alternative uses of these resources. These lost opportunities may be the most costly effect of poor regulation.

One of the most useful analyses of the costs and benefits was done by Robert W. Hahn, who wrote, "My analysis of federal regulations between 1990 and 1995 reveals that only 23 of the 54 regulations examined would pass a cost-benefit test based on the government's numbers." In his book on the subject,[1] Hahn estimates that by not implementing regulations failing this cost-benefit test, more than $100 billion could be saved. (The study examined regulations from many agencies, not just the Environmental Protection Agency.) This analysis is especially effective. Using the government's own numbers, Hahn finesses the usual argument over whose numbers are the "right" ones to use. (Had more neutral numbers been used, it is very likely more regulations would have failed the test.)

Without at all detracting from the good work being done in calculating costs and benefits, it is well to contemplate other approaches that consider the thoughts about statistical analysis expressed by Sir Josiah Stamp, of the Inland Revenue Department of England at the turn of the century: "The Government are very keen on amassing statistics. They collect them, add them, raise them to the nth power, take the cube root and prepare wonderful diagrams. But you must never forget that every one of these figures comes in the first instance from the village watchman, who just puts down what he damn pleases." The validity of all analysis depends on the reliability of the data, but it also depends on the analyst. Another skeptic said, "If you torture numbers long enough, they will confess to anything."[2]

Is Environmental Protection More Important than Everything Else?
To begin to decide how far we should go with regulation, and to do so without leaning on statistics, we should ask: Is there anything more important than more environmental protection? If there is not, we should keep on the track of ever-more stringent air quality and emission standards. We should not concern ourselves about the cost; all harmful substances should simply be banned. Also, we should not only attempt to stop the emission of any pollutant that might cause discomfort or aggravate a preexisting condition; we should stop any activity that might disturb the world in its natural state.

But environmental protection, of course, is not more important than everything else. Life is not that simple. Preventing murder is also important. We know, for example, that around 400 people a year will be murdered in the nation's capital city, but we do not attempt to overwhelm the city with more police or agree to deny civil rights to keep the potential perpetrators off the streets. We know that just under 2 million people each year will suffer injuries by falling on stairs, landings, or floors but we do not drop everything else to deal with this problem. We have too many drunk drivers, too many unsafe and poorly run schools, and too many children without loving parents. All these and many more needs command at least some of our attention and resources. We sort out our governmental priorities by trying to provide all "special interests" the opportunity to promote their causes and by giving our elected representatives the authority, within limits, to act, along with the flexibility to change priorities as events require. If our representatives don't do the right thing, we have the option of throwing the rascals out.

Traditionally, we have not attempted to enact federal laws that bind all parties to a priority that takes precedence over all others. The Clean Air Act, unfortunately, does just that. As the law of the land, in effect it establishes the regulation of air pollution as the most important priority for America. Under the terms of the act—as interpreted by the courts—if there is *any* adverse health effect attributable to air pollution, there is no limit on what should be spent to eliminate that threat. Within this framework, the EPA has determined that more strict control of ozone and particulate matter should have this kind of priority.

Cost Cannot Be Considered! The officials who determine the requirements of air quality standards are not obliged to take into account other needs. They need not be concerned with whether the money spent to eliminate the last bit of nitrogen oxides or volatile organic compounds from auto exhaust, or to cut back on the permissible levels of particles, could be spent more wisely—perhaps on water purification, medical research, traffic safety, health care, crime prevention, investment in job-creating businesses, or a hundred other things. This is not a trivial matter. As we have seen, billions of dollars are involved. These are billions that cannot be used for other purposes.

Incredibly, Congress, at least as interpreted by the courts, has forbidden regulators to take cost (or technological feasibility) into consideration in setting air quality standards. Section 109(b)(1) of the Clean Air Act requires the EPA administrator to set air-quality standards, "the attainment and maintenance of which in the judgment of the Administrator, . . . allowing an adequate margin of safety, are requisite to protect public health." The courts, as a result of a lawsuit brought by the National Resources Defense Council, interpreted this to mean that the only consideration allowed is the effect of pollution on health. The U.S. Court of Appeals for the District of Columbia made this clear, saying: "Under section 109 . . . the Administrator *may not consider* cost and technological feasibility." The emphasis is in the original. The court went on to say:

Where Congress intended [the EPA] to be concerned about economic and technological feasibility, it expressly so provided . . . . The absence of any provision requiring consideration of these factors [when setting NAAQS] was no accident; it was the result of a deliberate decision by Congress to subordinate such concerns to the achievement of health goals.[3]

Since the Clean Air Act specifies that all suits challenging the EPA's national ambient air quality standards must be filed in this D.C. circuit court, and since the U.S. Supreme Court generally refuses to review complex administrative law cases, the only relief from this unrealistic requirement will have to come from Congress. No help can be expected from the EPA. Testifying before Congress, Mary D. Nichols of the EPA said, "Under the law, we are not to take costs into consideration when setting these standards." She added, "We believe this approach remains appropriate."[4] With the Clinton-Gore administration taking this position, it is time for Congress to answer the question: "Is the environment more important than everything else?"

Unfortunately, the number of Americans who understand that there is a requirement in the Clean Air Act to ignore cost and technological feasibility in setting air quality standards is somewhere very near zero. If asked, it is doubtful that any would say that zero tolerance of ozone or particles has a higher priority than all other national goals or programs. In fact, when Princeton Research polled Americans in 1995, only 1 percent said that the environment (all of it) is the country's most pressing problem.

The national ambient air quality standards set by the EPA in the 1970s have already resulted in the expenditure of billions of dollars to clean up ozone and particulate matter. One lawsuit by professional activists resulted in a decision confirming that a nonsensical law says that cost and technology do not count and shall not be considered. Now another lawsuit brought by professional activists has required the EPA to review its air quality standards. The question is whether the EPA feels obliged to attempt to eliminate *any* effect of air pollution, no matter how slight, on the incidence of eye irritation, asthma attacks, or any other health problem.

If a substance produces adverse health effects, should we rush to ban it entirely? If smog causes any adverse effect at all, will the EPA ultimately require zero emissions of the pollutants that make up smog?[5] That is certainly the direction in which regulators and professional activists are taking the country, at least insofar as motor vehicle emissions are concerned. But does it make sense?

The sixteenth-century Swiss physician Paracelsus offered some excellent guidance on this point: "In all substances there is a poison, and there is nothing without a poison. It depends only upon the dose whether a poison is poison or not."[6] Every day we make compromises about the health effects of what we eat, drink, and do. We compromise as individuals and as governments. One thing we do several times a day serves to demonstrate the point. We have a drink of water. In almost every instance, that water contains something that can cause adverse health effects, depending on the dose. Most of us know that and drink anyway. Government agencies know it and let it happen and even contribute to it. As Paracelsus said, it's the dose that counts.

Government-Approved "Pollution"

Chlorine is classified as having carcinogenic effects. Activist groups have even called for its ban. Nevertheless, citizens and local governments throughout America pour heavy doses of chlorine not only into our swimming pools and hot tubs but also into our drinking water, to make it safer to drink than it would be without this dose of "poison." Despite chlorine's potential adverse health effects, society finds it acceptable to drink some every day. This happens simply because there is no sensible alternative. A ban would take away the means by which 98 percent of America's drinking water is disinfected. As a result, not only is there not a ban; there is a federal standard requiring a minimum level of chlorine, if it is used as a disinfectant.

Every day, the Food and Drug Administration wrestles with decisions about approving drugs that have unhealthy side effects. Every day hundreds of thousands of people take aspirin, which, taken to excess, can cause severe stomach problems and even death. A dab of iodine can disinfect a cut, but drinking a little bottle of it can result in death. Similarly, too much salt can kill.

In these instances, there are some benefits to be derived from the use of a potentially harmful substance. But that is not a necessary criterion for government approval of certain levels of pollutants. For example, despite treatment with chlorine, filtration, or other means, most water we drink is "contaminated," and the presence of certain amounts of the contaminants is condoned by the EPA. For example, the standard for *Giardia lamblia* (from human and animal waste) requires a treatment technique that removes all but 0.01 percent (100 parts per million) of the contaminant. (The EPA reports that more than 2,700 water systems affecting nearly 12 million people are violating this standard.) The maximum contaminant level (MCL) for asbestos permits the presence of 7 million fibers per liter in our water. The MCL for arsenic permits 0.05 milligrams per liter of water. In these cases, the EPA determined that some pollution or contamination is acceptable, even when there are no benefits to be derived from its presence. While zero tolerance might be preferable, it is a matter of common sense that this goal is not always feasible.[7]

Common sense finally prevailed in eliminating what the EPA has called the Delaney paradox. For years, the Federal Food, Drug, and Cosmetic Act (FFDCA) prohibited setting an acceptable tolerance level for any pesticide that caused cancer in laboratory animals. This zero-tolerance rule had the paradoxical effect of encouraging the use of alternative pesticides that posed higher but noncarcinogenic risks for food safety. In 1996, the FFDCA was amended to eliminate the zero-tolerance rule.

Unpleasant as it may seem in the abstract, this practice of accepting certain levels of "poison" enables society to enjoy many benefits. We have affordable water that is reasonably safe to drink. We also have a plentiful and reasonably affordable food supply that is generally safe. We have miracle pharmaceuticals that, taken as directed, heal with very rare side effects. We also have billions of dollars to use for other purposes that might have been depleted to ensure the absolute purity of all water and food.

Comparative Regulation: The Radon Case. When considering what should be done about ozone and PM, it is instructive to compare the EPA's attitude about those pollutants with its approach to radon gas. According to the EPA, "There is no doubt that radon gas is a known human lung carcinogen."[8] The EPA estimates that radon contributes to between 7,000 and 30,000 lung cancer deaths each year.[9] It is estimated that one out of every fifteen homes in the United States has radon levels higher than the level at which the EPA recommends corrective action. This is a gas that you cannot see, smell, or taste, and according to the government, its effects do not simply make a preexisting condition worse or bring discomfort while exercising. Radon, says the EPA, is a killer.

In the face of this health threat, what regulatory actions are being taken by the government? What standards must be met? What concentrations are permissible? The answer is, there are no regulatory actions, no standards, no ambient air concentration caps. In 1996, President Clinton established a National Radon Action Week and signed a letter addressed to "everyone participating." He wrote about making "great strides in educating the public" and "encouraging families across America to test for radon in their homes." He added that "we must do all we can to combat this serious health threat." The president concluded with this sole call to action: "I urge you to test your homes and schools today. Working together, we can ensure a safer, healthier world for future generations."

This action plan is hardly comparable to the EPA proposals for ozone and particulate matter. Either the EPA suspects that it is wrong about the health risks of radon, or it is not politically attractive to attempt to deal with the radon problem. Since radon cannot be regulated by requirements placed on cars or factories, it is handled through "awareness" letters and voluntary action.

Zero Tolerance for Ozone and Particulate Matter

While government regulators tolerate "poisons" in water and contaminants in food and take a laid-back approach to radon, common sense is abandoned when it comes to pollution in the air. While the government supported the elimination of the Delaney zero-tolerance rule for pesticides, the EPA maintains that there is no "maximum tolerated dose" of ozone and particulate matter. This has been made official by the EPA in proposing its 1997 national ambient air quality standards for ozone and particulate matter. In this process, the EPA has concluded that "there is no discernible threshold below which no adverse health effects occur."[10] In other words, any dose of ozone or PM, no matter how small, is considered to have adverse health effects. If this view holds, then, under current policies, there is no natural stopping point in setting more stringent standards. In the best of all possible worlds, where there would be no limits on money or talent, this approach might be wonderful. If we had the funds and other resources needed to attack all our problems with equal vigor, it would be understandable to attempt to eliminate all pollution. Unfortunately, this is not the kind of world we live in.

Nonetheless, the law of the land sets health effects as the sole consideration in devising a control program. It appears that, ultimately, the goal of the EPA must be a zero concentration of ozone or particulate matter in the atmosphere. This is especially so since the standards must protect the public health with "an adequate margin of safety." The EPA believes this means that the ambient air quality standard must protect 99 percent of the sensitive population from any health effects, including short-term discomfort. This is a laudable sentiment, but it is hardly a sound judgment on which to set priorities and to budget scarce resources.

· 13 ·

THE EPA'S 1997
AIR QUALITY
STANDARDS

The Clean Air Act requires the Environmental Protection Agency to reevaluate its national ambient air quality standards (NAAQS) every five years and either confirm the existing standards or propose changes.

In early 1994, the American Lung Association (ALA) sued the EPA to compel the agency to complete its review of the NAAQS for particulate matter (PM). The ALA prevailed, and subsequently the courts ordered the EPA to announce its decision by June 1997. For reasons not entirely explained, the EPA also decided to review the ozone NAAQS as well, even though there was no requirement to do so.[1] Both proposals stirred deep concern among industries, labor unions, farm groups, and small businesses.

A New Standard for Particulate Matter

The current national ambient air quality standard for particulate matter (PM) covers particles measuring 10 microns or fewer in diameter. The standard, commonly called PM10, sets a limit of 150 micrograms of these particles per cubic meter of air for a twenty-four–hour average, and 50 micrograms per cubic meter of air for an annual average.

When the EPA complied with the court order to review the PM10 standard, it could have decided to extend the existing standard. Despite controversy about the state of scientific knowledge about health effects, the EPA decided to propose an annual PM2.5 standard set at 15 micrograms per cubic meter ($\mu g/m^3$), with a twenty-four–hour limit at 50 $\mu g/m^3$, while leaving in place the PM10 standard. The purpose of the added requirement was to concentrate more effort on the control of very fine airborne particles. (The diameter of PM2.5 is approximately 1/30th the thickness of a human hair.) The concern is that these particles can become deposited deeply in the lungs, with deleterious effect. (A supplementary argument for the general advisability of keeping one's mouth shut is the fact that nasal breathing can screen out particles down to PM1, while combined nasal and mouth breathing results in screening of particles down to PM10.)

In brief, the PM10 standard placed limits on both coarse and fine particles. Coarse particles include windblown dust, dust from construction sites and demolitions, and other particles that are the result of mechanical processes, such as crushing or grinding. They also include fly ash from the combustion of coal and oil, metal oxides of crustal elements, pollen, mold spores, and plant and animal fragments. Fine particles are generally formed through chemical processes and by industrial, residential, and vehicular combustion of fuel. As Mary Nichols of the EPA testified before Congress, "The implementation of these new standards is likely to focus on sources like cars, trucks, buses, power plants, and cleaner fuels."[2]

OAQPS and CASAC. The EPA's reevaluation of the PM10 NAAQS (and also of the ozone NAAQS) began with the preparation by EPA staff of a criteria document that attempts to evaluate all existing science relevant to the issues. This material was then reviewed for policy implications by the EPA's Office of Air Quality Planning and Standards (OAQPS), which prepared a document know as the OAQPS Staff Paper. Next came a review of the issue by EPA's Clean Air Scientific Advisory Committee (CASAC).

When the courts set the June 1997 date for a decision by the EPA, the CASAC found that the deadline "did not allow adequate time to analyze, integrate, interpret, and debate the available data on this very complex issue."[3] In other words, the EPA and the committee could not do the job properly under the court's time constraints. As they approached their task, several members of the CASAC panel of experts were concerned with the "unanswered questions and uncertainties associated with establishing causality of the association between PM2.5 and mortality."

The result of the CASAC review was a "diversity of opinion" among committee members about the course of action the EPA should take. Some members supported a specific PM2.5 standard. Several endorsed the concept of a standard but did not support a specific level or range. Some supported no standard. The panel was unanimous, however, in urging that the agency "immediately implement a targeted research program to address these unanswered questions and uncertainties."

One important complication relates to the fact that the particulate matter NAAQS is the only one not chemically specific. That is, the standard is based not on the chemical properties of the particle but on its size. The toxicity of individual particles may vary widely, and although the biological response to particles may also vary with the size of the particle, it is the toxicity about which there is the most concern. The fact that particulate matter is regulated solely by the size of the particle and not by its health effects is a major weakness of the standard. PM10 and PM2.5 are not specific chemical entities. They differ in their makeup and may be composed of several major constituents and hundreds of trace constituents. As a result, it seems logical to control the specific chemical constituents, which may be directly related to health effects, rather than to attempt to control all particles, whether they are associated with mortality or not.

In support of the new air quality standard, the EPA says it will save lives. More specifically, Browner says that it will prevent 15,000 "premature deaths annually." (On April 2, 1997, the EPA acknowledged that it had a "data glitch" and lowered by one-fourth its earlier estimate that 20,000 deaths would be prevented each year.)[4] This estimate is highly questionable.

What Is a Premature Death?

Preventing a premature death is not necessarily the same as saving a life. Determining just how premature a death may be is elusive, especially if it is the death of the terminally ill, aged, and others in delicate health. Definitions are necessary to pursue the issue and to make serious judgments about the benefits of measures aimed at preventing premature deaths. When asked for a definition, the EPA headquarters presented the following:

> We checked with the EPA Office of Air Quality Planning and Standards for your request about the EPA definition of "premature death" as used in literature about ozone or particulate matter. According to Dr. David McKee and others in his office with whom we checked, there is no official EPA definition of the term "premature death." It is considered to be "self-defining" and no particular time periods have been standardized as indicating a premature death time period.[5]

Voltaire was wise when he said, "If you wish to converse with me, define your terms." He would not have had a satisfactory conversation with the EPA on this issue. Justification for the extremely stringent ambient air standards for particulate matter and ozone—and the emission standards that follow—is based on preventing premature deaths. There is good reason why the EPA does not provide a definition. No method exists to identify 15,000 individuals who have died as a result of ozone or particulate matter. This number is the result of epidemiology studies and is generated by statistical analysis. Roughly speaking, mortality rates in different locations are compared with PM concentrations and, if there are higher mortality rates in those locations with higher concentrations, they are attributed to PM.

Adjustments in these studies are made for some, but by no means all, confounding variables. For example, a key study used by the EPA in setting its PM standard, entitled "Particulate Air Pollution as a Predictor of Mortality in a Prospective Study of U. S. Adults," was prepared by the econo-mist C. Arden Pope III and others.[6] The study focused only on fine particles and found a high correlation between these and mortality. Unfortunately, the limited nature of the study prevented analysts from knowing whether any other factors might have been responsible. It has been suggested that since high levels of pollution usually occur during periods of very hot weather, the death of a vulnerable person may be more closely linked to heat stress and humidity than to pollution.[7] It is no surprise that a major criticism of the EPA's new particulate standard is that it is based on very limited research—essentially epidemiology studies that have themselves come under critical scrutiny.

Although useful, epidemiology studies are not adequate.[8] The OAQPS Staff Paper pointed up a major problem, saying,

> It is important to emphasize that, at present, available toxicologi-cal and clinical information yields no demonstrated biological mechanism(s) that can explain the associations between ambient PM exposure and mortality and morbidity reported in commu-nity epidemiologic studies. Thus, any discussion of possible mechanisms linking ambient PM exposures to mortality and morbidity effects is necessarily limited to hypotheses derived from animal or human studies conducted at exposure levels of PM con-stituents far higher than found in ambient air.[9]

The Staff Paper for PM is also candid in saying,

> The relationship between precursor emission reductions and am-bient PM2.5 is nonlinear in many aspects: thus, it is difficult to project the impact on PM2.5 arising from expected changes in PM precursor emissions [sulfur dioxide (SO_2) and nitrogen ox-ides (NO_x) and certain other organic compounds] without air qual-ity simulation models that incorporate treatment of complex chemical transformation processes. In general terms, one would expect that emission reductions of SO_2 should lead to reductions in sulfate aerosol, but reductions will vary by season, depending on both emission fluctuations and changes in prevailing meteo-rology and photochemistry.[10]

In other words, benefits from reducing precursors such as sulfur dioxide are not predictable.

In any event, under the acid-rain rules, the EPA already regulates emis-sions of sulfur dioxide, which are transformed in the atmosphere into small acid sulfate particles that in turn are major components of fine particles—PM2.5. So we have a major source of PM2.5 already being regulated by the same EPA that has proposed to get at this same set of emissions by regulating *all* PM2.5, whether all such particles are toxic or not. Furthermore, no "biological mechanism" has been discovered that relates ambient PM exposure to mortality or morbidity, and there is no linear relationship between reduction in the precursors of the PM2.5 and reductions in PM2.5.[11]

This gap in our knowledge leaves major questions unanswered. The Staff Paper addresses them as follows:

> While a variety of responses to constituents of ambient PM have been hypothesized to contribute to the reported health effects, there is no currently accepted mechanism(s) as to how relatively low concentrations of ambient PM may cause the health effects that have been reported in the epidemiologic literature. Therefore, there is an urgent need to expand ongoing research on the mechanisms by which PM, alone and in combination with other air pollutants, may cause adverse health effects.[12]

The sensible path for the EPA to have followed in these circumstances would have been to take the advice of its own Staff Paper and the CASAC and get on with the research program needed to address the uncertainties and unanswered questions. The EPA should not go forward with a costly new PM regulatory program without getting the data from such a program. It could and should satisfy the court order by reaffirming the current PM10 standard, with some adjustments recommended by CASAC. Given the importance of the issues and indications of health effects of certain small particles, research should go forward promptly, but new standards should not be implemented on the basis of the data now available. If the EPA does not of its own initiative follow this path—and all indications are that it will not— then Congress should pass the necessary laws to ensure that it does so.[13]

Reaching for a New Ozone NAAQS

Not content to deal only with the court-ordered action on PM, the EPA voluntarily began a rulemaking process on the NAAQS for ozone. In the early 1970s, the first ozone NAAQS was set at 0.08 parts of ozone per million parts of air. In 1977, as a result of its review and reevaluation, the EPA loosened the standard to 0.12 parts per million (ppm). The test procedure called for no more than three exceedances in three years. (If the air contained more than 0.12 ppm of ozone for more than one hour four times in three years, the area would be officially designated as "in nonattainment.") In 1993, after its review, the EPA reaffirmed that this standard adequately protected human health.

Although another review was not due until 1998, the EPA decided to propose a new ozone NAAQS of 0.08 ppm, averaged over eight hours. If the three-year average of the third highest ozone reading each year were to exceed 0.08 ppm, the area would be in nonattainment. When an area is found to be in nonattainment, the state would be required by the EPA to revise its plan for implementing the federal clean air requirements. The revised state implementation plan would have to demonstrate, to the EPA's satisfaction, how the state would get itself into attainment. (Failure to reach attainment could result in the federal government's withholding certain funds, including highway trust funds, for the state. This is a foolish punishment. It is well recognized that traffic congestion creates more pollution from idling vehicles. Denying highway funds can only create more congestion, and therefore more pollution.)

What Are the Health Benefits? The EPA's scientific advisory committee, CASAC, after its review of the EPA staff recommendation for a 0.08 ppm ozone standard, found that there would be no significant health benefit to adopting the stricter standard. The CASAC panel advised Administrator Browner that the "evidence indicates that there in no threshold concentration for the onset of biological responses due to exposure to ozone above background [natural] concentrations." Furthermore, the panel found that "there is no 'bright line' which distinguishes any of the proposed standards [including the current standard] . . . as being significantly more protective of public health." In other words, there was no significant difference in health benefits between the current 0.12 ppm standard and the proposed 0.08 ppm standard. Also, the EPA's own cost-benefit study (which Administrator Browner says was conducted even though cost cannot be considered under the Clean Air Act) found that it was difficult, at best, to justify a stricter standard.

In testimony before U.S. House of Representatives subcommittees, Mary D. Nichols of the EPA acknowledged as much, saying, "For the proposed ozone standard revision, the annual costs of partial attainment by the year 2007 were estimated to range from $600 million to $2.5 billion, compared with quantifiable annual benefits ranging from $100 million to $1.5 billion." She hastened to suggest that this study was inadequate and would be revised—and issued "with the final standards revisions."[14]

The effects of air pollution on health are even more difficult to determine than are the costs of controlling emissions. A major problem occurs in attempting to determine exactly what causes a health problem. In their work on this subject, researchers for the Health Effects Institute asked: "Can automotive emissions adversely affect human health under conditions of human exposure?" They concluded that finding the answer to this first question "can be confounded by the transformation of primary pollutants and the generation of new chemical species," and added that "the 'molecule of interest' and its concentration are not always readily identifiable."[15] This is a scientist's way of saying that the complexity of air chemistry confounds (confuses or frustrates) the effort to pin down the effects of specific emissions in the form, time, and place that humans are exposed to them. They asked a second question: "Do human ailments or physiological malfunctions result from exposure to automotive emissions?" In answer, they found that "the contribution of other agents capable of inducing disease makes the assignment of attributable risk to automotive emissions more difficult." In other words, there are so many other factors affecting disease that it is difficult to attribute specific risk to auto emissions.

In its review of the NAAQS for ozone, the EPA's Office of Air Quality Planning and Standards developed the OAQPS Staff Paper, dated June 1996. This document is the EPA's assessment of current scientific and technical information, including the 185 ozone-related studies that the EPA says provide the basis for its decision to propose a new standard.

The OAQPS assessment of ozone health effects actually contains some good news. For example, it reports that "there remains little or no evidence of association between ambient O_3 [ozone] exposures and carcinogenicity and/or genotoxicity at this time." Also, surprisingly, it reports that "controlled human exposure studies of O_3 have demonstrated that at concentrations reported in ambient air, O_3 alone does not induce eye irritation."[16]

On the down side, it reports that heavily exercising children and adolescents may experience decrements (reductions) in lung function when exposed to 0.12 ppm of ozone for one to three hours, in studies using smog chambers. Heavily exercising adults also demonstrate lung function decrements. These decrements or reductions are measured by having a person exhale forcefully into a spirometer, which measures expiratory flow rates. Most notably, these decrements are transitory, and when ozone concentrations are lowered, the lung function returns to its previous capacity. The Staff Paper says that "the data suggest that acute O_3 exposures can impair the host defense capability of both humans and animals." But it reports that "there is no single experimental human or animal study or group of studies which proves that respiratory infection is worsened by exposure to O_3."[17]

Trouble with the Research

It would seem reasonable to assume that repeated reduction of lung function would have long-term effects. In evaluating this phenomenon, the Staff Paper says, "it has been necessary for researchers to utilize the results from both epidemiology and animal toxicology studies." They find that "epidemiology studies do not provide clear causal relationships due to the presence of confounding variables (e.g., heat, humidity, other pollutants)." As for animal studies, the researchers found some evidence of causal relationships, "but lack of a full understanding of species sensitivity differences between humans and animals limits the extent to which results of toxicology data can be extrapolated to human health effects." The Staff Paper further reports that "most studies investigating this association [between long-term O_3 exposures and chronic respiratory effects in humans] . . . have been compromised by incomplete control of confounding variables and inadequate exposure information."[18]

Finally, the Staff Paper finds that epidemiology studies "lack good information on individual O_3 exposure and are frequently confounded by personal or co-pollutant variables." These studies find "a biologically plausible basis for considering the possibility that repeated inflammation associated with exposure to O_3 over a lifetime may result in sufficient damage to respiratory tissue such that individuals later in life may experience a reduced quality of life, *although such relationships remain highly uncertain*" (emphasis added).[19]

On mortality and ozone, the Staff Paper cites a 1988 study that was reanalyzed in 1991. The authors of the reanalysis wrote that "the possible mechanism linking O_3 with mortality is speculation based on known acute pulmonary effects." The Staff Paper says these authors "further emphasize that, although statistically significant associations have been detected among mortality and environmental variables, one cannot conclude with complete confidence that such associations are causal based on results from an observational study." The Staff Paper also reports that the EPA's *Criteria Document* summarizing science on ozone "concludes that although an association between ambient O_3 exposure in areas with very high O_3 levels and daily mortality has been suggested, the strength of any such association remains unclear at this time." Again, the researchers of today, like those of 1988, find the answers to key questions are "confounded." This Staff Paper, with all its uncertainties, represents the strongest case that can be made for a new standard. Clearly, the case it succeeds in making is the need for conducting more research before confounding problems can be resolved and conclusions can be drawn.[20]

There is no argument about whether ozone and particulate matter should be regulated. Both are stringently regulated now, and no one is seriously suggesting the removal of all regulation.[21] The question at issue is whether even more stringent regulation is needed (the evidence is not persuasive), or whether there may be more important priorities. The concern about asthma illustrates the problem.

The Bioaerosols and Asthma

In contrast to the confounding problems in establishing low-level ozone health effects, the effects of what are called bioaerosols are increasingly clear. Bioaerosols are microscopic living organisms or pieces from living things that are suspended in air. Examples are bacteria, amoebas, viruses, dust mites, cockroaches and their debris, fragments of human or animal skin, molds, mildews, fungi, spores, and pollen.

The relationship between these pollutants and asthma is instructive. In recent years, there has been a significant rise in asthma incidence; at the same time, the air became cleaner. Ozone was down. The number of days with poor air quality in ninety-four of the nation's largest urban areas dropped by nearly 61 percent between the 1986–1988 period and the 1990–1995 period. Auto-related pollutants have been drastically cut. All this progress—and yet asthma incidence has increased. One might almost think that cleaner air causes more asthma attacks. That is foolishness, of course, but it does seem that reducing the pollutants now being regulated is not helping, or at least not helping much.

Asthma is a condition that can vary among individuals from a grave illness to an occasional discomfort. It may be caused or aggravated by allergy to pollen and other bioaerosols. Aspirin and aspirin-like drugs can cause or aggravate asthma. Nearly 10 million Americans have asthma. Experts say it is seen most often in children and is usually an inherited condition.[22] Some researchers suggest that the "tight-building syndrome," encouraged by the government during the energy crises of the 1970s, is a factor. Poor interior air quality is attributed to the sealing up of homes and offices from outside air to save energy used for home heating and cooling. Other studies point to an infestation of the indoor dust (or house) mite as a cause for the increase in asthma incidence. Dust mites are spider-like organisms too small to see with the naked eye. They are a major cause of allergies and are found in blankets, pillows, mattresses, carpets, upholstery, stuffed animals, and elsewhere. They feed on the scales shed from human skin. It is their excretion to which people are most allergic.

Researchers William O.C.M. Cookson and Miriam F. Moffatt of Oxford University recently published their findings about the increase in asthma incidence. "For asthmatics," they found, "the most important source of allergens is the house dust mite. These mites thrive in warm, moist conditions and are ubiquitous in human bedding. There is a dose-response relation between exposure to mite antigens and asthma, and a plausible but unproven case can be made for increasing levels of mites in modern heated homes. In Japan, asthma has increased just as the population has moved away from the traditional bare and well-ventilated house to Western-style buildings."[23] A pamphlet from the Asthma and Allergy Foundation of America entitled "How to Reduce Exposure to Allergens" proclaims, "The bedroom is your first line of defense." It outlines the ways to avoid the major causes of allergic action—dust mites and the other bioaerosols found in bedding, drapes, carpets, and other household hideouts. Ozone is not mentioned.

Cookson and Moffatt found that "air pollution may aggravate existing asthma but is not responsible for the asthma epidemic." They wrote that the prevalence of asthma in "clean Munich" was higher than in "highly polluted Leipzig" in former East Germany. Similar results were found in comparisons of Poland and Sweden. They reported that respiratory and other infections are more common among children in former Eastern Bloc countries, and these "infections may, paradoxically, protect against asthma." They talk of the "complexity of the environmental contribution to asthma," and suggest that "the relevant factors" need to be identified to resolve the epidemic. This conclusion is not unlike that of the Health Effects Institute in 1988.

In February 1997, the National Asthma Education and Prevention Program, sponsored by the National Institutes of Health, issued updated guidelines. Recommended actions included allergy testing, avoiding smoke, controlling dust mites, keeping the humidity low in the home, and forgoing furry or feathered pets.[24] A paper published by North Carolina State University reports that 10 to 15 percent of people are allergic to dust mites, the most common allergens in indoor air. Also, 40 percent of all people who have other allergies are also allergic to dust mites.[25]

For some people, it is better to be outside with the ozone than inside with the dust mites and cockroaches. The poor quality of indoor air as a result of bioaerosols and other pollutants casts further doubt on the validity of more stringent regulation of ozone and other "traditional" pollutants. According to the *Washington Post* report of the study, "Numerous experts emphasized . . . that relatively small expenditures in cockroach control could pay substantial public-health dividends." Nonetheless, the EPA seems determined to keep on doing what it has been doing.

In a Rut. As with most institutions, the EPA, as it grows older, is falling into the rut of resistance to change. It knows how to regulate a handful of auto companies and the plants of industrial companies. It knows how to overcome resistance to regulation from those elements of the economy. It has no experience, however, in dealing with dust mites, or even everyday pollen. The EPA's leaders know that taking on the problems these and other bioaerosols cause would stir up new antagonists in the clean air debate. They also know that the professional activists would call for their heads if they did not keep on doing what they have been doing. The result: whether it makes sense or not, the EPA is going after the last little bit of their old and defeated foes, ozone and particulate matter—and ignoring what are likely to be much more serious problems. They will use up resources that could be more effectively directed toward dozens of other problems, or even, heaven forbid, left in the pockets of the taxpayer.

What President Clinton, Vice President Gore, and Administrator Browner are doing with the air quality standards they announced is to get as close to a zero concentration of pollutants as they believe may be tolerated by the public, once the full effect of the standard is understood. In his July 16, 1997, memorandum to EPA chief Browner approving the new NAAQS, President Clinton stressed that no areas would be designated as out of compliance with the ozone standard until the year 2000. For the particulate standard, he said no area would be designated as out of compliance until after 2002, when the EPA will have reviewed the PM2.5 requirements. By doing so, the president apparently hopes to avoid a crisis during his term and before Gore officially becomes a candidate for the presidency in 2000. This approach is reminiscent of the comment to Mme. de Pompadour attributed to King Louis XV of France in the mid-1700s: "*Après moi le déluge*" (After me, the deluge). The French revolution ensued, and Louis XV's grandson and successor, Louis XVI, lost his head to the guillotine.

These new standards for ozone and particulate matter are the EPA's answer to the need to eliminate all adverse health effects of these pollutants and to provide an "adequate margin of safety." Both these NAAQS involve motor vehicle emissions and, therefore, are very important to the future of the automobile and personal mobility. Under the court's interpretation of the intent of Congress, the EPA could conceivably be forced, by lawsuits from groups such as the American Lung Association or the NRDC, to propose an air quality standard of zero ppm, or zero tolerance. Everyone would know that it would be impossible to achieve, since there are natural sources of ozone precursors, most notably, trees. (Yes, trees!)[26] In fact, the "background" ozone levels—meaning levels that would be present without any human-caused emissions—are between 0.03 and 0.05 ppm during the summer in the United States.[27] The EPA's new NAAQS for ozone would set a 0.08 ppm limit. This means that on a day when the background level is at 0.05 ppm, all human activity could produce no more than 0.03 ppm.

The next step, of necessity, would be emission standards designed to eliminate any human-caused pollutants that would drive atmospheric concentrations of those pollutants above background or natural levels. There would be no rationale for anything but zero-emission standards. This, of course, would mean the end of the car and truck as we know them.

The End of the Car and Truck?

Of course, this will not happen. The current drive toward zero tolerance of ozone and particulates, and the subsequent requirement of zero emissions for all vehicles, will not succeed. At some point, enough people will wake up to the realities and put a stop to such irrational requirements. In the meantime, unfortunately, we must go through the charade of bureaucratic rulemaking and political maneuvering.

If there were an affordable substitute that could provide the kind of personal mobility we now have, perhaps such a radical change would be only a financial problem, not a technological one. That is not the case. The only vehicles available today that produce zero emissions are electric. The electricity needed for charging vehicle batteries, however, is mostly generated from power plants burning oil, natural gas, or coal. As a result, these plants emit VOCs and NO_x, the precursors of ozone. In this sense, electric vehicles are not emission-free (unless the electricity for recharges is generated by nuclear plants).

Every responsible authority in the world knows that electric vehicles, fun as some are to drive, are not now able to substitute for vehicles powered by the internal combustion engine. Their range is too low and their cost is too high. Most of the electric cars on the road today are still powered by the same type of battery—lead-acid—used in the electric vehicles at the beginning of the twentieth century. The nickel-metal hydride battery is reportedly close to being technologically feasible. At this point, however, it would be too costly to be considered economically viable for wide application. In any event, the limited additional range it provides makes it an interim step toward the development of a more useful battery. While intense research has been directed toward finding a breakthrough battery, it has not yet been developed.

It would be irresponsible and ultimately politically suicidal to legislate that Americans must switch from their current vehicles to ones that have an effective range of around 100 miles, can carry only two people and virtually nothing else, and cost as much as today's luxury, six-passenger cars. The electric car may well have a future, especially if clean nuclear power can be the recharging power source, but there is no guarantee that the necessary breakthroughs will come about to make it appeal to any more than a small, niche market. This is not a hypothetical issue. California, New York, and Massachusetts have attempted to put electric cars on their roads by commanding auto manufacturers to sell them—even if the consumers do not want them.

In view of the unique conditions in the Los Angeles area, the Clean Air Act permits California to set its own auto-emission standards. In doing so, in the mid-1990s, California set a requirement that starting in 1998, 2 percent of new vehicles sold in that state by each automobile manufacturer must be zero-emission vehicles, with the requirement increasing to 10 percent for the year 2003. There was no rule that anyone had to buy these vehicles; the manufacturers simply had to find a way to sell them, even if it meant losing money on every sale.

To show they were not to be outdone, New York and Massachusetts also put in place a zero-emission vehicle (ZEV) requirement, under a section of the law permitting other states to enact requirements that were exactly the same as those of California. Subsequently, however, California's

Air Resources Board convened a panel composed of experts who found that consumers were not ready to buy the numbers of zero-emission vehicles the state regulators planned. After much hand wringing and rhetorical combat, the state eliminated the 1998 requirement and called for a "voluntary" sale of vehicles through 2000, and a target for 2003 requiring 10 percent of all sales by each manufacturer to be zero-emission vehicles— meaning electric.[28] New York and Massachusetts refused to change their rules, and the matter is in litigation. There is much confusion about the future.

As state and federal governments push for zero-emission vehicles, there is inevitably a cost to the consumer. Hundreds of millions of dollars have been spent on electric vehicle research—not just by General Motors, which has a passenger car on the market, but also by other automakers, as insurance that they will not get caught short by government requirements for such vehicles. The costs involved in these efforts ultimately are borne by the consumer or investor. There is likely to be a role for the electric car in the future, but it is impossible to judge where, in their wisdom, consumers will place it in the larger market. And it is in the marketplace that the decision should be made—not in the political arena. Andrew Card, president of the U.S. automakers trade association, said, "The technology and the free market should determine when electric vehicles will be ready for the marketplace, not government mandates." Politics, of course, trumps the market on this issue.

Other approaches are also on the horizon, most notably the hybrid, employing both an electric motor and a gasoline engine. They obviously are not zero-emission vehicles, and their two power sources add complexity and cost. They also are not yet projected for the mass market. There is, in fact, not a vehicle available or about to be available that can come close to matching the utility and value of the current car powered by the internal combustion engine. The day will come when the vehicle as we know it today will be replaced, but that day is not yet in sight. People, the economy, the environment, and certainly personal mobility will be better served if we can let the market determine how that change will occur and not try to guess at the best technology, with a high risk of mandating a mistake.

How to Choose Environmental Targets. The government may have a hands-off approach to radon and a common-sense acceptance of small doses of pollutants in water and food, but when it comes to emissions from cars, common sense about health risks flies out the window. There are at least two reasons for this. First, in the 1960s, cars and trucks were major sources of lead, hydrocarbons, carbon monoxide, and nitrogen oxides. The dose, as Paracelsus would say, was very high. Also, early control systems were reasonable in cost.[29] It made sense to cut emissions significantly. The auto industry agreed on the health issue, and it agreed that the government should have a role in getting the job done. The result was that these vehicle emissions were slashed, leaving only 4 to 10 percent in comparison with the emissions from pre-control cars.

The second reason why autos are so heavily regulated is political. The auto industry is an easy target for politicians, and this condition invites more regulation. This sounds cynical or even paranoid, but there is no doubt that regulating the car has been the path of least political resistance for Congress and the bureaucracy. There are only three major U.S. manufacturers left (regulation having had a hand in the demise of American Motors and other smaller competitors), along with a handful of foreign producers who sell in the U.S. market. The so-called Big Three do not take any political popularity prizes. They lost favor when foreign competitors, with favorable cost structures and excellent quality, took big bites out of their market share. They were the constant target of professional activists, who heaped personal abuse on industry executives.

More important, perhaps, the industry does not command a big voting bloc.[30] Executives are concerned (with good reason) about their relationships with politicians and government regulators, who wield tremendous power with a potential to affect seriously the corporate bottom line. They are also fearful of appearing to be negative about environmental protection and other public policy issues, and as a result they sometimes fail to contest the substance of regulatory proposals. This reluctance to engage in political fights is a powerful disincentive for legislators and others in government to take up their case. In sum, they are easier to push around than are most other sectors involved in the control of air pollution.

Foreign car manufacturers are politically unloved as well, especially by the U.S. unions that have generally failed to organize their U.S. plants. Also, they are concerned, with good reason, about possible efforts to limit their imports of vehicles or parts. More important, they are in a position to be classic free riders in the public policy arena. Since they have traditionally concentrated on producing smaller vehicles (appropriate for their home markets), they have had an easier time meeting fuel economy and emission standards. This advantage has often given them the opportunity to sit back and let the U. S. manufacturers take the heat for fighting unreasonable rules and timetables. (It has been a perfectly good business strategy, but as they move deeper into the production of larger cars and as standards become more stringent, this edge will diminish.) The result of these factors is that regulation of motor vehicle emissions is more stringent—and therefore more costly—than public policy priorities or common sense would justify.

· 14 ·

WHAT TO DO

There is something the government can do now to reduce up to 50 percent of the remaining amount of pollution from cars and light trucks. The way to do this has been known for some years. The political will to do it has been absent, and the public has been apathetic, at best.

The High Emitters

Studies show that 10 percent or fewer of the vehicles on the road generate more than 50 percent of the auto-produced pollution. In 1992, the Environmental Research Consortium of the United States Council for Automotive Research (USCAR) gathered pollutant readings on more than 40,000 vehicles on two Michigan roadways. The results showed that 6 to 7 percent of the vehicles produced more than 50 percent of the pollution. When these vehicles were repaired, carbon monoxide and hydrocarbon emissions from the "high emitters" were reduced by roughly 95 percent.

In a comprehensive paper published in 1993, four engineers and scientists wrote, "It has become increasingly apparent that most of the mobile source emissions are caused by a small percentage of the vehicles. A compelling body of remote-sensing and roadside data shows, more or less regardless of locale, that about 50 percent of the CO and HC emissions come from 10 percent of the vehicles."[1] Up to 30 percent of these "high emitters" are the result of "tampering" by the owners or mechanics, who make adjustments to improve drivability. Some are the result of a "poisoning" of the catalyst by the use of leaded gasoline in past years. Fuels vary considerably and may also contribute to high emissions, and malfunctions of key components such as the airflow meter or exhaust gas oxygen sensor can do the same.

The authors of the 1993 paper saw remote sensing as the way to address the problem. They said, "The remote monitoring of tailpipe emissions of passing cars allow the identification of high emitters, which can then be targeted for repair." They concluded that "the combination of remote-sensing programs with IM [inspection and maintenance] programs to focus inspection resources on the high emitting vehicles is an especially attractive strategy."

Writing in *Car and Driver,* Patrick Bedard says it more colorfully. "About one in ten cars on the road is a gorilla." He adds, "If just one-tenth of the fleet stayed home, and they were the gorillas, the air would be 50 percent cleaner—a miracle. Air pollution would no longer be an issue. If the goal is clean air, then the facts point to the target."[2]

Remote sensing is a possibility. Donald Stedman, a chemistry professor at the University of Denver, has invented an instrument to measure hydrocarbons and carbon monoxide from cars as they drive down the road, past the monitoring site. Hughes, a subsidiary of General Motors, also has a remote sensor called the "smog dog" that is being tested in Arizona, Taiwan, and elsewhere. A version of the device called a "clean screen," developed by a Toronto firm, would with a quick, twenty-five second check identify and excuse the clean cars from the routine, time-consuming inspections. Ideally in combination with a video camera, the emissions reading of a passing car could be recorded along with the make, model, and license number. The owners could be asked to bring them in for a dynamometer test and repair, if needed. The system may need further development to improve feasibility, but finding the high emitters one way or another makes good sense.

Adding more cost to all cars to cut emissions closer to zero amounts to a subsidy for the 10 percent of vehicles that are high emitters and produce 50 percent of the pollution. (Also, correcting the high emitters would relieve the owners of the other nearly 180 million motor vehicles in the United States of the burden of taking them in for emissions inspection.)

Politics Beats Science? All productive work—whether it is farming, publishing a newspaper, baking bread, making computers, or trucking products to market—creates waste and pollution. By striving to make any amount of pollution intolerable, environmental zealots in effect convert what has been honorable work into what may be the only act accepted as a sin in our secular world. In a society where tolerance—even promotion—of past taboos is now politically correct, lumberjacks, miners, farmers, road builders, manufacturers, and countless others are viewed by many in the government, the media (especially the entertainment media), academia, and elsewhere not as productive members of society but as polluters and destroyers of the environment. Paul Bunyan, John Henry, Old MacDonald— all are now politically incorrect.

In these circumstances, using common sense in dealing with pollutants of any kind is difficult. The demagoguery is on the side of the regulatory extremists. The public, when uninformed about the science or economics involved in these matters, is too vulnerable to manipulation. If something is a pollutant, why not ban it from the face of the Earth? That is the position almost automatically taken by the professional activists, the sensationalist media, and too many politicians who see political benefit in such a position.

"In a Role Reversal, GOP Courts the 'Greens'" is the headline on a *New York Times* article reporting on a shift in Republican rhetoric about the environment as evidenced by "a parade of Republican governors who sound like tree-huggers as they trumpet their environmental records."[3] Who, pray tell, wants to become the defender of pollution? What manufacturer wants to try publicly to justify the effluent of his product? What politician looks forward to saying, "Let's keep a little of this pollutant around"? The consequence is a great reluctance on the part of politicians, or even industrialists, to challenge the demand for the most stringent of pollution-abatement legislation. Politicians do not want to be labeled as anti-environment, and business leaders do not want to appear to be uncaring. Even scientists are reluctant to speak out once the advocates have succeeded in establishing the received wisdom about an environmental issue. They do not want to become part of what the critics call "a handful of scientists" who do not agree with them; nor do they want to miss out on government research funds, very little of which go to skeptics of government programs. The result of this timidity in the face of intimidation is regulatory extremism and wasted resources.

The Breyer Analysis

Stephen Breyer, now a justice of the U.S. Supreme Court, wrote an excellent book on the subject of regulatory extremes. He described three major problems in the regulatory process. The first is what he calls "tunnel vision," or "the last 10 percent." "Tunnel vision, a classic administrative disease," he wrote, "arises when . . . conscientious performance effectively carries single-minded pursuit of a single goal too far, to the point where it brings about more harm than good. In the regulation of health risks, a more appropriate label is 'the last 10 percent,' or 'going the last mile.'"[4] As an example, Judge Breyer wrote about litigation over cleaning up the last bit of a New Hampshire toxic waste dump, at a cost of $9.3 million, to make the dirt clean enough for children to eat small amounts of it for seventy days each year—an unlikely occurrence under any circumstance. And as it turned out, there were no children playing in the area; it was a swamp.

Another problem Judge Breyer described is "random agenda selection." He lamented that "one cannot find any detailed federal governmental list that prioritizes health or safety risk problems so as to create a rational, overall agenda . . . that would seek to maximize attainable safety or to minimize health-related harms."[5] One result of this absence of priorities and the proliferation of regulatory agencies is that the most politically attractive regulations most often command the field.

The third problem the judge mentions is inconsistency in the different ways agencies estimate the effects of their regulations. Inconsistency is also a problem when one agency ignores the effects of its regulations in areas over which another agency has jurisdiction. An excellent example (not in the judge's book) is the EPA's insistence on going forward with regulations requiring cars to be equipped with on-board refueling vapor–recovery systems (ORVR), known also as on-board canisters. These devices capture vapors flowing from the fuel tank when it is refilled. The alternative was a fueling pump, at the gasoline service station, engineered to capture the vapors during refueling. The auto industry opposed the canister. The oil industry opposed the pump system, known as Stage II.

The Clean Air Amendments of 1990 directed the National Highway Traffic Safety Administration (NHTSA) to advise the EPA on the safety of these devices before it could mandate their use. NHTSA advised that "fire risks will increase with ORVR," and that "ORVR systems increase safety risk and Stage II does not." NHTSA concluded, "Control of gasoline vapors at the fuel pump (Stage II) is a viable alternative to ORVR." ORVR systems cause an increased safety hazard from fire because the system would require plumbing and a container that would collect and hold these highly flammable vapors. The EPA, one of whose employees had been awarded a government bonus for developing an on-board canister, favored the canister and ordered its installation.[6] The courts upheld the decision.

Does Anybody Care?

Judge Breyer recognized the difficulty of breaking the vicious circle that results in overly zealous regulation. The inclination to "err on the safe side," he says, may lead the public to press Congress to enact standards and set up agencies that, in turn, encourage strong actions to regulate substances or activities that "catch the public eye." These congressional reactions provoke further public concern, and "all of the above makes it more difficult for agencies to resist overkill and random agenda setting." This is an excellent description of how the EPA operates.

Solutions do not come easily. Judge Breyer urges the development of a "depoliticized regulatory process" staffed by civil servants with experience in health and environmental agencies, Congress, and the Office of Management and Budget, with interagency jurisdiction and with the protection of political insulation. The group, he presumes, would have the prestige of a highly capable staff and would be given the authority to achieve results. He is pessimistic about stimulating the public to call for restraint in such matters. As he writes, "To speak of the need for improved communications with the public, or a more responsible press, or a more disciplined Congress is to call spirits from the vasty deep. One can call them, but will they come?" This, indeed, is the critical question. Will the public become sufficiently involved to protect its own interest—or will it leave this interest in the hands of the activists and their political allies?

As the saying goes, "Never underestimate the public, but never overestimate their information." It is hard to be optimistic about the public having enough good information to make informed judgments about complicated regulatory matters. How does the public educate itself, for example, about ozone standards, and how can it determine the priority to assign to various levels of control, if all public health and safety needs were prioritized? Judge Breyer calls rather plaintively for "a Socratic notion of virtue—the teachers teaching well, the students learning well, the judges judging well, and the health regulators more effectively bringing about better health."[7] He is correct. We need such virtues. We can speak of these needs, but to do so may be "to call spirits from the vasty deep." Will they come?

American businesses, industrial companies, and unions bear a heavy burden in improving the regulatory process. They are the repository of the most relevant information about their products and the problems or benefits these products provide. They know a great deal about the externalities, and it is they who will develop the best technological approaches to these problems. They will know the costs and will have to pay them—and then pass them on to the consumer, or take them as a loss. The companies and their employees (and the employees' unions) have the first and most direct interest in what the regulators require of them. This being so, these companies also have the duty to share their information, not only with the regulators, but with the public as well.

Unless the private-sector companies undertake the mission of educating the public about the problems, their solutions, and the costs involved and unless they are ready to inform the public about the potential harm of overzealous regulation, these companies will continue to be the villains in the public-health–and–safety debate and will continue to be saddled by excessively costly requirements aimed at addressing "the last 10 percent" of problems selected from an old and random agenda determined by emotion, fear, and politics.

To be effective on air pollution issues, auto companies must focus not just on tailpipe and evaporative emissions. They must know as much and more about atmospheric concentrations of pollutants and their health effects as do the professional activists and political antagonists. They must concentrate on demonstrable air quality needs and how to meet them. They must understand what the public interest requires.

Auto companies spend billions on research related to product and manufacturing process, but they spend little on public policy research—as if the government were not now as deeply involved as the companies are in determining the kinds of vehicles the companies may sell. As long as the government is so deeply involved, it is in the interests of the shareholders for companies to be deeply involved in understanding public policy and how it is determined—and to participate in that process. A hands-off or temporizing position will bring neither peace nor affection. It will result in more regulation, needed or not. Decisions in our democracy are not made in an antiseptic vacuum. They are the result of a clash of ideas and interests, and ultimately they are made by the people, on the basis of what they know and want. It is in the public interest for private companies to share what they know with the people.

The public wants to know that it is not in danger. Over several decades, auto emissions have been characterized as major villains of air pollution. People will be satisfied about vehicle pollution only when they know that (1), whatever the auto is emitting is doing them no real harm, or (2), if there is harm, an effective program is underway to remove that harm. This does not mean that the last few grams of emission must be eliminated, but it does mean that an operative majority of the public must be satisfied that the last few grams pose no significant health problem. Because the industry has such limited political leverage, until these questions are satisfied, cars and trucks will be vulnerable to more stringent regulation, which means car buyers will be paying more for less.

Industry, public officials, and other interested parties have responsibilities for good public policy, but ultimately it is up to the public itself to become informed and insist on sound policies that meet the public need. Personal mobility is too important to be left in the hands of the government—or the industry, for that matter.

Editorializing on the problem of deciding whether the proposed ozone and PM standards should be enacted, the *Washington Post* opined, "Our own sense is that the science in a case such as this is never going to solve the problem entirely. . . . No EPA administrator can ever be sure that a given level or regulation is enough to protect the public health, or too much, or sometimes that it is even aimed at the most important cause. . . . And the economic projections that accompany such decisions are often little more than glorified guesswork."[8] In a classic example of one of Judge Breyer's concerns, the *Post* went on to say, "It's a choice of risks. Do you want to go down in the record books as someone who imposed no extra cost at some possible risk to public health, or the other way around?" The *Post* took the err-on-the-safe-side route and said the proposed standards ought to take effect. The vicious circle has not yet been broken.

Time to "Reengineer" the EPA. In addition to regulatory improvements derived from an educated public or a depoliticized, experienced, and empowered regulatory staff, there is another action that might help—restructuring of the EPA. Today, that sprawling agency has more power over more American lives than has any other government agency (with the possible exception of the Treasury, with its Internal Revenue Service). It controls most environmental research. It determines what is or is not an environmental problem. It develops the regulations (some more complex than much legislation) to address the problems. It promotes these regulations within the government and then with the public (or vice versa). It approves these regulations and promulgates them, giving them the force of law. It investigates violations. It "tries" and "convicts" the violators. It determines the punishment and inflicts it.[9]

The EPA's power extends beyond its effect on industry, business, farming, and individuals. It has told the Department of Energy's Nuclear Regulatory Commission (NRC) that its recommended maximum level of 25 millirems of radiation annually for deactivated nuclear plants and research facilities is unacceptably lenient. The EPA says the maximum level should be 15 millirems, and it accused the NRC of treating radiation as a "privileged pollutant."[10] To put both levels in perspective, the EPA says that a person moving from sea level to Denver would receive an additional 53 millirems of radiation annually. A woman getting a mammogram, according to the EPA, receives a 30-millirem dose. Radon in the average home in the United States produces a dose of 200 millirems annually. The EPA also took on the defense establishment by telling the Defense Department that the use of lead bullets at firing ranges in certain locations is unacceptable.

Of more serious concern is the fact that the EPA has threatened a sovereign state of the Union that, under the terms of the Clean Air Act, it might take over the state's enforcement of environmental laws.[11] The federal EPA threat to seize control came after a change in governors and a reorganization of the staff by a new head of the Virginia Environmental Protection Agency. The seizure of state authority by the central government for whatever reason no doubt would have Virginia's Thomas Jefferson turning in his grave.

The environment, obviously, touches every aspect of our personal and business lives. To protect it, the EPA has been given the legislative, executive, and judicial functions that the designers of the U.S. Constitution so carefully separated. It does the research, writes the rules, administers the rules, and punishes the wayward. The agency serves as prosecutor, judge, and jury, a concept that is anathema under our judicial procedure. There is a clear need to break up this dangerous concentration of power. The professional activists and their political allies will say such a proposal will "gut" environmental protection—a favorite slogan—but, properly done, it will result in better environmental regulation, not worse.

With "separation of powers" as the principle, a reorganization of the EPA is not difficult to imagine. First, transfer the research function. There are good people involved in research for the EPA, but the organization of their efforts has come under criticism. Writing in *Nature,* David L. Lewis of the EPA's National Exposure Research Laboratory in Georgia says, "The EPA now has about a third fewer scientists, and their time is largely consumed by administrative red tape, overseeing contracts and other funding agreements."[12] Commenting on the EPA's Office of Research and Development, he says, "By late 1993, the organization charged with ensuring that U.S. environmental regulations are scientifically sound became hopelessly gridlocked." He expressed concern about any agency that loses its scientific knowledge, "takes their best guesses," and then codifies their "guess work and conservative safety factors into costly regulations for which noncompliance carries fines and imprisonment." He says, "this is basically what happens when environmental regulations are being promulgated and enforced without knowledge of how most living organisms interact with environmental changes."

A Little Reorganization

It is time to take a very close look at how the federal government is conducting the research upon which so many costly and disruptive environmental regulations are based. Such a review can mean that Americans will get better environmental protection for less cost and less disruption. It does not mean that evildoers are out to gut the program. That is the charge that will be made, of course, by all the organizations with vested interests in keeping the EPA exactly as it is.

While the ability to select subjects for research should stay with the EPA, the conduct or supervision of the research itself should be assigned to a public research institute, independent from any regulatory agency, with supervision over all federal environmental research programs. This separation could remove the temptation of regulators to guide their research along the lines of their own preconceptions. It could facilitate the prioritization of all research programs (whether they involve radon gas or dust mites) and thereby, to some extent, the prioritization of regulations themselves. In such an institute, research could take into consideration more than one set of goals or one agency's mission. Of course, all agencies would fight hard to retain their research programs. Research is an instrument of power; it can provide the rationale for more programs. It also brings a certain degree of prestige and dignity to a regulatory agency. The fight put up by the agencies to retain control very likely would be matched by the opposition from congressional committees with jurisdiction over agencies and their research. The path would not be easy, but it would be worthwhile.

Another useful step would be to require regulatory agencies to include an analysis of benefits and costs in all regulatory proposals, using prescribed methodologies and common economic assumptions. While these analyses are greatly limited by the subjective nature of the judgments involved, the process of justifying costs would be a healthy exercise for regulators, and it would provide data that are useful in setting priorities among the proposals of the various agencies.[13]

The next step would be for Congress to take back some of the responsibility it has delegated to the EPA. Many of the regulations promulgated by the EPA are more far-reaching than are laws passed by Congress. Congress may find it convenient to pass broad authorizing legislation that delegates implementation power to agencies. By so doing it achieves some insulation from the responsibility for applying regulatory mandates directly on citizens and businesses—their constituents. But it also loses control of the hundreds of billions of dollars spent by regulated companies and individuals to meet regulatory mandates. And, in the process, accountability for these mandates is further diminished.

A simple approach would be to expand the Congressional Review Act that became law in March 1996. The act, in effect, "gives back" to Congress some of the legislative powers it has passed off to the federal bureaucracy over the years. Under the act, Congress may reject, by a resolution of disapproval, any new rule issued by any federal agency (with the exception of the so-called independent agencies, such as the Federal Trade Commission). Congress has sixty days to act after receipt of the rule from the agency, which, if requested, must also send to the General Accounting Office (GAO) a cost-benefit analysis, if any has been prepared, and other relevant analyses. For "major" rules, the GAO must provide Congress an assessment of the agency's analyses. Major rules are those having an effect of $100 million on the economy; or those that cause a major increase in costs or prices for consumers; or those that adversely affect U.S. competitiveness.

It would boggle the minds of the founding fathers that Congress has delegated its responsibility for writing and passing laws (that is what regulatory rules are) that have effects of this magnitude. Any C-SPAN viewer knows that Congress spends its time and energy on many things of lesser consequence. The argument is made that Congress does not have the expertise to craft the level of detail found in these regulations. That argument in itself suggests that the regulators have reached too far in their attempts to run our economy and our personal lives.

Congress could avoid the issue of its competence with detail by reclaiming a little more of the legislative power it has passed off. Instead of having only veto power over a new regulation, Congress should require that no major regulation will go into effect unless it passes a resolution of approval. A regulation that has more than a $100 million effect on the economy or one that significantly affects costs to consumers or American competitiveness is not trivial. [14] The EPA should not be promulgating regulations of such magnitude when our elected representatives cannot understand and are not willing to approve them.

Whether this "simple" amendment of the Congressional Review Act is adopted or the process remains as it is, there should be more restrictions on the use of taxpayers' money to promote the adoption of regulations. A carefully drawn rule is needed to permit the necessary information flow to the public, but without the propaganda. The extent of the problem is reflected in an item in the *Washington Post's* government gossip column, "The Regulators," which reports: "Carol Browner, Environmental Protection Agency administrator, is on the smog and soot circuit, promoting EPA's proposal to tighten standards. . . . Last Friday, Browner gave the keynote address to the Children's Environmental Health Network Research Conference. Last Monday, it was on to the John F. Kennedy School of Government for more pumping of the standard. Another promo expected on March 10 at San Francisco's Commonwealth Club."[15] Is this promotional tour really the kind of thing federal regulators should be doing?

We have had forty years of experience with the need for government intervention to protect the environment, and dramatic progress has been made in cleaning up the air and water. More can be done. But in some areas we have also stepped beyond the bounds of common sense and sound policy. Professional environmentalists have exploited the deep concern we Americans have for the well-being of the world we live in. In a sense they have abused the power they have been given by going after the last 10 percent of every pollutant that politics will permit them to regulate. They have seized the advantages of their popular public agenda to dominate the public health agenda.

The last half-century has seen the greatest intrusion of central government into the lives of Americans and their businesses since the founding of the republic in 1789. A virtual tidal wave of regulations has poured out of Washington, D.C., covering every aspect of our lives. There is no reliable count of how many there are. There is no way of judging their real cost or their value. Worse yet, there is no mechanism for judging the priorities that should be assigned to our many goals and problems. Washington has become a city of dozens of regulatory fiefdoms, each with a cadre of officials dedicated to the retention and expansion of its powers. Each sees its mission as promulgating ever more regulations and enforcing them more strictly. None is more aggressive than the EPA.

Summing Up

The air is clean and getting cleaner, but the good news cannot be heard above the din of melodramatic end-of-the-world warnings. The government helped clean up the air when markets did not deal with the externalities—namely, air pollution. But having succeeded to the point of reaching its goals, the EPA proposes to reinvent itself and extend its reach by redefining clean air as dirty. Its proposed air quality standards would add 229 U.S. counties to the dirty list and tell 48 million more Americans that they should fear the sky. Billions of dollars would have to be spent to reach this movable EPA finish line, assuming it is technologically feasible.

Unbelievably, the Clean Air Act, the courts say, forbids the government from taking into consideration either cost or technology when air quality standards are involved. Scientists say there is no threshold concentration for the onset of health effects from ozone that is above background levels. The EPA is charged to eliminate *all* adverse health effects, and to add a margin of safety. This, as two-time EPA administrator William Ruckelshaus says, is "an impossible standard of perfection." Ultimately, this unworkable and wasteful provision of the act, if not reinterpreted by the courts, must be amended.

Cars and trucks now have emission-control equipment costing somewhere between $1,500 and $2,000. Costs may double as federal and state vehicle-emission regulations already on the books are implemented. If the new national ambient air quality standards are implemented, the emission standards that follow would mean even higher vehicle costs. Government regulation by all agencies is estimated to cost our economy somewhere around $600 billion a year. That is money that cannot be spent for education, medical care and research, safer cities, or anything else. The EPA's new rules would add substantially to this cost, although experts cannot agree on what the new standards would cost the economy or, for that matter, what the benefits would be worth.

Identifying the air-related health needs is not an easy task. The EPA's own review of the science reveals many "unanswered questions and large uncertainties." Experts suggest that dust mites inside the home may be worse for asthma sufferers, but there is no dust-mite control program. The EPA says radon gas is a killer, but it has no real radon regulatory program. The government permits and even encourages the use of a well-known contaminant—chlorine—in our water, because it makes sense. Federal rules permit the presence of small amounts of asbestos, arsenic, and even *Giardia lamblia* in our drinking water. But with ozone and particles, the government is headed toward zero tolerance. That makes no sense.

If more is to be done with car and truck emissions, we know of a way to cut them by up to 50 percent—now. Studies show that 10 percent or fewer of the cars on the road emit 50 percent or more of the vehicle emissions. Remote sensing may be able to identify those vehicles; in any event, inspection and maintenance programs will reveal them. Owners can take them in for repairs and up to half the emissions would be gone—a miracle! Of course, it would take political courage to implement that policy, and people would really have to care about emissions to support it.

American businesses and industries, including especially the automakers, are struggling with the aftermath of the Clean Air Act Amendments of 1990; if they succeed in meeting all the requirements of that monumental compilation of complex requirements, the air will be cleaner yet. What the nation needs now is a regulatory timeout during which a coordinated, rationalized, and above all prioritized approach to regulation can be developed. As part of that effort, Congress could perform a public service by directing the EPA to retain the national ambient air quality standards as they are, and to get on with research to determine what else needs to be done. This would make common sense. So would a little reform of the EPA and a "take-back" by Congress of some important legislative powers it has given away to the bureaucracies over the years.

Unfortunately, common sense is too rare a virtue in regulatory Washington. Perhaps this is so because America is so rich that it can absorb high regulatory costs, while most Americans can still have what they want and need. In these circumstances, there is little motivation to become exercised over excessive regulation. But when their needs and wants do become threatened, Americans will react. A little common sense now could avoid an excessive backlash later. More important, many Americans' needs are *not* being met today. They might benefit if a smaller portion of our resources went to marginal or unnecessary regulatory programs. Unfortunately, their voices—the voices of small business, labor, farmers, and the poor—are not being heard in this debate.

· 15 ·

EPILOGUE

How we "get around" in the future is tied directly to the issues discussed in the preceding chapters: the regulation of automobile fuel economy, the proposed international regulation of carbon dioxide through energy rationing, and the control of automotive emissions. How we deal with these issues will determine the future of the motor vehicle as we know it.

Fuel Economy. Corporate average fuel economy (CAFE) regulation is a classic case of government failure, accompanied by harmful, unintended consequences. Conceived in the heat of a temporary crisis to achieve the elusive objective of energy independence, CAFE not only failed in its goal but has resulted in the production of cars that are lighter, smaller, and consequently less safe. Vehicle-fuel economy is best determined by the marketplace, leaving unrestricted the customers' right to buy cars that meet their needs, as they see them, and not cars that the government deems are good for them. CAFE puts the government between the citizen and the car of his or her choice. It should be repealed.

Global Warming. Global climate change (specifically global warming) is the new rationale for CAFE. The proposed international treaty to attempt to regulate the world's climate is testimony to the ego and delusion of those who believe they are ready and able to do so. It is admirable, even essential, to endeavor to understand the incredibly complex interactions among the Earth's atmosphere, biosphere, and oceans and the relationship of these systems to the sun. Assertions that these relationships are clearly enough understood, that climate disaster is upon us, and that we can avoid climate change by implementing a radical, internationally administered program of energy rationing (affecting mainly the United States) strain both common sense and the imagination. To invest the central government and interna-

186

tional regulators with the power to prescribe who may use carbon-based fuel (which represents 90 percent of the world's energy source) is a frightful prospect, lined with contesting special interests and the promise of disastrous unintended—and intended—consequences. A full-blown campaign is underway to "educate" us about the horrors that will come without this plan. This campaign has the full force of the U.S. government behind it. To counter it will take the kind of sustained effort the private sector is hesitant and generally unprepared to undertake. The potential effect on the national and world economy, on jobs, and on the way we live, along with the overwhelming uncertainties about the science, should ensure that this plan is rejected—but only if the facts are broadly understood by enough people.

Climate change has always been with us. Research, however, is warranted. It is good to expand our understanding. It is not good to sign on to a premature action plan that will mean the greatest leap yet into government regulation.

Vehicle Emissions. Motor-vehicle emissions are classic externalities. They create costs (health effects), but since the market provides no "invisible hand" to ensure that these costs are paid or eliminated, some outside intervention appears to be necessary to control emissions at an appropriate level. The problem of defining the appropriate level, however, presents intractable differences. The government has been regulating emissions for more than thirty years, and auto emissions have been more than 95 percent eliminated. The problem is not whether governments should have a role—it is that governments, and all those other interests whose futures are tied to the pursuit of the regulatory process, do not know when to declare victory, or cannot, for their own welfare, afford to do so. Zero emissions becomes the holy grail, no matter the costs, the feasibility, or, most important, the need. Before any additional regulation of emissions from the automobile is considered, independent research of the need is warranted: specifically, research into the nature and effects of particulate matter. When compared with other social and economic needs, does further expenditure of resources on auto emissions make sense? There is presently no reasonable case for more regulation.

Implementation of more stringent emission standards or fuel-economy rules for any reason, including the need to meet international treaty agreements to reduce carbon dioxide emissions, could mean the end of the motor vehicle powered by the internal combustion engine. This outcome would be comparable to a government rule in the early 1800s that would have outlawed the horse. The horse was replaced not by a government mandate but by the ingenuity of private inventors and developers. The role of the government was not to impede the use of the horse or of its successor, the automobile. Fortunately, efforts to block the new technology, with the Red

Flag Act and other regulation, were defeated by the overwhelming enthusiasm of humankind for this new technology that gave them mobility as they had never before experienced it. The inevitable replacement for the automobile as we know it today should arise through the same process. For government planners to drive the current technology off the road and to pick the winners and losers among competing technologies is a prescription for mischief.

Two Additional Key Issues

Two other issues crucial to the future of the car have not yet been discussed in this volume. They are not directly related to the internal combustion engine, and they will continue to require attention no matter how vehicles may be powered. The first is safety; in terms of deaths and injuries, it is by far the most important of all five. The last of the five is the roadway. Without adequate roads and streets, the vehicle, as General Motors' Albert Bradley once said, is as useless as a canoe in the desert. These issues require a separate volume, but it is appropriate to discuss them briefly.

Motor Vehicle Safety. The United States has one of the lowest traffic fatality rates in the world—1.8 deaths for every 100 million miles of vehicle travel in 1994. Only Great Britain and Sweden had slightly lower rates than had the United States. (Japan's rate is 2.6, Germany's is 2.9, Poland's is 9.1, and the rate in some countries is in the double digits.) Nonetheless, in the United States, more than 40,000 people die in traffic accidents annually. These are not statistically estimated deaths. They are the deaths of family members, friends, and neighbors—people we know. More than 65 percent are under forty-five years of age. These deaths are tragedies.

With the enactment of the National Highway Safety Act of 1966, the federal government took on the responsibility for regulating traffic safety. The law originated as a proposal by President Lyndon B. Johnson. It took on national momentum after a notable corporate public affairs debacle when, in early 1966, General Motors learned that trial lawyer Ralph Nader was about to publish a book attacking its small, innovative car, the Corvair. With home-office tunnel vision (there was no Washington government affairs staff), lower-level GM staff set off a chain of events that had inept private investigators tailing Nader into a Senate office building. The upshot was an apology from the president of GM, a settlement of a lawsuit by Nader for $425,000, and a more intrusive law than otherwise might have passed.

Was an intrusive law warranted? The traffic safety record is instructive. In the period from 1933 to 1937, the traffic-fatality rate averaged 15.55 per 100 million vehicle miles traveled. This dropped to an average of 11.49

in the 1937–1942 period. The 1943–1947 average rate was 10.52. By 1965, the rate had dropped to 5.54. This happened even as the numbers of vehicles on the road and number of miles traveled soared.

The lesson here is that dramatic progress in safety was made without government regulation. It happened because there were major improvements in vehicles and roads (and some improvement in driver skills). Huge advancements were made in brakes, structural integrity, lighting, handling, glazing, tires, and every other aspect of the vehicle. Competitive forces worked well, as cars evolved from rigid boxes to energy-absorbing structures; from experiencing frequent blowouts to having almost fail-safe tires; from using dangerous hard glass to using laminated glazing that gives way; from having dim lights to being equipped with sealed-beam headlights; from having open occupant compartments to offering enclosed, air-conditioned cabins (yes, safety is enhanced when the driver is cool)—and much more. All this happened before the professional activists were born and before a government safety bureau was a gleam in LBJ's eye.

Today, there are more than fifty major safety standards and some 1,400 to 1,500 requirements under those standards that must be met by manufacturers. Cars are safer today than they were in 1965, but most of the advances (for example, antilock braking systems) are not the result of regulations; many (for example, high-mounted rear stop lights) probably would have come without government regulation. Most safety standards were originally developed with the full cooperation of auto industry safety experts and were codifications of existing or emerging technology. Auto executives and engineers drive their own products with their own families, and it is foolish to suggest that they are not personally interested in greater safety. It is also foolish to suggest that safety has not been a competitive factor from the 1890s onward. From the time cars were first introduced, customers have looked for more safety features.

There is one prominent example, however, where government involvement has made a major difference, saving tens of thousands of lives. There is no doubt that state and federal government hastened the installation and increased the use of safety belts. The auto companies were slow to install belt systems. Designers found them aesthetically difficult. More important was the belief, supported by experience, that motorists would resist using safety belts, making them a useless expense. A few 1956 models came equipped with lap belts, and they were offered as options on others. They became standard equipment on the 1964 model-year passenger cars produced by major car makers, but usage rates were in the single digits.

"Consumer activists" led by Nader were not interested in belts. Nader wanted a car that assumed full responsibility for protecting the occupants. While it is theoretically possible to have a completely passive protection system, it has not turned out to be practical or workable. Nader was convinced the air bag was the answer. Not only is an air bag much less effective than belts; it turns out to have tragic, unintended consequences. While industry and government experts estimate that the air bag, as a supplement to belts, can reduce fatality risk by an estimated 10 percent, the National Transportation Safety Board says that government databases "preclude a proper evaluation of the effectiveness of air bags" because the information is not comprehensive or because the sample size is insufficient. We do know that, in some circumstances, air bags can kill occupants, belted or unbelted. The most vulnerable are children and adults of small stature. From 1990 through mid-1997, the deaths of eighty-three persons—forty-five of whom were children—have been attributed to air-bag deployments.

The entire air-bag issue needs and is undergoing an intense and continuous review—of the kind it was receiving before it became thoroughly politicized and the industry was driven to include air bags in its vehicles as standard equipment. The Harvard Center for Risk Analysis says that air bags are saving seventy-five drivers for every one killed by an air bag. The most vulnerable are short drivers and elderly drivers. For passenger side bags, the center says the best estimates are that a life (usually a child's) is lost for every five lives saved. Air bags should not be a mandatory requirement for vulnerable occupants. Deciding how to manage a device that saves lives but may also be lethal for members of an identifiable group is "sort of a Godly call that we normally leave to deities much more potent than ourselves," said Representative Billy Tauzin, chairman of the House Subcommittee on Consumer Protection, where hearings on air bags were held.[1]

Air bags should also not be fodder for those trial lawyers who seize on every opportunity to reach into the deep pockets of the productive elements of our economy. (Safety measures are in danger of being driven more by legal liability considerations than by what is good for the occupants.) Air bags have saved lives, but as devices that must explode to work, they are also intrinsically dangerous. Ultimately, it seems likely that better systems will be developed, perhaps as part of the intelligent vehicle–intelligent highway effort now underway, which is dedicated to the avoidance of accidents—clearly a preferable outcome.

The most important safety measure available to society today is the increased use of safety belts. According to the National Highway Traffic Safety Administration (NHTSA), lap-shoulder belts, properly used, reduce the risk of fatal injury to front-seat–passenger vehicle occupants by 45 percent. Failure to use belts results in an estimated 10,000 deaths and 200,000 injuries each year.

All states but New Hampshire have belt-use laws, but only eleven authorize primary enforcement that permits the police to cite car occupants for not wearing belts without first stopping them for another infraction. There is still resistance to belt-use laws as a limitation on personal freedom. As a Michigan doctor wrote, "What a strange kind of freedom this is. It's the freedom to risk fractures, paralysis, fatal bleeding, disfigurement, blindness, lifelong idiocy, and hopeless dependency. . . . to leave one's family grieving or worse, to become a hopeless perpetual burden upon them."[2] He went on to say that society is expected to see to it that, if injured, these freedom lovers are attended by emergency medical services, transported to hospitals, and treated in emergency rooms, perhaps displacing others who were less complicit in their injuries.

It seems reasonable to ask whether anyone not having sense enough to wear safety belts has sense enough to drive. Belt-use laws do limit freedom, just as do licensing requirements for drivers, stop signs, and other rules of the road. We should examine all such limits critically, but if they make good sense we should accept them. Effective belt-use laws make much more sense than do other government mandates that cost more and do less but are "passive." Belt-use laws are not prohibitions; they do not force us to forgo something we want or force us to do a disagreeable act. They do save lives and do not take any. The country ought to get on with strengthening the use laws on the books in forty-nine states. (As other states upgrade their use laws, perhaps New Hampshire, the Live Free or Die state, will serve to provide data on additional fatalities in a state with low belt use.)

There are other safety measures that need attention. Ricardo Martinez, head of NHTSA, says that aggressive driving is responsible for around two-thirds of traffic fatalities. (Aggressive driving is a staple of American movies; heroes and villains alike show us how it is done.) Alcohol is involved in about 40 percent of all traffic fatalities. (No one knows the degree to which the use of marijuana and other drugs is involved, but in a Tennessee study of crash-injured drivers, drugs other than alcohol were detected in 40 percent. In a Los Angeles study, marijuana and alcohol were detected in one-third of 440 drivers, aged fifteen to thirty-five, who were killed in crashes.)

Excessive or unsafe speed accounts for 16.5 percent of nonalcohol-related fatalities. Traffic accidents are the leading health problem for teenagers aged sixteen to nineteen, and 25 percent of those killed in that group were intoxicated. The accident rate for sixteen-year-old drivers is higher per mile driven than for drivers of any other age—and their accidents are much more likely to be serious. Seniors also pose safety problems. Reaction times slow with age, and nighttime glare becomes worse. Teenagers and drivers over seventy-five have the highest accident rates, with the teenagers at 11.8 percent and the seniors at 5.2 percent. Some states are having success with graduated licenses for beginning drivers—for example, good only for daytime driving for the first months. Special driving classes for seniors, with lower insurance premiums as the incentive, can help. Rigorous policing and sentencing, as well as preventive programs, are reducing the problem of drunk driving and are beginning to be used more aggressively with aggressive drivers.

It makes good sense to devote resources to these and other factors that are contributing to the deaths of more than 40,000 people annually. When the Environmental Protection Agency is stampeding the country into spending billions in a dubious program to address 15,000 "premature deaths," it should be the nation's business to redirect some of these funds to the very concrete problem of traffic safety.

Highways. When Moses was leading his people out of Egypt, the Bible tells us, he petitioned for permission to pass through Edom, assuring the king, "We will keep to the king's highway without turning right or left." The king refused permission, and there being no other road around Edom, Moses was obliged to lead his people through the wilderness. Of the many lessons derived from that account, one is that roads have been vitally important since the dawn of recorded history—not just since the coming of the car. Another lesson is that without adequate roads, our destiny may be to wander very slowly through the wilderness of near-gridlock congestion, finding our employment and social opportunities stifled by a lack of flexible transportation.

Archaeologists have found stone-paved streets in Ur dating back to 4000 B.C. and brick paving in India believed to date back to 3000 B.C. The Assyrians, around 1200 B.C., built a major road connecting their capital of Susa, via Nineveh, to Sardis in western Turkey. The Romans built and maintained an incredible road system from Britain to Jerusalem (until they were overrun by the Vandals, who put a stop to road building). Marco Polo traveled the Silk Road, the means for technology transfer between the Mediterranean and China for centuries. In parts of Europe, building and repairing roads and bridges were considered by the church as charitable acts.

In the New World, the fifteenth-century Incas built a road system running from present-day Peru to lower Chile that was later praised as superior to European roads of the time. In the United States, Jefferson's Treasury secretary, Albert Gallatin, proposed a program of building roads that "would become a clear addition to the national wealth" (this, without cost-benefit analysis). The National Road was begun in 1811, ultimately reaching Illinois (mired in contractor fraud). In 1892, the League of American Wheelmen (bicyclists) combined with the farmers of the National Grange to found the National League for Good Roads.

The Assyrians, Romans, Incas, and perhaps Moses would have said that one of the primary reasons for having a government was for it to build and maintain roads and bridges. The farmers and bicyclists of America felt the same way. Road building in America was a principal activity of local, county, state, and national government, fully supported by the people.

Woodrow Wilson, an ardent motorist (Edith Bolling Galt accepted the widowed president's marriage proposal on a ride through Rock Creek Park in the White House Pierce-Arrow), supported a plank in the Democratic platform adopted in 1916 that said, "The happiness, comfort and prosperity of rural life, and the development of the city, are alike conserved by the construction of public highways."[3]

In 1955, President Dwight D. Eisenhower, credited with getting the Interstate Highway System underway, said, "Together, the united forces of our communication and transportation systems are dynamic elements in the very name we bear—United States. Without them, we would be a mere alliance of many separate parts." Surprisingly, at a June 26, 1996, dinner commemorating the fortieth anniversary of the Interstate Highway System, Vice President Al Gore praised President Eisenhower, saying, "He came home [from World War II] and then helped pave the way so Americans could be freer still, enjoying among other freedoms the freedom to travel America on modern highways that are safe and that are now the marvel of the world."

Unfortunately, this "marvel" is rapidly deteriorating. By the government's own analysis, about 33 percent of the rural Interstate Highway System and about 40 percent of the urban interstate is in poor or mediocre condition. Another 24 percent of each is in fair condition. Counting the interstate, America has a total of 3.9 million miles of streets, roads, and highways, of which 28 percent are in poor-to-mediocre condition and another 31 percent are listed as fair. Good roads save lives. The fatality rate on the interstate is 0.86 per 100 million vehicle miles, compared with 1.99 on all other roads. Having more lanes is important. In 1995, 77 percent of fatal crashes occurred on two-lane roads. About 32 percent of the nation's 574,671 bridges (more than twenty feet long) are structurally or functionally deficient and in need of rehabilitation or replacement.

Between 1970 and 1995, private vehicle registrations in the United States went up by 35 percent. The number of licensed drivers rose by 58 percent. Vehicle miles driven increased by 67 percent. (A big chunk of this mileage was rolled up by women. From 1983 to 1990, miles driven by women grew by 49 percent. Miles driven by men grew by only 18 percent. It seems unfair that just as women are driving more miles, the roads are being permitted to deteriorate.) In that same period, miles of roadway in America went up all of 0.05 percent. The fact that about 30 percent of our major urban roads are rated as congested should come as no surprise. (Neither should it be surprising that Washington, D.C., is rated the second-most severely congested city in the country.)

Every man, woman, and child in America is dependent in some important way on the road system. It is the way we get to work, to school, and to virtually every place we want to go. Virtually everything we eat, wear, or use spent some time on the highway in a truck on its way to us. Yet we cannot maintain our roads, much less build additional ones. The reasons for this paralysis are varied. Most construction projects of any kind face the NIMBY (not-in-my-back-yard) challenge. People simply do not want the disruption of a highway project or other public works in their neighborhood. That is understandable, but it is also disastrous for our political system. If politicians will not bite the bullet and overcome the NIMBY obstruction, perhaps a court-appointed arbitration system with teeth could help more projects along.

Equally disruptive are the professional activists who see roads as just another way for people to drive their cars "needlessly." Their public arguments, however, take two basic forms. First is the assertion that building more road capacity just leads to more use of the roads. This is very much like saying that if you build houses, people will just fill them up. Or, if you make more clothes, people will just wear them. Or, if you grow more potatoes, people will just eat them. Somehow, when there is a demand for most of the good things in life, the supply increases. Why should that not be the case with roads? (The notion that we are "paving over America" is nonsense. The entire Interstate Highway System physically covers less than 0.08 percent of the 3.5 million square miles within our boundaries. France, the United Kingdom, Germany, and Japan each has more than twice as many miles of roads per square mile than has the United States.)

The second frequently made assertion is that new roads are not needed. Those assertions must be answered by the people who need more road capacity. That is not happening. Since the establishment of the Highway Trust Fund, the federal government has been taxing gasoline and other indicators of road usage (such as tires, trucks, trailers, and diesel). The more miles driven, the more of these highway-user fees the driver pays to fund the federal highway program on a pay-as-you-go basis. From these funds, the government allocates shares to the individual states (with much political heat being generated about the distribution formula) to build and maintain roads. This was the "contract with America" negotiated in 1956 by President Eisenhower and a Democratic Congress. It was the basis on which tax-loathing Americans bought into the gasoline tax. One result was the Interstate Highway System. Another result is that the American people began to assume that the roads they needed would come automatically from the trust fund, and from state funding through gasoline and other taxes or highway users. Since it was no longer necessary for voters to fight for roads, public pressure on elected politicians for other good things began to take precedence. It became a temptation for politicians to dip into the money collected from highway users.

Revenues from highway-user fees in 1996 were estimated at $31.5 billion, of which $6.5 billion went into the general fund to reduce the federal deficit. Another $2.6 billion was destined for mass transit funding. Smaller amounts were spent on bicycle paths and other programs—including new, federally financed granite curbs lining the potholed streets of Washington, D.C.; new roofs on horse barns at Indiana fairgrounds; restoration of artifacts from a ship salvaged off the Texas coast; and other such "transportation enhancements." As the diversions from highway purposes grew, public support for gasoline taxes dwindled. The contract was broken, and citizens had another reason to be cynical about government. Eventually they may again feel the need to fight for good roads. (The Washington-based Highway Users Alliance is a leader in focusing people on roadway improvements needed, as its slogan says, to Keep America Moving.)

The criticism of road-building programs as a subsidy of the automobile and truck deserves a response. The flippant answer is that roads no more subsidize the motor vehicle than they subsidized the sandal in the time of Moses or the horse for the next several thousand years. If the public road system represents a subsidy of any kind, it is, at least in the United States, a subsidy of virtually every man, woman, and child in the country. If something benefits all citizens and if it is a "good" that has been supplied by civil organizations since the beginning of history, can it be a subsidy? Even the very few citizens who may enter a car only rarely still depend on the roads for the transport of their food and everything else they use.

Nonmotorists who use rail mass transit are the truly subsidized. No such rail system comes close to paying for its operating costs, much less paying off the investment in its construction and maintenance. A study by Professor Martin Wachs of UCLA found that each time a rider boards the Blue Line in Los Angeles, the taxpayers contribute around $12 in subsidy. Worse yet is the Metrolink, a wonderful rail system radiating out from Los Angeles to Riverside and other cities. Each of its riders paid (at the time of the survey) $4.50 for a one-way trip, and the taxpayers picked up a tab of $26.50 in subsidy for the ride. Civil rights activists charged that the Los Angeles Metropolitan Transportation Authority was starving the bus lines that served minorities and the poor in order to subsidize "white, relatively wealthy rail commuters," according to the Environmental Defense Fund, which helped obtain agreement from the authority to reallocate funds to buses. Even with the subsidies, rail systems haul only a tiny percentage—about 1.5 percent—of America's commuters.

For those who would still question highway financing, a look at a few numbers may help. In 1994, the total amount of revenue collected by federal, state, and local governments from motor vehicle users was nearly $142 billion, according to an analysis by Rayola Dougher for the American Petroleum Institute. Most of this—$87 billion—came from traditional road-user taxes and fees, including fuel excise and sales taxes, vehicle license and registration fees, tolls, and so forth. Also, more than $55 billion was collected from vehicle sales taxes, vehicle property taxes, and miscellaneous fees. (Often these kinds of taxes are levied at a higher rate, and sometimes are exclusively levied, on motor vehicles.)

In the same year, road investments at the federal, state, and local level totaled only $82 billion. Capital outlays for roads took $42.4 billion; maintenance and traffic services claimed $23.6 billion; administration and research took $8.4 billion; and law enforcement and safety used $7.7 billion. These expenditures left nearly $60 billion for nonroad uses such as subsidizing mass transit, reducing the federal deficit, and general government funding. There is some road funding from general funds, but if all the highway user fees were dedicated to roads, no general fund or property tax funding would be necessary. In 1994, all federal, state, and local road investment could have been paid for from highway user fees alone, with $4.5 billion left over.

There are ways other than with government funding to build roads. In colonial America there was no funding for roads other than from tolls. Turnpikes were the only overland means of transporting goods or traveling until competition from the railroads forced them out of business. Toll roads came back in the late 1930s with the Merrit Parkway, the Pennsylvania Turnpike, and later, the New Jersey Turnpike and others. The Interstate Highway System, at congressional insistence, was funded on a pay-as-you-go basis from gasoline and other highway user taxes, and fees and toll roads again took a back seat.

Today, privately built toll roads are again appearing, with mixed success. Highly successful is the privately funded four-lane automated toll road built in the median of State Route 91 in Orange County, California. Around 26,000 drivers a day pay up to $2.75 to reduce their fourteen-mile–commute time from the north end of the Costa Mesa Freeway to the Riverside County line by about twenty minutes. (Americans may be easy spenders of resources, but they can be misers when it comes to time.) Using the congestion pricing concept, the California Private Transportation Company charges 25 cents to drive the road in the middle of the night and $2.75 during rush hour. In Virginia, a more ambitious project, the Dulles greenway, running fourteen miles from Dulles Airport through sparsely populated countryside to Leesburg, Virginia, was built by a private company after obtaining enabling legislation from the state and buying the right-of-way from private landowners. Not a financial success today, there is a reasonable expectation that, in a decade or so, the greenway may be heavily traveled.

Roads supply a public good, and the traditional supplier of that good— government—is not meeting the demand. While there is little reason to believe that toll roads will meet more than a fraction of the national needs, it should be the public policy of the states and the federal government to place no barriers in the way of private road building. Entrepreneurs have surprised the world too many times to count them out in this field.

Meanwhile, however, the government's road program needs attention. According to federal government reports, in 1997, the investment in highways will be $20 billion less than the amount needed to maintain their current status, and $40 billion less than is needed to improve them. At the same time, $12 billion of the federal user taxes collected for the Highway Trust Fund will not be allocated to the states. That money will be withheld to subsidize mass transit and to help cover the federal budget deficit. More than $20 billion of trust fund revenue has been withheld over the years to mask the true size of the deficit, which means that it exists only on paper. Although it is less well known, the Highway Trust Fund faces the same skepticism as the social security trust fund. Will it be there when it is needed? Or, like Moses and his people, will future generations be in a wilderness without the roads they need?

Future Mobility

The problems facing the American motorist—many of them government related—seem daunting. We may find, however, that some very good engineers and scientists are on the way to freeing us from the threats of doom of the would-be climate managers, permitting us to feel good about the sky again, developing ways to avoid accidents, and guiding us past the roadway impasse. In sum, if the government would not get in the way, we might have all these good things and our personal mobility at the same time.

Under the umbrella of something called "intelligent transportation systems" (ITS), many exciting innovations are emerging. ITS (formerly the Intelligent Vehicle–Highway System, IVHS) is a concept, not an organization. The U.S. Department of Transportation (DOT) has established an ITS Joint Program Office, and the government is spending about $250 million a year on related programs. At the same time, the private sector has organized the Intelligent Transportation Society of America (ITS America). It is officially a "federal advisory committee" to the DOT, with a board of directors that includes a mixture of private- and public-sector members. Nearly 100 private firms, the federal government and 118 state and local governments, and 30 universities are associated with ITS America. The amount spent by the private sector is unknown and probably unknowable, because so many proprietary activities also fit under the ITS umbrella.

The ITS mission is simple: to overcome congestion and get people to their destinations faster and more safely. Side benefits include lower emissions and higher fuel economy. Technologies range from low-tech improvements in street signs to the high-tech concept of turning your driving over to a "smart car" and a "smart highway."

Public transportation. One of the five areas of ITS activity is public transportation. In ITS terms, "route deviation" and "demand-responsive modes" hold significant promise. The flexibility of bus service permits route changes as demand shifts. Demand-responsive jitney services, local buses, and shared-ride taxis, used effectively in Manila, Mexico City, the Caribbean, and elsewhere, show promise but have been stifled by regulations or prohibitions designed to protect the monopoly status of public-transit systems or taxi-fleet operators. Breaking through these regulatory barriers is in the public interest.

Traffic management. Another major ITS activity, traffic management, attempts to establish the order and lanes in which cars, trucks, cyclists, and pedestrians may proceed most efficiently. Signaling is the most obvious tool for this purpose. While fixed signals such as stop signs, traffic lights, location identifiers, and lane markers can be improved by better placement and clearer messages, major innovations have been made in dynamic road signaling that can be adjusted as driving conditions change. Traffic engineers, receiving current traffic data, can send messages to travelers via electronically changeable road signs or message boards, by remote control. They can reset traffic-light timing, reverse directional signals to change two-way streets to one-way, and otherwise redirect traffic in keeping with ever-changing conditions.

Houston, Texas, does many of these things through its Transtar center, and other cities have similar programs. But too often public officials neglect these relatively simple technologies in their budgets—and commuters do not object. Peter Brown, editor of *Automotive News,* says "Americans could improve their [transportation] system by half tomorrow morning with just a little simple information at almost no cost." But, he says, "they show no demand" for it. "When they drive their cars," he adds, "Americans are sheep, albeit angry sheep."[4] The Institute of Transportation Engineers estimated that 74 percent of the signalized intersections in America's urban areas needed upgraded physical equipment or improved signal timing.

Surveillance of traffic by video can enhance remote control and can help with incident detection. Systems that detect an accident, pinpoint its location, and dispatch assistance not only assist the injured but also smooth the traffic flow by enabling swifter removal of disabled vehicles. Improved management of incidents is likely to provide the highest immediate payoff for ITS by reducing the effects of accidents on hundreds of thousands of road users.

Rigorous enforcement of well-conceived traffic codes is necessary but is often neglected by police, who are overwhelmed by felonies. In New York City, however, stepped-up enforcement and prosecution for petty crimes (including traffic violations) helped reduce the crime rate, both by setting a tone that discourages all crime and by finding that many perpetrators of petty offenses are often wanted for major crimes. But technology and laws are not enough. Ultimately, efficient traffic management depends on civility. There is no substitute for a culture in which respect for others and for the community will move people to do the right thing, even when not required by law.

Traveler information systems. The more exciting ITS activity is in traveler information systems. Navigation and communication systems, already offered in upscale vehicles, tie the driver into the global positioning system (GPS) satellite technology. The GPS enables the vehicle to retrieve information from a satellite that can establish exactly where it is at any time. With this information and through the use of computer databases, navigation systems can then tell the drivers exactly how to get to other specific locations. Just punch in the address and let the navigation unit tell you how to get there. When tied in with a cellular phone system, these units also make it possible to ask for and receive directions to avoid or escape from traffic bottlenecks and hazards. (Marital friction is also reduced, since there need be no husband-and-wife debates about stopping the car to ask for directions.) These units can signal when a vehicle is stolen and can assist the police by tracking it. When a crash occurs, they can automatically, or at the direction of the driver, summon emergency assistance or roadside help. This security feature seems to be the most attractive to American consumers.

Hundreds of thousands of car-navigation devices are sold each year in Japan, where traffic is heavily congested and street addresses difficult to find. In the United States, they are available on Cadillacs, Oldsmobiles, and Lincolns and soon will be more broadly offered as options. How many Americans will pay for the cellular-phone direct-link system or for the expensive liquid-crystal display (LCD), the databases, and the computer is still an open question. Marketing this technology will be much easier if current efforts are successful in adding the capability of receiving continuous, real-time information about traffic conditions and specific directions for getting to a destination in the most efficient way. When drivers can learn about traffic conditions and divert to uncongested routes, they will save fuel and time and will reduce emissions—and psychological wear and tear. This rerouting ability will enable Americans to use efficiently the vast network of uncongested streets and roads they pay for but are not using, for lack of knowledge or effective travel management.

Commercial vehicle operations. Trucks carry around 78 percent of the freight (by dollar value) in America and commercial vehicle operations will benefit from any ITS activity that provides for more efficient traffic and travel management. Additionally, technologies exist that can weigh trucks while in motion, pay tolls electronically without requiring a stop, and provide other electronic data interchanges that reduce paperwork. These measures make it possible to cover more "loaded miles," a significant savings to truckers and their customers.

Advanced collision avoidance systems. Safety belts, energy-absorbing structures, and other post-crash technologies are good, but it is better to avoid the crash altogether. This is the mission of advanced collision avoidance systems, using roadside and in-vehicle electromechanical and communications devices. Collision warning devices and blind-spot detectors are already on the market. Vehicle-control systems use sensors to gather information about velocities, travel paths, and conditions around the vehicle. Computers analyze the data and decide when to intervene by sending a signal to a control device that temporarily takes control of the vehicle—for example, by reducing speed or stopping the vehicle to avoid a crash. One system in use on some school buses is a radar-based unit that permits the driver to view the front and left side of the bus to ensure that no children are in the area. Another system now installed on some vehicles is "intelligent cruise control," which senses when the vehicle is too close to the traffic ahead and cuts off the device. A version of that system signals truck drivers when they come too close to another object. The critical factor in these systems is the sensor, which today is either laser- or radar-based. Cost is a major problem, and continuous research and development is key to making the systems affordable.

Automated highway system. Related to these control systems is the automated highway system (AHS), the most far-sighted project authorized by Congress under the ITS umbrella. The mission is to improve mobility so that people and goods may travel from their origin to their destination in an efficient, reliable, and safe way. Key objectives are virtually to eliminate fatalities, to reduce injuries while the vehicle is under automated control, and to double or triple highway capacity, with closer spacing and smoother flow (by eliminating "rubbernecking" and reducing the "accordion effect" in traffic). Mobility improvements are to come from more predictable trip times and more reliable travel in poor weather, and from permitting drivers to do other tasks while traveling. For the environment, eliminating speed-ups and slow-downs will cut pollutants significantly and will improve fuel mileage. What may make these objectives possible is uniform communication from vehicle to vehicle and from vehicle to infrastructure (highway).

No one sees automated highways as a substitute for the interstate. The plan is to make them available as options in selected congested areas for a motorist with a properly equipped vehicle who, when electronically checked in (perhaps after a pre-check of systems before leaving home), could enter the "smart" highway and turn the driving task over to the vehicle-highway system until he or she exits and, again, takes charge. The existing road system would be available for those who do not want to leave their driving to the computer.

To accelerate development, a cooperative agreement was signed in December 1994 between DOT's Federal Highway System and nine "core participants" (Bechtel, General Motors, Carnegie-Mellon University, Caltrans [California Department of Transportation], Delco Electronics, Hughes, Lockheed Martin, Parsons Brinckerhoff, and the University of California-Berkeley PATH Program), forming the National Automated Highway System Consortium (NAHSC).[5] Since then, 112 others have joined as associate participants, including Toyota and Honda (but not Ford or Chrysler), as well as the transportation departments in Colorado, Virginia, Michigan, California, and other states.

From August 7 through 10, 1997, the NAHSC conducted Demo '97, a demonstration project mandated by Congress to showcase advances in automated highway technology. The events included the "platooning" of a line of eight Buick LeSabres, driving 60 miles an hour only 21 feet apart, while the drivers had both hands off the steering wheel and their feet off the accelerator and brakes. This hands-and-feet–free drive was done on a 7.6-mile stretch of Interstate 15 outside San Diego, California, using lanes built years ago by California's transportation department (Caltrans) to be used as reversible high occupancy vehicle (HOV) lanes during rush hours and as a proving ground during the middle of the day and on weekends. For the demonstration, a system of magnets was imbedded in the road and used to guide the magnetometer-equipped Buicks, keeping them each a car-length's distance apart at highway speeds. The magnetometer detects the magnetic field and, using software, signals the steering device to keep the vehicle on the correct path. Proper spacing is maintained by using a microwave radar transmitter mounted in the front of the vehicle. Platooning may be key to efficient utilization of limited road space; it can potentially double or triple road capacity.

Related technologies demonstrated at Demo '97 included an adaptive cruise-control system that senses vehicles ahead and alters speed appropriately; obstacle-collision avoidance that employs radar to "see" obstacles and other vehicles and then warn the driver or actually brake the vehicle; and lane keeping, a system using video cameras or sensors to track magnets or radar-reflective tape attached to the road and warn drivers when the vehicle drifts across a lane boundary. Because vehicles today are equipped with cruise control, electronic brakes (antilock brake systems), and in some vehicles, electronic steering (drive by wire), the additional expense of AHS on-board communication systems should not be too great. The major addition will probably be a radar or laser device for detecting obstacles.

Putting electronic devices in cars is something the vehicle makers can do on their own, for profit. The vehicle electronics market, already large, is expected to burgeon in the years ahead. The smart highway, however, is another matter. Except in rare instances (such as California Route 91's privately financed lanes), highways are the preserve of state and local governments, with assistance from the federal government. Making them "smart" will require a hefty public investment, which means that politics will rule. Also, there is a chicken-and-egg dilemma. Car makers will not add complex and costly devices without a roadway that works with them, and governments will be loath to build those highways unless there is good reason to believe that people will buy the smart cars—and use them on the smart highway. Inevitably, the critical decision is political, and those wanting the benefits of the AHS will find it necessary to become politically active and make their case to the public.

More difficult than the technical problems may be the job of convincing people to give up control of their car. Americans may not stand for it. For most people, driving is not just a necessary task; they positively enjoy it. Editorializing eloquently on the subject, the *Washington Post* said, "For the truth is that driving has never been just another bit of drudgery—like washing clothes by hand—to be done away with at the first opportunity. It's a part of people's personality, a skill to be mastered, a duty even—although admittedly many people do a horrible job of it."[6]

Trust is also a problem. People will initially want a perfect, fail-safe system; unfortunately, perfection is unattainable. As *ITS World* magazine says, it is time to make the public aware that it already trusts automated transportation. As Robert Llaneras, who works on human factors with ITS America, told *ITS World*, "Many planes land on full automatic in adverse weather conditions," and are actually safer doing so.[7] (In view of the risks, nonetheless, law firms have been asked by ITS researchers to look into the issues of liability. No doubt the trial lawyers association is doing the same.) It may well turn out that the concepts being explored today will not be accepted in the marketplace, or that some technology we have yet to see will take us in entirely new directions. But that is no justification for inaction.

The automated highway may turn out to be an internationally competitive issue. The Europeans are concentrating on commercial vehicle operations in their Promote-Chauffeur program and are planning to demonstrate platooning technologies to move freight in convoys of trucks. The Japanese are moving ahead swiftly in their AHS program. According to U.S. AHS project manager James Rillings, the Japanese minister of construction has studied the U.S. program, set up a similar one, and obtained four to five times the funding. (Japan provided $105 million for AHS research for the 1997 fiscal year, as compared with U.S. funding of $22 million.) The Japanese have already platooned an eleven-car fleet, using collision avoidance and lane-departure prevention equipment, and they are looking at deploying a section of automated highway in the year 2005. With their love of electronics and gadgets—and their heavily congested roads—the Japanese consumers may pull their vehicle companies and drive their government faster than the Americans in this field. But when conditions become intolerable, the Americans are likely to move with great energy and determination. They will ultimately insist on having their personal mobility and the vehicles and infrastructure that give it to them.

Looking Ahead

There are dangers ahead. But the greatest threat to our personal mobility (and many other aspects of our lives) comes not from those things we read about in the newspapers or hear on television. The greatest threat comes from a fear of the future. Looking ahead, we have two options. One is to join with those who believe that we have reached the pinnacle of human development and that it is now necessary to put government restraints on all human impulses, including mobility. They agree with the Duke of Wellington that the "common people" should not "move about needlessly." These advocates believe it is also time to manage the allocation of our resources, not by permitting people to buy and sell at prices determined by markets but by means of government planning, regulation, and rationing. Their vision is that we must prepare for the end.

This hunker-down philosophy is dangerous not just because it would limit our standard of living or quality of life—which it would. It is also the wrong mentality for dealing with the problems these advocates fear: global climate change, the environment, resource limits, energy uses, and population growth. Hunkering down will not prepare us for the future. Reaching out with imagination and daring, searching the universe, plumbing the depths of the oceans, continuing to push at the boundaries of human knowledge: looking for new ways to accommodate, not contain, "the desire to know" is the way to ensure the future. It is the vision that will encourage the discovery and development of solutions to our technical problems and will find the political, economic, and social structures that will take the human race to new levels of material, social, and spiritual accomplishment. The inward-looking, fearful vision anticipates a long, slow slide into oblivion. The better choice is to go forward, relishing the challenges and embracing the future.

When it comes to the motor vehicle, the negative view appears to be strong in academia, the news media, and much of the government. The fearful, it seems, make the most noise and get the most attention. As James Q. Wilson says, "The automobile, the device on which most Americans rely for not only transportation but mobility, privacy, and fun, would not exist if it had to be created today."[8] The fearful and the control-obsessed would not permit it to happen. They would like to end its dominance today.

But, as Loren E. Lomansky has written,

> Because automobility is a mode of extending the scope and magnitude of self-direction, it is worthwhile. . . . Moreover, the value of automobility is strongly complementary to other core values of our culture, values such as the freedom of association, pursuit of knowledge, economic advancement, privacy, even the expression of religious values and affectional preference. . . . Automobile motoring is good because people wish to engage in it, and they wish to engage in it because it is inherently good.[9]

Personal mobility by automobile is good, but it is not an entitlement. Because mobility is a natural part of human life, people will insist upon it and, in the final analysis, will prevail. Before that happens, however, and until Americans find their voice on the issues of mobility, congestion could get much worse and regulation could further restrict our choice of vehicles and our ability to use them. If the American public wishes to continue to enjoy, without serious disruption, the benefits of mobility by automobile, it must make those wishes known to sitting and aspiring politicians, and must do so forcefully enough to make a difference. It can be done.

NOTES

CHAPTER 1: INTRODUCTION

1. The French Academy coined the word *automobile* to describe steam buses. Americans adopted the word to replace *horseless carriage*. A January 3, 1899, *New York Times* editorial attacked the word for "being half Greek and half Latin. [It] is so near indecent that we print it with hesitation." M. G. Lay, *Ways of the World* (New Brunswick, N.J.: Rutgers University Press, 1992).

2. John Lukacs, *Outgrowing Democracy* (New York: Doubleday & Company, 1984).

3. Robert Lacey, *Ford, the Men and the Machine* (Boston: Little, Brown and Company, 1986).

4. William Joseph Showalter, "The Automobile Industry: An American Art That Has Revolutionized Methods in Manufacturing and Transformed Transportation," *National Geographic Magazine*, October 1923. The article went on to say, "The motor vehicle has assumed the role of a highly efficient factor in our transportation system, touching the lives and promoting the welfare of America as few developments in the history of any nation have done."

5. Robert S. Lynd and Helen Merrell Lynd, *Middletown in Transition* (New York: Harcourt Brace and World, Inc., 1937), p. 265.

6. Alvin Toffler, *Future Shock* (New York: Bantam Books, 1970).

7. Steve Nadis and James J. MacKenzie, *Car Trouble* (Boston: Beacon Press, 1993), pp.1, 156, 171. This is one of a series of volumes constituting the World Resources Institute Guides to the Environment.

8. But as Brad Edmonson points out in *American Demographics*, June 1994, for many, "the trip from home or day care to the office is a rare opportunity to meditate in solitude, listen to music, or catch up with a book on tape." He added, "The truth is that work and home lives may be far more stressful than driving in heavy traffic."

9. B. Bruce-Briggs, *The War against the Automobile* (New York: E.P. Dutton, 1977).

10. *International Encyclopedia of the Social Sciences*, vol. 15 (New York: Macmillan, 1968), p. 270.

11. James Q. Wilson, "Cars and Their Enemies," *Commentary*, July 1997. Wilson is the Collins professor of management and public policy at UCLA.

CHAPTER 2: MILEAGE RULES

1. CAFE is one provision in an even more complex law—the Energy Policy and Conservation Act of 1975—which set up energy regulatory programs running from oil price controls to labeling water heaters and other appliances with energy consumption information.

2. Some CAFE advocates say there is no need to reduce vehicle size and weight. They say new technology will vastly increase mileage. Unfortunately, most technologies they suggest are already in use. Fuel injection, for example, was used in fewer than 1 percent of cars in 1975 and is now used in 100 percent. Front wheel drive went from fewer than 2 percent in 1975 to more than 80 percent by 1993. All manufacturers have used weight reduction to reduce fuel usage. If the advocates have found the magic formula for higher fuel economy, they should get it on the market, and make themselves rich.

3. These studies were not released as planned and, more than a year later, surfaced with a new "spin" suggesting that people driving larger vehicles are endangering those who are in smaller cars. The *New York Times* of June 11, 1997, headlined its story: "Sport Utility Vehicles Pose Growing Danger to Car Occupants." The implication is that everyone should "dumb down" and drive smaller cars, ignoring their vulnerability in all kinds of accidents, not just those with larger passenger vehicles.

4. Pietro S. Nivola and Robert W. Crandall, *The Extra Mile: Rethinking Energy Policy for Automotive Transportation* (Washington, D.C.: Brookings Institution, 1995), p. 41.

5. Ibid.

6. *Washington Times,* September 29, 1988.

7. *USA Today,* April 2, 1991.

8. *New York Newsday.*

9. *Orange County Register,* April 29, 1991.

10. *Detroit News,* February 24, 1992.

11. These activists and groups include Greenpeace, Center for Auto Safety, Worldwatch Institute, Friends of the Earth, the Sierra Club, the Natural Resources Defense Council, World Resources Institute, American Lung Association, Union of Concerned Scientists, Worldwatch Institute, and others.

12. Steve Nadis and James J. MacKenzie, *Car Trouble* (Boston: Beacon Press Books, 1993).

13. M.G. Lay, *Ways of the World* (New Brunswick, N.J.: Rutgers University Press, 1992), p. 138.

14. Daniel Carlson, with Lisa Wormser and Cy Ulberg, *At Road's End* (Washington, D.C.: Island Press, 1995).

15. Elsewhere in the city, he introduced one-way streets and, in effect, no-parking zones—evidence that congestion preceded the automobile.

16. Nicholas Cugnot of France is most often given credit for the first self-propelled vehicle. In 1771 he built a steam-powered tractor to move cannon for the military. Before that, in the 1600s, Fernando Verbiest, a Belgian Jesuit stationed at the Chinese imperial court in Beijing, was said to have demonstrated to the emperor the use of steam to blow on vanes attached to a wheel and thereby move a cart. Scottish inventor James Watt and others improved on steam power.

17. Peter Roberts, *Collector's History of the Automobile* (New York: Bonanza Books, 1978).

18. Ernest Henry Wakefield, *History of the Electric Automobile: Battery-Only Powered Cars* (Society of Automotive Engineers, Inc., 1994).

19. Ibid.

20. This early clash of the automobile with its critics had an odd result. Steam carriages were driven off the road but found a home on the rails. Tramways had existed for many years, with wooden rails accommodating horse-drawn cars. Now steam vehicles, developed first for the road, were adapted to iron rails. As some transportation historians have suggested, the automobile was not an offshoot of the railroad locomotive but was rather its ancestor.

21. In their book *New Deals* concerning the rescue of Chrysler from bankruptcy in 1979, coauthors Robert B. Reich (later President Clinton's first secretary of the Labor Department) and John D. Donahue wrote: "Since this measure [the oil price rollback] clearly would have destroyed any incentive to conserve fuel, Congress had tacked on a requirement that the auto companies improve their fleet average of gas mileage—the average mileage for all the cars they sold." They added: "Instead of letting higher fuel prices nudge consumers toward smaller cars and more parsimonious driving habits, Congress had assigned responsibility for oil conservation to the automakers."

22. *Christian Science Monitor,* May 22, 1985. Weidenbaum, a former chairman of the Council of Economic Advisers, is director of the Center for the Study of American Business at Washington University in Saint Louis, Missouri.

23. Signing EPCA was not helpful to Mr. Ford in his 1976 presidential election campaign in Texas and other oil states, which objected to the oil price rollback required by EPCA. Senator John Tower (R-Tex.) called it the "OPEC Relief Act of 1975." Governor Jimmy Carter took Texas and Louisiana and their 36 electoral votes. He won the presidency with 297 electoral votes, with 240 going to Ford. Without Texas and Louisiana, Carter would have had 261 and Ford would have won with 276. One more veto might well have helped his cause.

24. *Washington Post,* August 11, 1977.

25. *Automotive News,* March 24, 1997.

26. When President Richard Nixon announced his Project Independence in November 1973, he said, "Let us set as our national goal in the spirit of Apollo, with the determination of the Manhattan Project, that by the end of this decade we will have developed the potential to meet our own energy needs without depending on any foreign energy source." According to Daniel Yergen, "His staff had told him that the goal of energy independence by 1980 was impossible and suggested that it was thus silly to proclaim." Nixon, mired in the Watergate mess, went ahead with the announcement. See Daniel Yergen, *The Prize* (New York: Simon & Schuster, 1991).

27. Press release, Public Citizen, July 2, 1991.

28. In evaluating this "small is safer" theme, it is useful to note that in testimony before a U.S. House subcommittee (June 6, 1987), Dan Howell of the Center for Auto Safety said, "We don't have scientific or engineering staff. We are a citizens' group trying to evaluate the effectiveness of [NHTSA] just as any citizen might undertake to do."

29. *Scientific American,* vol. 271, December 1994.

30. The studies in this and the subsequent four paragraphs are the work of Leonard Evans and others, summarized in Evans's article, "Small Cars, Big Cars: What Is the Safety Difference?" from *New Directions for Statistics and Computing,* a journal of the American Statistical Association, Summer 1994. Evans is a safety engineer with General Motors and the author of *Traffic Safety and the Driver* (New York: Van Nostrand Reinhold, 1991).

31. Robert Q. Riley, *Alternative Cars in the 21st Century* (Warrendale, Pa.: Society of Automotive Engineers, Inc., 1994).

32. The most effective safety measure available is proper use of the safety belt. By buckling the lap and shoulder belt system, a driver reduces his or her fatality risk by around 42 percent, and does so without posing any serious side effects. Amazingly, Ralph Nader opposed state laws requiring people to buckle up (now in effect in forty-nine states) because, as he explained, he thought belt use laws might distract from his goal of requiring air bags. His priorities were badly flawed. (See *Barrons*, July 31, 1989.)

33. This seriously reduces the utility of the vehicle, especially for the soccer mom who may not be able to carry all her charges in the back seat. Small-statured adults are urged to sit as far back from the steering wheel as possible—hardly the best position for good driving control. For the expectant mother, the risk of being seated in front of an air bag is "being investigated," according to a June 13, 1997, *Washington Post* report.

34. People with limited incomes may still obtain the protection of size and weight by purchasing large used cars or used trucks, but if CAFE remains in force, the stock of large used cars will diminish over time.

35. With candor, Rick Wagoner, president of General Motors's North American Operations, says, "We have some products that inherently don't make money. It's not unique to us. Small cars are not profitable." *Automotive News,* January 13, 1997.

36. *Woman's Day*, October 24, 1989.

37. Peter Pestillo, Speech, Meeting of the Society of Automotive Engineers, April 1995.

38. *Automotive News,* May 26, 1997.

39. *Seattle Times,* June 18, 1996.

40. Since it was purchased by Ford Motor Company, Jaguar has not had to pay fines. Under the CAFE law, the mileage of the Jaguars sold in the U.S. is averaged in with the mileage of other Ford products produced abroad and sold in the U.S.

41. American car manufacturers have believed that the law requires them to file a product plan with the government that will result in meeting the CAFE standards and that, in our litigious society, planning to fall short of the standard would make them vulnerable to lawsuits. Foreign manufacturers have believed they would not have that problem and have regularly paid fines. The law also provides for a manufacturer to "earn" credits from past or anticipated exceedances of the standard and apply them, under specific rules, to make up for CAFE shortfalls in other model years.

42. Nivola and Crandall, *The Extra Mile.* The authors point out that "the fuel taxes required to reduce fuel consumption would not have as deleterious an effect on motor-vehicle safety as does the CAFE system. Higher fuel prices would reduce vehicle miles traveled, thereby reducing the need for as much downsizing as the CAFE law requires to obtain a decrement of fuel consumption. Lower VMT [vehicle miles traveled] and somewhat larger cars would combine to provide fewer fatalities than the current regulatory apparatus permits."

CHAPTER 3: CAFE, IMPORTS, AND JOBS

1. The slogan at General Motors, originated by long-time CEO Alfred P. Sloan, was, "A car for every purse and purpose."

2. Ed Gray, *Chrome Colossus* (New York: McGraw-Hill Book Company, 1980), p. 485.

3. Quoted in *Resources,* Spring 1995.

4. *Providing for Energy, Report of the Twentieth Century Fund Task Force on United States Energy Policy* (1977).

5. *Economist,* January 5, 1974. The article also suggested that muddled American energy policy was responsible for much of the problem. It said: "People forget that from 1963 right up to the early 1970s the 'oil question' in America meant that you should not allow Texan oil millionaires to make so much money. Indeed, it was this trendy populism in America in the past decade which created much of the present temporary energy 'crisis.'"

6. Ironically, human rights advocates helped prepare the way for the fundamentalist revolution by their strident criticism of the shah's government for being backward in such things as women's rights. When the shah left Iran on January 16, 1979, the women's rights that had begun to take hold in Iran were immediately reversed by the new regime.

7. Karl Hausker, "Automobile Fuel Efficiency Stalls in the 102d Congress," *Journal of Energy and Development,* Spring 1991. Hausker went on to say, "However, beginning in the early to mid-1980s, CAFE standards became binding and raised fuel economy above what would have been market-induced levels."

8. General Motors, News Release, July 9, 1980.

9. David Glasner, *Politics, Prices, and Petroleum* (San Francisco: Pacific Institute for Public Policy Research, 1985), p. 182.

10. Ibid.

11. Marina v. N. Whitman, Testimony, Senate Committee on Energy and Natural Resources, Subcommittee on Energy Regulation and Conservation, May 14, 1985.

12. Alfred C. Decrane, Jr., Speech, Executives Club of Chicago, November 17, 1995.

13. Chrysler, having just gone through the near-bankruptcy wringer and the government "bail-out," had dropped production of its large cars and did not face the same problems with CAFE. American Motors had CAFE and other problems and was near the end of its rope.

14. James J. MacKenzie and Michael P. Walsh, *Driving Forces* (World Resources Institute, 1990).

15. American Automobile Manufacturers Association.

16. Hausker, "Automobile Fuel Efficiency," p. 177. While U.S. manufacturers were reducing the size and performance of their luxury cars, the Japanese began bringing in larger, more powerful and less fuel-economical vehicles. Some, including the Nissan Infiniti, were legally classified as "Gas Guzzlers" under the U.S. tax laws.

17. Exchange rate fluctuations have a huge effect. For example, in November 1995, Toyota predicted that the dip in value of the yen from Y89.1 to Y100 to the dollar would increase its profits by $800 million in the second half of that year.

18. With their concentration on what the government was "commanding" in this period, U.S. manufacturers took their eyes off what the customer wanted. They built some cars that were not as good as they should have been and did so at great cost to their reputations.

19. MITI officials were not all unhappy with the restraints. As the principal "guide" for the Japanese private sector, MITI found that the VERs gave them substantially more power over the Japanese auto industry, something Japanese "industrial policy" advocates had long wanted. This was especially so since Honda had refused to stay out of the car business when MITI thought the industry was overcrowded in the 1960s.

20. The Japanese also brought highly efficient assembly and manufacturing processes with them, enabling more production with fewer workers. In the past decade, the high

value of the yen drove up the cost of Japanese-sourced components and the transplants increased their sourcing of components in the United States, thus increasing their U.S. employment. In more recent years, the rising value of the dollar has brought in more imports. The Japanese are well positioned to adapt to exchange-rate fluctuations and are flexible enough to do so. They have not been hospitable to American and other foreign manufacturers' efforts to secure the same positioning in Japan.

21. *Economist*, May 10–16, 1997.

22. *Washington Post*, January 30, 1985.

23. In the 1997 J.D. Power Initial Quality Survey (IQS), which measures problems reported in the first ninety days of ownership, the Chevrolet Lumina and Mercury Sable were in the top ten. Fewer than 1.5 problems per car separate the best from the worst in the total survey. The span of difference in quality when the IQS began was 3.4. Vic Doolan, president of BMW of North America, says, "The IQS is no longer of value to the customer." *Automotive News*, May 12, 1997.

24. The Japanese did not abandon their voluntary quotas until 1993. With their increasing U.S.-based production, the quotas had long since ceased to have any real effect. The Japanese, however, found value in announcing their continuance each year, which was dutifully, and naively, heralded in much U.S. press as another concession of the Japanese to American automakers.

25. Takashi Kitaoka, Speech, CEO Club of Boston, April 16, 1997.

26. *Washington Post*, July 16, 1997.

27. An international system of open trade can endure only when it is reciprocal. If any trading partner persists in keeping its market restricted, the system will eventually erode.

28. *Wall Street Journal*, April 1, 1997.

29. Professional activists see things differently. In an advertisement in the *Washington Post* of August 12, 1997, Greenpeace called on the CEO of Mobil Oil and on other oil companies to adopt the motto "No new oil." Greenpeace claimed to be "leading the fight to stop the oil companies from further exploration." Perhaps this view of the world is the reason membership in Greenpeace has dropped sharply in recent years.

CHAPTER 4: TURMOIL IN THE INDUSTRY

1. *Detroit News*, July 5, 1996.

2. *Tampa Tribune*, April 10, 1996.

3. *Detroit News*, April 8, 1996.

4. *New York Times*, March 19, 1997.

5. Robert B. Reich and John D. Donahue, *New Deals, The Chrysler Revival and the American System* (New York: Times Books, 1985).

6. Ibid.

7. *WARD'S Auto World*, December 1977.

8. *Seattle Times*, June 18, 1996.

CHAPTER 5: NEW GENERATION OF VEHICLES

1. With all regulatory programs, it is inevitably the consumer who is regulated, directly or indirectly. In her 1971 book *The Regulated Consumer*, Mary Bennett Peterson made this point in detail.

2. While it never got off the ground, President Jimmy Carter attempted to begin a joint research program with the auto industry. In May 1979, he met with leaders of the

American auto industry to discuss a program that would focus on such fields as thermo-
dynamics, combustion, structures, materials, control systems, friction, and wear. Agreement on the framework for the program could not be reached among the parties before
the end of Carter's term as president.

3. These statements are taken from the agreement accompanying a White House
press release on September 29, 1993.

4. Antitrust laws inhibited cooperation among competitors, including for research,
until 1993, when the National Cooperative Research and Production Act (NCRPA) was
passed, reducing antitrust risk for joint ventures of competitors working together on
precompetitive research and development projects.

5. *Public Citizen,* May-June 1994, p. 24.

6. WMAL-AM Radio, September 29, 1993.

7. In March 1997, Vice President Gore presented medals to members of a PNGV
team for progress they made in reducing oxides of nitrogen emissions from the diesel
engine, a long-time barrier to its use.

8. *Detroit News,* July 24, 1997.

9. *Los Angeles Times,* August 13, 1997.

10. *Automotive News,* April 21, 1997.

11. *Los Angeles Times,* August 13, 1997.

12. Since a fuel cell produces electricity and any fuel cell vehicle will be electric
powered, the experience gained by GM with its EV-1 should be useful in its fuel cell
program.

13. Robert Q. Riley, *Alternative Cars in the 21st Century* (Warrendale, Pa.: Society of
Automotive Engineers, Inc., 1994).

14. This determination by the joint government-industry PNGV should put to rest
any daydreams about the ability to increase fuel-economy requirements substantially
without substantial weight reduction.

15. *Los Angeles Times,* May 2, 1997. Professor Clark was responding to enthusiast
Amory Lovins, who foresees progress through "boldness, not incrementalism."

CHAPTER 6: THE FEAR VACUUM

1. Carbon dioxide is a natural product of the combustion of all carbon-based fuels
such as coal, oil, natural gas, and wood. When fuel combustion is not complete, other
products such as carbon monoxide, hydrocarbons, oxides of nitrogen, and particulate
matter are also emitted. They are already under strict government regulation. Up to 98
percent of these pollutants are removed from vehicle exhaust by control equipment such
as catalytic converters. Reduction of carbon dioxide emissions would require a reduction in the use of carbon-based fuel, such as, gasoline.

2. The Earth's atmospheric composition is estimated at around 75 percent nitrogen,
20 percent oxygen, 1 percent argon, 1–3 percent water vapor, and trace amounts of
carbon dioxide, hydrogen, neon, helium, krypton, and xenon.

3. Intergovernmental Panel on Climate Change, *Climate Change 1995: The Science
of Climate Change* (Cambridge, England: Cambridge University Press, 1996), p. 56.

4. *Emissions of Greenhouse Gases in the United States 1987–1994,* Energy Information Administration, October 1995. DOE/EIA-0573(87-94).

5. Carbon dioxide can be converted into carbon units by dividing by 44/12, or 3.67.
Most of the references in this book are in carbon or carbon equivalent.

6. *Washington Post,* August 20, 1997.

7. U.S. Department of Energy, *Emissions of Greenhouse Gases in the United States 1995*, Energy Information Administration, October 1996.

8. These numbers are based on IPCC estimates and are found in ibid.

9. IPCC, *Climate Change 1995*. This was the contribution of Working Group I to the Second Assessment report of the Intergovernmental Panel on Climate Change.

10. Intergovernmental Panel on Climate Change, *Climate Change 1994: Radiative Forcing of Climate Change* (Cambridge, England: Cambridge University Press, 1995), p. 30.

11. *New York Times*, March 25, 1997. Researchers from the California Institute of Technology and the Rand Afrikaans University in South Africa say that one of the key questions raised by "Snowball Earth" is how it thawed. When they ran the problem through current climate models, the models showed no way out of the frozen state. One of the lead researchers, Joseph L. Kirschvink, said this "makes you sit back and worry a little bit about what the models are predicting." He added, "If you don't know whether the Earth can survive an ice catastrophe, your models are not complete."

12. *Science*, vol. 272, May 24, 1996.

13. Get used to this new alphabet soup. New international agencies are likely to become as familiar as the EPA or the IRS.

14. IPCC, *Climate Change 1995*.

15. *Nature,* vol. 383, September 5, 1996.

16. This is a common problem with models (including impressive computer simulations), whether they are used to make economic predictions or to project climate change. They "work" if they provide predictions that are useful. As time goes by, if their predictions have not tracked what actually happened, they will be "tuned" to correspond to what happened or will be abandoned for a model that gives better predictions.

17. While at first he was well received in Rome, Galileo came to difficulty over his insistence that Copernicanism be recognized as truth, while the Church was willing to consider it as a hypothesis. Also, he exceeded his portfolio and engaged in reinterpreting Scripture, a function strictly reserved by the Church to the Church.

18. *Time*, December 18, 1989.

19. Senate Joint Resolution 88, March 16, 1989.

20. Henry Lansford, "A Climate Outlook: Variable and Possibly Cooler," *Smithsonian*, November 1975.

21. Lowell Ponte, *The Cooling* (Englewood Cliffs, N.J.: Prentice-Hall, Inc., 1976).

22. Rachel Carson's 1962 book *Silent Spring* is often cited as the first popular call for environmental action. It dealt with the effects of DDT and other pesticides.

23. Gregg Easterbrook, *A Moment on Earth* (New York: Viking, 1995).

24. Despite concerns about his doing so, President Bush attended the proceedings in Rio. The apparent assumption was that by attending and agreeing to the treaty (without goals and timetables), he could satisfy the major desires of the environmentalists and show his own concerns for the environment. This assumption ignores the agenda of the professional activists, who would lose their reason for existence if they appeared satisfied.

25. The Kellogg-Briand Pact, signed in 1928 by nearly all the nations of the world to "renounce war as an instrument of national policy," came just a few years before the most horrendous war in world history. We should learn from these experiences or the past will continue to be prologue.

26. Al Gore, *Earth in the Balance: Ecology and the Human Spirit* (New York: Houghton Mifflin Company, 1992). See especially p. 302.

27. Gore, *Earth in the Balance,* p. 360. Gore was especially harsh with the coal industry. Not surprisingly, the mine workers union is deeply concerned about the effect this issue will have on the jobs and lives of their members.

28. *Science,* vol. 268, April 14, 1995.

29. The developed nations will be expected to pay for this privilege. The environment minister of India called on them to contribute $100 billion a year to developing nations as "environmental rent" for "freeloading" on the backs of the third world. While there was no action taken on this demand, it was a reminder that hopes formed at Rio for financial aid for the developing countries have not been realized at the level anticipated and that demands will continue.

30. *China 2000,* April 1997.

31. *New York Times,* April 17, 1996.

32. A joke among national security experts in Washington is that when Jiang Zemin and Bill Clinton had parted, Jiang called his interpreter back and asked, "All right now, what did he really say?"

33. *Economist,* April 8, 1995.

34. Oil produces less carbon dioxide than coal, per unit of energy, and natural gas produces less than oil.

35. *Washington Post,* March 31, 1995.

36. *Financial Times,* March 13, 1997. Talking about winter storms and floods occurring in 1997, Karl said, "They reflect the types of events we expect to become more frequent as global temperatures increase." Not a crystal-clear formulation.

37. Testimony of Bill Cunningham, economist, AFL-CIO, before the Senate Subcommittee on International Economic Policy, June 26, 1997.

38. *Energy Daily,* June 20, 1996.

39. President Chirac did not add that unemployment in France has been more than twice as high as in the United States.

CHAPTER 7: SCIENCE OF CLIMATE CHANGE

1. "Experts Confirm Human Role in Global Warming," *New York Times,* September 10, 1995. Typical of the sensational treatment of this subject by journalists, or at least by headline writers, the story did not support the headline. It reported that the IPCC draft said data "suggest" that global warming "is unlikely to be entirely due to natural causes."

2. Intergovernmental Panel on Climate Change, *Climate Change 1995: The Science of Climate Change* (Cambridge, England: Cambridge University Press, 1996).

3. It is important to note that any estimates of atmospheric concentrations of carbon dioxide and other greenhouse gases before the 1950s or 1960s are based on analysis of the air found in small bubbles in ice cores drilled in a small number of sites in Russia and elsewhere. These are relatively new measuring techniques and almost certainly will be refined and improved.

4. *Consumer Reports,* September 1996.

5. Letter to the Editor, *Wall Street Journal,* January 15, 1996.

6. *Science,* vol. 271, February 2, 1996.

7. *Consumer Reports,* September 1996.

8. John R. Christy, e-mail to author, December 4, 1996.

9. Scientists can pay a price for dissent from the party line. Patrick J. Michaels at the University of Virginia writes that he took exception, in a *Washington Post* article, to the cataclysmic interpretation of climate change and said, "I was genuinely taken aback

when, within one day, my simple and obvious piece prompted a great deal of personalized invective at an EPA meeting. Senator Albert Gore, Jr. (D-Tenn.), to whom I gave generally favorable reviews, wrote a nasty little attack in the July 7 *Post*, and I began to realize that people were, shall we say, touchy about the issue." In Patrick J. Michaels, *Sound and Fury, the Science and Politics of Global Warming* (Washington: CATO Institute, 1992).

10. There is no record that anyone in 1890 correctly anticipated the changes in all these variables—especially in technology—that have occurred over the past 110 years. Of course, our experts today are much smarter than those back then and no doubt see these things clearly for the next 110 years!

11. Lester R. Brown, undated fund-raising letter from the Worldwatch Institute president, received November 1996.

12. While characterizing the Santer study as "probably one of the most convincing pieces of work done to date," Tim P. Barnett of the Scripps Institution of Oceanography says, "I'm not 100 percent convinced" that the greenhouse signal has been detected. He adds, "There's still a number of nagging questions." *Science*, July 5, 1996.

13. *New York Times*, November 5, 1991.

14. *Science*, August 4, 1995.

15. Sallie Baliunas, Testimony, Senate Committee on Energy and Natural Resources, September 17, 1995.

16. James Hansen, *Research & Exploration*, National Geographic Society, Spring 1993.

17. *Science*, March 17, 1995.

18. Ronald Bailey, ed., *The True State of the Planet* (New York: The Free Press, 1995).

19. Robert Cass, in Richard A. Kerr, "Greenhouse Forecasting Still Cloudy," *Science*, May 16, 1997.

20. This enigma brought to a friend's mind the 1960s popular song by Joni Mitchell: "I've looked at clouds from both sides now/ From up and down, and still somehow/ It's clouds' illusions I recall/ I really don't know clouds at all."

21. Jessica Mathews, *Washington Post*, September 3, 1996. Mathews, a former official of World Resources, Inc., made this point in her comments on "the sequencing of the entire genome of a strange organism" discovered near a vent on the ocean floor. "This eccentric beast," she writes, "flourishes at near boiling temperatures under pressures of 200 atmospheres, far beyond the sun's reach. All it needs to live is nitrogen, carbon dioxide and hydrogen, from which it makes methane (natural gas.)" She speculates that this discovery "might make it possible to produce natural gas as a renewable energy supply."

22. Francis Bretherton, *Oceanus*, vol. 32, Summer 1989.

23. Taro Takahashi, Pieter P. Tans, Inez Fung, *Oceanus*, vol. 35, Spring 1992. This is one of the most readable and helpful papers available on global warming.

24. The estimate of carbon dioxide released annually from the oceans was rather arbitrarily reduced by 10 billion tons from the estimate reported in the previous year's edition of this report. This reduction—larger than the total human-induced release—is another indication of how preliminary our understanding of these issues is.

25. Energy Information Administration, *Emissions of Greenhouse Gases in the United States 1995*, U.S. Department of Energy, October 1996. Natural processes in the oceans and land biosphere absorb all but 3.2 to 3.6 billion tons.

26. James D. Watkins, *Science*, August 1, 1997.

27. R.S. Nerem, *Science*, May 5, 1995.

28. Jessica Mathews, *Washington Post*, September 3, 1996.

29. In this certainty, environmental activists are not unlike some overly zealous guardians of national security, who attempt to keep the public from getting information that may not compromise security but might cause public opposition to pet projects.

30. Stephen Schneider, *Discover*, October 1989.

31. Kerr, *Science*, January 27, 1995.

32. Bretherton, *Oceanus*, vol. 32, Summer 1989.

33. Taro Takahashi, "The Carbon Dioxide Puzzle," *Oceanus*, Summer 1989.

34. Arthur Fisher, "The Model Makers," *Oceanus*, Summer 1989.

35. Ben Wattenberg, *Washington Times*, March 27, 1997.

36. Thomas R. Karl, "Global Warming Debate," *Research & Exploration*, vol. 9, Spring 1993.

37. Robert Repetto, *Washington Post*, June 12, 1997.

CHAPTER 8: JUST-IN-CASE MEASURES

1. *Washington Post*, January 14, 1996.

2. Many analysts attribute the relatively good U.S. record of economic growth to cheap energy. This is another factor cited against raising the price through taxes.

3. John Fedkiw, "The Evolving Use and Management of the Nation's Forests, Grasslands, Croplands, and Related Resources," U.S. Forest Service, United States Department of Agriculture, September 1989.

4. President's Council on Sustainable Development, *Sustainable America, A New Consensus*, U.S. Government Printing Office, February 1996.

5. Literacy, however, seems to have a negative effect. It takes slightly more than a million trees to produce the newsprint (seventeen trees per ton) used for America's Sunday newspapers alone.

6. Fedkiw, "The Nation's Forests."

7. Trees that become lumber used in construction of homes and other structures or used to make furniture also sequester large amounts of carbon dioxide. It is released only if the wood is burned or allowed to rot.

8. Linda A. Joyce, ed., *Productivity of America's Forests and Climate Change*, USDA Forest Service, General Technical Report RM-271, September 1995.

9. Energy Information Administration, U.S. Department of Energy, *Emissions of Greenhouse Gases in the United States 1995*, U.S. Government Printing Office, October 1996.

10. Carbon dioxide is not sorted out in the atmosphere by source. It is all essentially the same. Reference to "industrial carbon dioxide" is shorthand for the assumption that all this gas in the atmosphere that exceeds the amount recaptured by the oceans and biomass is human-induced.

11. Taro Takahashi et al., "Balancing the Budget, Carbon Dioxide Sources and Sinks, and the Effects of Industry," *Oceanus*, Spring 1992.

12. *Science*, July 18, 1997.

13. Intergovernmental Panel on Climate Change, *Climate Change 1995: Impacts, Adaptations and Mitigation of Climate Change: Scientific-Technical Analyses* (Cambridge, England: Cambridge University Press, 1996). This is the contribution of Working Group II to the Second Assessment Report of the Intergovernmental Panel on Climate Change.

14. James MacKenzie of the World Resources Institute, however, has suggested that

the world has already consumed one-third to a little less than half of its ultimately recoverable oil reserves, according to the "Hydrogen and Fuel Cell Letter," April 1996.

15. *Emissions of Greenhouse Gases in the United States 1995*, EIA, DOT.

16. Godfrey Hodgson, ed., *Handbooks to the Modern World, the United States* (New York: Facts on File, 1992).

17. *Washington Post*, December 3, 1995.

18. Lester R. Brown et al., *Vital Signs* (New York: Worldwatch Institute, 1996).

19. Philip H. Abelson, "Nuclear Power in East Asia" (editorial), *Science*, April 26, 1996.

20. Eric Felten, "With a Bang, Not a Whimper," *Weekly Standard*, August 5, 1996.

21. James Trefil, "Phenomena, Comment and Notes," *Smithsonian*, December 1996. The first fertilization experiment was not considered a success. Trefil attended the meeting when those results were announced and wrote, "I was really taken aback by the reaction to them. . . . What surprised me was the reaction of the environmental scientists present. It was almost as if there were a collective sigh of relief, as if the prospect that humanity might find an easy way out of the greenhouse problem was just too much for them to bear."

22. Office of Technology Assessment, Congress of the United States, *Saving Energy in U.S. Transportation*, U.S. Government Printing Office, July 1994. To know that Paris is closer to Moscow than Denver is to Philadelphia helps explain why Americans travel more.

23. Energy Information Administration, *Emissions of Greenhouse Gases 1995*.

24. This is the undated document entitled *Submission of the United States of America under the United Nations Framework Convention on Climate Change*, printed by the Government Printing Office, ISBN 0-16-045214-7.

25. *Washington Post*, October 13, 1997.

26. IPCC, *Climate Change 1995*, p. 681.

27. Ibid.

28. It would be interesting to be able to calculate whether the energy produced by solar panels would displace enough fossil-fuel combustion to offset the heat retained by their capture of additional solar radiation.

29. The study was funded by the American Petroleum Institute. Professional activists claim that any industry-sponsored study is tainted—while arguing that their own numbers are without bias. All studies depend on assumptions, and minor changes in these assumptions can have major effects on the outcomes. All studies should be taken with some salt, but established research institutions of good repute are less likely to manipulate the assumptions—consciously or unconsciously—than are parties with an immediate interest in the outcome.

30. IPCC, *Climate Change 1995*, p. 52.

31. "Our Changing Planet, the FY 1997 U.S. Global Change Research Program," a supplement to the president's fiscal year 1997 budget prepared by the Subcommittee on Global Change Research, Committee on Environment and Natural Resources of the National Science and Technology Council established by President Clinton on November 23, 1993.

32. U.S. Congress, Office of Technology Assessment, *Climate Treaties and Models: Issues in the International Management of Climate Change*, U.S. Government Printing Office, June 1994.

33. *Washington Post*, June 12, 1997.

34. U.S. Congress, *Climate Treaties and Models*.

35. *Wall Street Journal*, July 16, 1997.

36. Janet Yellen, Testimony, House Commerce Subcommittee on Energy and Power, July 15, 1997.

37. *Economist*, June 28, 1997.

38. *Science*, February 10, 1989.

39. In his text, Moore adds "richer is healthier" to this conclusion, emphasizing the obvious fact that the people of wealthier nations are healthier for having the resources to provide superior medical care, nourishment, shelter, and the other things that contribute to health. Deep cuts in energy use to reduce carbon dioxide emissions reduce economic well-being, which in turn not only adversely affects health but also reduces our ability to deal with disasters of any kind.

40. Lester R. Brown et al., *Vital Signs 1995*, Worldwatch Institute, 1995.

41. "Our Changing Planet, the FY 1997 U.S. Global Change Research Program," a supplement to the president's fiscal year 1997 budget prepared by the Subcommittee on Global Change Research, Committee on Environment and Natural Resources of the National Science and Technology Council, established by President Clinton on November 23, 1993.

42. IPCC, *Climate Change 1995*.

Chapter 9: Where Do We Go?

1. Al Gore, Speech, Tokyo, March 24, 1997.

2. *Wall Street Journal*, March 10, 1997.

3. Some of these 120 are: Allied Signal, Boeing, Chrysler, Dana, Emerson Electric, Ford, General Motors, Halliburton, Ingersoll Rand, Johnson Controls, Kennecott, Lear, Motorola, Norfolk Southern, Ohio Edison, Phillips Petroleum, Reynolds Metals, Southern Pacific, TRW, USX, Virginia Power, and Whirlpool.

4. *Washington Post*, February 15, 1997.

5. *Washington Post*, October 6, 1997.

6. Press release, Global Climate Information Project, October 2, 1997.

7. Partial transcripts were released by the White House Press Office, October 6, 1997.

8. In a speech in Australia (August 20, 1997), Congressman John Dingell (D-Mich.) summed up the EU position, saying, "Germany wants credit for closing inefficient plants in the former East Germany. Great Britain wants credit for its shift from coal to gas. France doesn't much care, because it gets most of its electric power from nuclear plants."

The EU plan calls for a "bubble concept" that would treat the emissions of the fifteen-nation bloc as a whole, permitting some countries to increase or maintain current emission levels. The 15 percent cut would be made up by the large reductions made by Germany and Britain for reasons unrelated to climate change.

9. Bureau of National Affairs, *Daily Report for Executives*, October 7, 1997.

10. *Washington Post*, October 13, 1997.

11. *Washington Post*, October 24, 1997.

12. In one of the slickest (and most cynical) political moves in recent history, the Clinton administration, when confronted with a Byrd-Hagel Senate resolution calling on the president not to sign the Kyoto treaty if the developing countries were not committed to reducing greenhouse gases and if the treaty would be harmful to the U.S. economy, at first planned a counter-resolution. When sixty-six Senators signed on to the Byrd-Hagel resolution signalling certain victory, the administration simply said that

was exactly what it wanted, and the resolution passed the Senate 95–0. Since it is advisory only, the administration can simply "interpret" its terms and say that those terms have been satisfied when the treaty is negotiated—and put on a national scare campaign to attain Senate approval.

CHAPTER 10: BAD NEWS, GOOD NEWS

1. An estimated 229 counties in twenty-nine states will be added to the Environmental Protection Administration's nonattainment list.

2. These data are taken from the *1995 National Air Quality: Status and Trends*, published annually by the U.S. Environmental Protection Agency Office of Air & Radiation, and from an EPA news release of December 17, 1996.

3. These data are taken from the twenty-fifth anniversary edition of *Environmental Quality*, the annual report of the White House Council on Environmental Quality.

4. *Washington Post*, December 18, 1996.

5. EPA, *1995 National Air Quality*, October 1996.

6. EPA's *Trends Report, 1995*.

7. "Your right to breathe is on the line," says the lead sentence in a letter from Deb Callahan, president of the League of Conservation Voters, soliciting money to help "defeat anti-environmental Members of Congress." She asks that, "With the imminent threat to our health and our environment, I hope you'll support our work with a contribution of $50, $100 or more." The letter is undated but came in July 1997, as EPA announced its new national ambient air quality standards.

8. Americans tend to lay too much blame for their frustrations with government on the career bureaucracy. They forget that both the policies and the bureaucracies created to implement them are the creatures of their elected officials. Elections do matter!

9. James Boswell, Scottish author and biographer.

10. Deb Callahan's fundraising–political action letter (see note 7 above) also asks readers to "help mobilize voters to throw out Members of Congress who pander to polluters and ignore the health of the American people!"

11. Cranking up the rhetoric, U.S. Interior Secretary Bruce Babbitt, in a radio interview of July 21, 1997, said that the oil and coal industries "have joined in a conspiracy to hire pseudo-scientists to deny the facts." He went on to say, "What they're doing is un-American." Referring to an article appearing in the *Washington Post* by the CEO of Chrysler Corporation, Babbitt said, "It is a deliberate attempt to distort the facts and to mislead." Perhaps Secretary Babbitt would like for Congress to set up an Un-American Activities Committee to look into these matters!

12. Al Gore, *Earth in the Balance* (Boston: Houghton Mifflin, 1992), p. 275. Reminder: a principal instrument of the enemy for Gore is the automobile, whose effect, he says, "is posing a mortal threat to the security of every nation that is more deadly than that of any military enemy we are ever again likely to confront," p. 325.

13. There are more than thirty components in vehicle powertrains alone that are affected directly by EPA regulations, and they must be covered by the manufacturer's warranty to perform accordingly. There are eight such components in the fuel-management systems, twenty-four in the air-management systems, ten in the ignition system, thirty-eight in other systems, and countless pipes, hoses, valves, belts, connectors, and more.

14. Calculating gross domestic product and the government's percentage thereof is fraught with pitfalls, exceeded only by those encountered in calculating costs and ben-

efits of government regulations. The numbers used here come from table 517 of the *Statistical Abstract of the United States, 1995*, not always considered to be adequate by many economists.

15. What triggered the removal of lead from the air, arguably the most successful environmental cleanup to date, was not government action but the announcement in the early 1970s by Ed Cole, president of General Motors, that the engines in GM cars beginning in model year 1974 would have reduced compression ratios that would permit the use of lead-free gasoline. The market followed. Lead-free gasoline became available almost immediately.

16. Volatile organic compounds from motor vehicles are primarily unburned gasoline in the form of hydrocarbons.

17. As emission standards got closer to zero, it became important to reduce them through every means. One result was reformulated gasoline, now required in severe ozone areas by the federal and California governments. By controlling the content of gasoline (for example, olefins, sulfur, and aromatics) and the Reid vapor pressure, and by selective additions of oxygenates, vehicle emissions have been cut. This improvement was largely the result of the Air Quality Improvement Research Program (AQIRP) conducted by the petroleum and auto industries. For details, see the AQIRP Final Report of January 1997. Gasolines still vary so greatly in quality that Joseph Colucci of Automotive Fuels Consulting asks why there shouldn't be a Gasoline of the Year award, just as there are awards for the Car of the Year. It could be an incentive for better performance and lower emissions.

18. The study was conducted by Energy and Environmental Analysis, Inc., Arlington, Va.

19. U.S. General Accounting Office Report to the Congress, "Environmental Protection: Meeting Public Expectations with Limited Resources," June 1991.

20. U.S. General Accounting Office, "Regulatory Reform, Information on Costs, Cost-Effectiveness, and Mandated Deadlines for Regulation," March 1995.

21. American Automobile Manufacturers Association.

22. Patrick Bedard, *Car and Driver*, April 1995.

23. As the first emission standards were coming into force in the late 1960s and more were on their way, auto companies suggested that they might list the cost of meeting the standards along with the suggested retail price of the car on the window label, as a way for the public to know what they were paying as a result of the legislation. Privately, congressional staff made it clear that if the companies did so, ways would be found to make them regret doing so. The power of some congressional staff is such that the companies took the communication very seriously and dropped the idea.

CHAPTER 11: THE GOVERNMENT'S ROLE

1. The Automobile Manufacturers Association was later renamed the Motor Vehicle Manufacturers Association and, more recently, the American Automobile Manufacturers Association.

2. Testimony before the U.S. Senate Subcommittee on Air and Water Pollution, February 20, 1967, Detroit, Michigan.

3. The auto companies came close to being indicted in the 1960s for their cooperative work in reducing emissions. Antitrust law was amended in 1984 to reduce antitrust liability for some kinds of research and for joint ventures for development. Congress further amended the laws to permit production joint ventures in 1993. Such work is

progressing under the umbrella of the United States Council for Automotive Research, formed in 1991 by Chrysler, Ford, and General Motors.

4. An example of business interests favoring regulation is provided by an advertisement run in the January 26, 1995, edition of the *Washington Post* by the Oxygenated Fuels Association, Inc., which talks about people with asthma and other respiratory problems, and adds, "And virtually all of us are at risk of cancer and heart disease caused or aggravated by toxics from car exhaust." The advertisement was promoting the use of oxygenates in gasoline. It is no surprise that the membership of the association includes producers of these additives. In its 1996 annual report,WMX Technologies, Inc., better known as Waste Management, states, "The company believes that in general it tends to benefit when government regulation increases, which may increase the demand for its services."

The *New York Times* on November 21, 1976, reported an earlier example. In the congressional battle that year over auto-emission standards, the *Times* reported "a contribution of $10,000 to one of the Clean Air Coalition member organizations—from the catalytic-converter multinational. The money was earmarked specifically for plane tickets and hotel rooms to enable amateur lobbyists to freshen the Washington scene with homegrown, spontaneous demand for cleaner air—and, incidentally, more catalytic converters."

5. This was the English law of 1865 that required self-propelled vehicles to be preceded by a man on foot carrying a red flag by day and a lantern by night to warn the populace. This law stopped the use and therefore the development of the automobile in Great Britain.

6. Robert S. Lynd and Helen Merrell Lynd, *Middletown in Transition* (New York: Harcourt Brace and World, Inc., 1937).

7. For their part, the public agencies could have used the command-and-control regulatory approach and fined each householder for dumping his or her effluent in the street, hoping, thus, to end the practice. They chose, instead, to "tax" the effluent indirectly by placing a fee on each house and using the proceeds for a public work to handle it.

8. One unintended consequence, ironically, of blocking steam power was the added incentive this action by "public interests" and the government gave to the development of the internal combustion engine.

9. M. G. Lay, *Ways of the World* (New Brunswick, N.J.: Rutgers University Press, 1992).

10. A lesson illustrated by the Boston Commons, a field dedicated to the use of all Boston citizens in the colonial period, was that when something of value is owned by everyone to use as each pleases, it will be abused or neglected. The same is true when no one owns something of value, such as the air.

11. See Dr. Hugh W. Ellsaesser, "The Misuse of Science," a Heartland Policy Study. Internet, December 8, 1995.

12. In 1984, approximately 4,000 people died in Bhopal, India, when a pesticide plant accidentally released methyl isocyanate (MIC). This tragedy was not the result of air pollution from the normal emissions of plants or cars but from a failure in a manufacturing process.

13. Paul R. Ehrlich, *The Population Bomb* (New York: Ballantine Books, 1968). Ehrlich's most optimistic scenario, one he says "has considerably more appeal," called for food rationing to begin in the United States in 1974, subsequent famine and food riots in Asia, Africa, and Latin America, and a "die-back" of world population to two billion by 2025.

14. Al Gore, *Earth in the Balance* (New York: Houghton Mifflin, 1992), p. 109.

15. The Watergate and Whitewater investigations resulted in the conviction of several high officials, including Attorney General John Mitchell in the Nixon administration and Associate Attorney General Webster Hubble in the Clinton administration. There are other types of corruption, such as arrogant or abusive behavior, or tenured incompetence.

16. This is at the heart of the controversy over campaign contributions. Putting limits on contributions—the equivalent of price controls—will not solve the problem. As long as the value of the "commodity" in question—the elective office and its power—continues to be so high, ways will be found to circumvent the rules and pay the price—at least as often in the attempt to avoid ill will as to receive some benefit.

17. Some external problems can be handled effectively in the courts by using the laws governing nuisances. If someone dumps waste into a stream and it damages the interests of someone downstream, the aggrieved party may get satisfaction in court. This approach, however, does not adequately cover many externalities—air pollution, for example.

18. When the government does intervene, it is more effective when it uses market-reinforcing policies as opposed to command-and-control regulation. One such approach is to establish emission limits for the emitting companies and to permit the trading of credits earned by companies that reduce emissions below their limit. Companies unable to attain the required levels could buy these credits to offset their excess emissions. If the price of these credits is higher than the cost of emission reductions, then an incentive exists to make further reductions and sell the credits. A more complex form of this approach was authorized under the Clean Air Act amendments of 1990 to reduce sulfur dioxide emissions. While this approach is more efficient than tradional command-and-control, it is the setting of emissions limits that establishes the value of the credits, and that is still a political act.

19. The United States and some other countries have gone to much trouble and expense to protect stratospheric ozone by banning the use of chlorofluorocarbons (CFCs) for air conditioning, propellants in aerosol cans, and other applications. This ban, of course, has led to a black market, as well as to the smuggling of CFCs made in countries less dedicated to the environment.

20. The word "smog" was first used in Los Angeles when people originally thought—erroneously—that the yellow-brown haze was a combination of smoke and fog; hence, smog. Ozone is a principal ingredient of smog, but smog also contains other gases and particles, which give it its color, among other attributes.

21. Everett Carll Ladd and Karlyn H. Bowman, *Attitudes toward the Environment* (Washington, D.C.: AEI Press, 1995), p. 1.

22. Ibid., p. 18.

23. Californians further eroded their credibility as environmentalists in the 1996 elections by approving a ballot proposal authorizing them, in certain circumstances, to inhale the smoke from burning weeds (marijuana).

24. As a graduate student in Los Angeles in the mid-1950s when smog was at its worst, I can attest that the air brought tears to my eyes and irritation to my throat on many days of the year. On some, it was difficult to make out the buildings down the block at high noon. Worst yet were my high school days in the late 1940s, when I earned spending money lighting and tending smudge pots in San Bernardino Valley citrus groves to keep the fruit and trees from freezing during winter nights. The only sight similar to the one at daybreak was the smoke from the fires Saddam ordered set in the Kuwait oil fields during the Persian Gulf War.

25. *Washington Post,* February 23, 1997. Maryland's "violations" had not been egregious. The state exceeded the ozone NAAQS for an average of not quite ten days during each of the past three years.

26. Particulate matter is measured by the size of the particles involved. PM10 involves particles that are roughly ten microns in diameter. A human hair is about seventy microns in diameter.

27. In rural areas, most volatile organic compounds are products of plant life and other natural sources; in urban areas, human-induced VOCs dominate.

28. The auto manufacturers had great difficulty in adjusting to heavy regulation and understanding the political process that drives all government decisions. While the companies appeared to have a broad constituency with their plants throughout the United States, their political support was essentially concentrated in Michigan. Plant managers generally do not engage the politicians as readily or as effectively as do heads of local businesses, industries, and other local interests, including auto dealers. In Washington, the auto industry is generally referred to as "Detroit."

29. Reacting to a bill introduced by President Lyndon B. Johnson, Congress passed the National Highway Traffic Safety Act of 1966. This came after extensive hearings in which the industry was vigorously attacked by Ralph Nader, Senator Bobby Kennedy, and others. It was unprepared and did not distinguish itself in its response.

30. An example of this trap came early in the consideration of air pollution legislation. A top executive of General Motors, a very enthusiastic engineer, met with a key senator to dicuss what was feasible in pollution control. The auto executive told the senator that the engineers were "just this far from being able to meet" the proposed oxides of nitrogen standard. He held his thumb and forefinger slightly apart to demonstrate. The senator saw this as an opportunity to "help" the industry "stretch" a little, and successfully advocated the enactment of the standard under discussion. Unfortunately, the technology did not come as fast as the auto company executive hoped, and subsequently the law had to be amended, after a very painful legislative struggle, to give the engineers more time to invent and refine.

31. Administrator Browner ignores the fact that the industry took an enormous gamble by putting these devices on every new car without the normal field and durability tests. There were no guarantees that the catalyst would work. Early on, some facilities even banned catalyst-equipped cars from their property, fearing these very hot devices would set fires. Senator Ed Muskie, author of the Clean Air Act, reportedly believed these devices were the wrong technology.

32. Environmental Protection Agency.

33. In the 1996 elections, the professional environmental activists claimed success in electing all their "Earth list" candidates and defeating six on their dirty dozen list. Of course, like other groups wanting a good track record, they chose their lists carefully. For example, freshman house member Michael P. Flanagan (R-Ill.) was on the dirty dozen list. He was elected in 1994 because his opponent, incumbent Representative Dan Rostenkowski, was under indictment. There was virtually no chance for Flanagan's reelection in that traditionally Democratic district. Environmental issues had nothing to do with his defeat, but the activists attempt to wield them like a club.

34. *New York Times,* November 11, 1976. Alexander, an amateur among professionals, was active with the Maine League of Women Voters and had been brought to Washington to assist the National Clean Air Coalition, formed to support the Muskie bill. For the true believers among the activists, there can be no compromise. Their champions must hew to the line or pay the consequences.

35. Representative Waxman's attitudes about air pollution are not only related to the fact that his district shares the smog common to the Los Angeles area. He also pines for the chairmanship of the House Commerce Committee, with its jurisdiction over energy, health, the environment, telecommunications, finance, and commerce, among other areas. The ranking Democrat on the committee and the former chairman is John Dingell of Michigan, who has opposed excessively stringent approaches to environmental issues.

36. For his efforts on behalf of his fellow auto workers, Woodcock was thoroughly denounced by the professional activists, including Nader.

37. Auto dealers are good at politics. Ramsay Gillman, president of the National Automobile Dealers Association, said, "Dealers need to realize how much clout they have. . . . They can get a more immediate response from their congressmen than [can the automakers]. *Automotive News,* January 13, 1997. Dealers generally use their political clout on issues directly related to their retail business, sometimes in conflict with the manufacturers. When they fully engage in broad public policy issues, they can be very effective.

38. *Washington Star,* October 2, 1976.

39. *New York Times,* July 30, 1977.

40. *Washington Post,* April 24, 1990.

41. Representative Henry A. Waxman (D-Calif.) is another perpetrator of the myth that the auto engineers always complain but then meet any standard the political "engineers" devise. In his op ed piece in the *Washington Post* on February 5, 1997, entitled "False Alarms on Clean Air," he wrote about the 1979 change in the NAAQS, saying that GM and others claimed that widespread inflation and unemployment would follow adoption of the proposed rule. "EPA adopted the rule," Waxman wrote, "and calamity did not follow." He apparently forgot that the rule relaxed the standard from .08 to .12 ppm, and it was Carter White House economists who had been concerned about the economy.

CHAPTER 12: HOW FAR TO GO?

1. Robert W. Hahn, ed., *Risks, Costs and Lives Saved* (Washington, D.C.: AEI Press and Oxford University Press, 1996).

2. Attributed to Charlie Thayer by the *Washington Post,* "In the Loop," June 30, 1997.

3. *NRDC v. EPA,* 902 F. 2d 962 (D.C. Cir. 1990); *Lead Industries Ass'n v. EPA,* 647 F. 2d 1130, 1148-51 (D.C. Cir. 1980); *American Petroleum Inst. v. Costle,* 609 F. 2d 20 (D.C. Cir. 1979).

4. Testimony of Mary D. Nichols, assistant administrator of the EPA for Air and Radiation, before the Subcommittees of Health and the Environment and Oversight and Investigations of the Commerce Committee of the U.S. House of Representatives, April 17, 1997.

5. The state of California attempted to require a phase-in of "zero-emission" cars, but since only electric cars qualify and they are not ready for the mass market, California postponed its deadline for the requirement—but only until 2003, when 10 percent of the sales of each car maker must be zero-emission vehicles, whether customers want them or not!

6. Ann Y. Watson, Richard R. Bates, Donald Kennedy, eds., *Air Pollution, the Automobile, and Public Health* (Washington, D.C.: National Academy Press, 1988).

7. In an entirely different area, Congress and government regulators found it acceptable to require the installation of something in motor vehicles that will kill a certain

number of people, most of whom fall into specific categories. Air bags, which were mandated by Congress, turn out to have some very unfortunate, unintended consequences. Nonetheless, this mandate has been maintained in the face of a growing number of fatalities of children and adults of small stature, some properly belted, as the direct result of air bag deployment.

8. Environmental Protection Agency, "Basic Facts about Radon (Rn)," fact sheet, modified October 10, 1996. Internet, February 4, 1997.

9. Environmental Protection Agency, *Radiation: Risks and Realities*, Report 402–92-004, August 1993.

10. Environmental Protection Agency, "EPA's Proposal on the Ozone Standard," fact sheet, November 29, 1996.

CHAPTER 13: AIR QUALITY STANDARDS

1. In his memorandum directing the EPA to implement the 1997 NAAQS for ozone and PM, President Clinton said there is "a linkage between these two pollutants and their precursors and regional haze problems." Is haze to be the next multibillion dollar target?

2. Mary D. Nichols, assistant administrator for Air and Radiation, U.S. Environmental Protection Agency, testimony before Subcommittees on Health and the Environment and Oversight and Investigations, Committee on Commerce, U.S. House of Representatives, April 17, 1997. But doubts about the effectiveness of reducing fine particles by controlling VOCs and NO_x precursors have been raised by scientists. See Z. Meng, D. Dabdub, and J. H. Seinfeld, "Chemical Coupling between Atmospheric Ozone and Particulate Matter," *Science,* July 4, 1997.

3. Letter from George T. Wolff, chair, Clean Air Scientific Advisory Committee, to Carol M. Browner, administrator, EPA, June 13, 1996.

4. *Washington Post*, April 3, 1997.

5. EPA Headquarters Information Resources Center, April 15, 1997, e-mail.

6. The Natural Resources Defense Council, on the basis of this same study, claims that 64,000 premature deaths are attributable to particulate pollution.

7. For an extensive discussion of the Pope study and other such studies, see Michael Fumento, *Polluted Science: The EPA's Campaign to Expand Clean Air Regulations* (Washington, D.C.: AEI Press, 1997).

8. Statistical studies are tricky. Some wit has noted that there is a correlation between the sale of ice cream cones and excess deaths in the summertime. No one would suggest, however, that the deaths were the result of the cones and not the heat.

9. Environmental Protection Agency, Office of Air Quality Planning and Standards Research, Triangle Park, North Carolina, *Review of National Ambient Air Quality Standards for Particulate Matter, Policy Assessment of Scientific and Technical Information,* OAQPS Staff Paper, EPA-452\R-96-013, July 1996.

10. Ibid., p. IV-11.

11. It is also worth noting that some scientists assert that the presence in the atmosphere of particulates and aerosols is the reason there has not been more global warming. There is a general agreement that they do reflect solar heat back to space, thus having a cooling effect.

12. OAQPS Particulate Matter Staff Paper, July 1996, p. V-8.

13. Commenting on July 30, 1997, about the PM and ozone air quality standards, Representative John D. Dingell (D-Mich.) said, "I am willing to undertake what is in all

probability going to be a very nasty fight to save EPA from its own folly." On the same subject, on July 17, 1997, Representative Fred Upton (R-Mich.) called the EPA action "Washington at its worst." He added, "They [the EPA] haven't taken into account an ounce of reality while writing these rules." House Commerce Committee Chairman Tom Bliley (R-Va.) called the standards "a sharp rebuke to the thousands of mayors, local and county officials, governors, and state legislators." He added, "It is also a major setback to those like the U.S. Conference of Mayors, the National Black Chamber of Commerce, and many within the president's own inner circle of advisers who have predicted that these new standards will lead to significant layoffs."

14. Mary D. Nichols, assistant administrator for Air and Radiation, U.S. Environmental Protection Agency, testimony before Subcommittees on Health and the Environment and Oversight and Investigations, Committee on Commerce, U.S. House of Representatives, April 17, 1997.

15. Ann Y. Watson, Richard R. Bates, Donald Kennedy, eds., *Air Pollution, the Automobile, and Public Health* (Washington, D.C.: National Academy Press, 1988).

16. Environmental Protection Agency, Office of Air Quality Planning and Standards Research, Triangle Park, North Carolina, *Review of National Ambient Air Quality Standards for Ozone, Assessment of Scientific and Technical Information,* OAQPS Staff Paper, EPA-452/R-96-007, June 1996, pp. 24, 33.

17. Ibid., pp. 26, 38.

18. Ibid., p. 45.

19. Ibid., p. 51.

20. Ibid., pp. 41, 42. There is much more in the nearly 400-page Staff Paper on health effects. The excerpts here were selected because they raise questions about the scientific basis for new standards.

21. For example, the motor vehicle share of the emissions that form ozone has been drastically reduced; highway-related volatile organic compound (VOC) emissions were cut by 31.2 percent between 1986 and 1995. At the same time, VOC emissions from other sources increased by 4 percent. Cars and trucks are doing the most in cleaning up ozone.

22. Mayo Clinic, *Family Health Book, Respiratory Allergies,* CD-ROM, IVI Publishing Inc., 1993.

23. William O.C.M. Cookson and Miriam F. Moffatt, "Asthma: An Epidemic in the Absence of Infection?" *Science,* vol. 275, January 3, 1997.

24. *New York Times,* February 26, 1997.

25. Sandra A. Zaslow and Mary Beth Genter, North Carolina Cooperative Extension Service.

26. "Trees That Pollute?" *Urban Ecologist,* 1997. The article reports, "Recent studies show that some species emit organic compounds such as isoprene which actually contribute to photochemical smog." High emitters include the weeping willow, the European oak, and the palm oil tree. This environmental journal laments that, "Unfortunately, little work has been done to screen all the nation's tree species for emission levels." Trees are great for taking up carbon dioxide, but some, it seems, are "polluters" when it comes to ozone.

27. Ozone levels as high as .072 ppm have been reported in North Dakota's remote Theodore Roosevelt National Park.

28. General Motors is leasing its electric car, the EV1, through Saturn dealerships in California and Arizona. Showing once more that actions count more than do people's reported intentions, fewer than 200 had been leased by April 1997 in California, a state

where enthusiasm had been strong—verbally. Other manufacturers have had even less success. It is, of course, too early to predict future demand, especially if a better battery is developed, providing more range at reasonable cost.

29. The first emission-control equipment captured crankcase vapors, drawing them into the engine cylinders where they are burned. This eliminated about 20 percent of all hydrocarbons produced by the car and cost only $3.00 per vehicle—a great bargain. Costs have since escalated, and the cost of eliminating the last small percentage of vehicle emissions left uncontrolled is incalculable at this point, especially since it may not be possible without a drastic change in the vehicle's power plant.

30. Although they have improved in providing data on public policy issues to their employees, customers, suppliers, and others with a stake in the regulations, the U.S. manufacturers find it hard to stay on a steady course of rallying their constituencies to become involved in public debates. In contrast, the professional activists are fully committed to continuous political action.

CHAPTER 14: WHAT TO DO

1. J. G. Calvert, J. B. Heywood, R. F. Sawyer, and J. H. Seinfield, "Achieving Acceptable Air Quality: Some Reflections on Controlling Vehicle Emissions," *Science*, July 2, 1993.

2. Patrick Bedard, *Car and Driver,* April 1995.

3. *New York Times,* July 2, 1997. The Environmental Defense Fund (EDF) applauded the possibility of "a new dynamic," while the Sierra Club, true to form, concluded that the "Republicans have drawn a smiley face on their poison." The EDF is virtually alone among environmental groups in sometimes using the soft approach. Any politician or business person who believes he or she can reason with the professional activists or ingratiate himself with them will almost certainly get the Sierra Club "poison" treatment in return.

4. Stephen Breyer, *Breaking the Vicious Circle: Toward Effective Risk Regulation* (Cambridge, Mass.: Harvard University Press, 1994), p.11.

5. Ibid., p.20.

6. Predictably, today the pump is also being required in jurisdictions around the country. According to the *New York Times,* July 21, 1997, as the canister regulation takes effect, drivers are experiencing difficulty in filling their gas tanks with these pumps. More important is the *Times* report that the "safety experts worry about hazards." The lawyers will be fighting that battle for decades to come. With the device now mandated for every car, the manufacturers—and the consumers—are stuck again with any problems that arise.

7. Breyer, *Vicious Circle,* pp. 55, 81.

8. *Washington Post,* February 21, 1997.

9. In political power, the EPA is moving into the place so long occupied by the national security establishment. Its operatives and constituents are quite willing to wield the "polluter" label with the same abandon as some used the "security risk" label in the past.

10. See EPA, *Radiation: Risks and Realities*, August 1993.

11. A counter demand by a Virginia official was that the federal government shut down on pollution-alert days to cut pollution from commuter traffic generated by 272,000 federal employees in the area. A federal spokesperson replied, "This air quality thing, while serious, doesn't seem to justify the cost of shutting down the government." That judgment should be useful for the cost-benefit analysts.

12. David L. Lewis, "EPA Science: Casualty of Election Politics," *Nature*, vol. 381, June 27, 1996, p. 731.

13. For an excellent discussion of the pros and cons of such requirements see Robert W. Hahn, ed., *Risks, Costs and Lives Saved* (New York: AEI Press and Oxford University Press, 1996). See especially chapter 10, "Regulatory Reform: What Do the Government's Numbers Tell Us?"

14. The major fear of many regulatory advocates is that such a rule would slow down the further encroachment of government into our personal and economic lives. It would slow the rapid growth of a fourth branch of government—the regulatory branch—not contemplated by Jefferson, Madison, Adams, Washington, and other founders. But for most Americans, that would be very a good thing.

15. *Washington Post*, February 28, 1997.

Chapter 15: Epilogue

1. Preliminary hearing record, Subcommittee on Consumer Relations, Fall 1997.

2. Joseph D. Mann, M.D., Kent County Medical Society Bulletin, Grand Rapids, Michigan, July-August 1983.

3. Democratic Party Platform, 1916.

4. Peter Brown, "Smart Highways? Americans Really Aren't Ready for Them," *Automotive News,* August 18, 1997.

5. The Web site for NAHSC is http://nahsc.volpe.dot.gov.

6. *Washington Post,* July 28, 1997.

7. *ITS World* magazine, July-August 1997.

8. James Q. Wilson, "Cars and Their Enemies," *Commentary,* July 1997.

9. Loren E. Lomansky, "Autonomy and Automobility," Competitive Enterprise Institute, June 1995.

INDEX

ABOUT THE AUTHOR

James D. Johnston is a resident fellow at the American Enterprise Institute. He was vice president of General Motors for Industry-Government Relations and special assistant to the president of the Automobile Manufacturers Association. Earlier he was a career foreign service officer, serving at the Department of State in the Bureau of Far Eastern Affairs and at the U.S. Embassies in Mexico and Nicaragua. He was special assistant to the under secretary of state for economic affairs. He lives in Washington, D.C., with his wife Margaret.

A NOTE ON THE BOOK

This book was edited by
Cheryl Weissman of the publications staff
of the American Enterprise Institute.
The index was prepared by Nancy Rosenberg.
The text was set in New Baskerville.
Electronic Quill set the type,
and Edwards Brothers, Incorporated,
printed and bound the book,
using permanent acid-free paper.

The AEI Press is the publisher for the American Enterprise Institute for Public Policy
Research, 1150 Seventeenth Street, N.W., Washington, D.C. 20036; *Christopher DeMuth,*
publisher; *Dana Lane,* director; *Ann Petty,* editor; *Leigh Tripoli,* editor; *Cheryl Weissman,*
editor; *Jennifer Lesiak,* editorial assistant (rights and permissions).

www.ingramcontent.com/pod-product-compliance
Lightning Source LLC
Jackson TN
JSHW011934131224
75386JS00041B/1372